Literary Awakenings

Literary Awakenings

Personal Essays from the *Hudson Review*

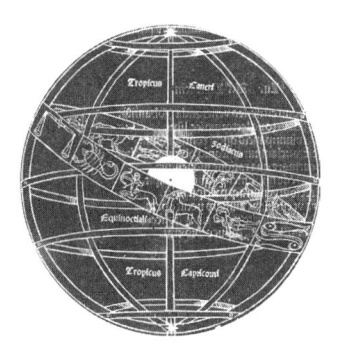

Edited by **Ronald Koury**

With an Introduction by William H. Pritchard

Syracuse University Press

Copyright © 2017 by Syracuse University Press
Syracuse, New York 13244-5290

All Rights Reserved

First Edition 2017
17 18 19 20 21 22   6 5 4 3 2 1

∞ The paper used in this publication meets the minimum requirements of the American National Standard for Information Sciences—Permanence of Paper for Printed Library Materials, ANSI Z39.48-1992.

For a listing of books published and distributed by Syracuse University Press, visit www.SyracuseUniversityPress.syr.edu.

ISBN: 978-0-8156-3487-4 (hardcover)   978-0-8156-1078-6 (paperback)
978-0-8156-5385-1 (e-book)

Library of Congress Cataloging-in-Publication Data
Available from the publisher upon request.

Manufactured in the United States of America

To my parents, George and June Koury, with love

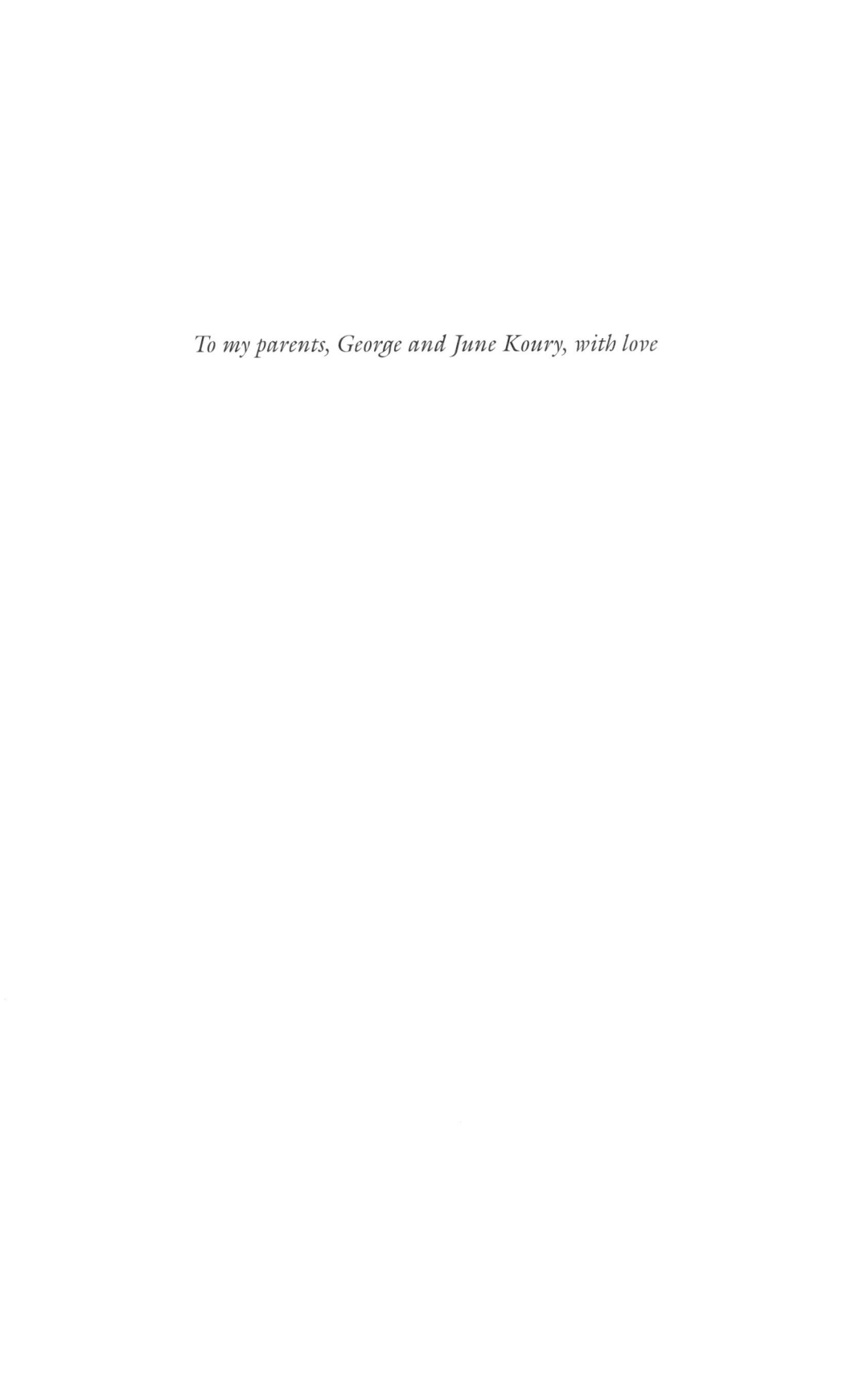

Photograph by Jane Bishop

Ronald Koury, a graduate of Columbia College with a degree in English, joined the *Hudson Review* in 1981 and has been its managing editor since 1985. He has been a speechwriter for the delegation of the Permanent Mission of the Kingdom of Bhutan to the United Nations. He lives in New York.

Contents

Preface | RONALD KOURY ... ix
Introduction | WILLIAM H. PRITCHARD ... xi
Listening to Virginia | JEFFREY HARRISON ... 1

PART ONE. Awakening to Literature

A Double Education | ANTONIO MUÑOZ MOLINA ... 5
"Apt Admonishment"
   Wordsworth as an Example | SEAMUS HEANEY ... 18
The Poem and the Path | ANDREW MOTION ... 34
Waterloo, the Story of an Obsession | LOUIS SIMPSON ... 58
Writer and Region | WENDELL BERRY ... 67
The Poetry of Life and the Life of Poetry
   | DAVID MASON ... 84

PART TWO. Students and Teachers

Talking Back to the Speaker
   | CLARA CLAIBORNE PARK ... 103
Before I Read *Clarissa* I Was Nobody
   Aspirational Reading and Samuel Richardson's Great Novel
   | JUDITH PASCOE ... 128
Learning from Robert Fitzgerald | DANA GIOIA ... 144
A Pilgrimage to Santayana | IRVING SINGER ... 164

PART THREE. Tributes

Last Days of Henry Miller | BARBARA KRAFT — 177

Prophet against God
   William Empson (1906–84) | GEORGE WATSON — 191

Who's Afraid of Virginia Woolf?
   A Memoir | RICHARD HORNBY — 204

Horatio Hornblower | IGOR WEBB — 215

PART FOUR. Facing the Text

Nell and I | JOYCE ZONANA — 239

My Roommate Lord Byron | THOMAS M. DISCH — 258

Flannery O'Connor Resurrected | SUSAN BALÉE — 264

The Pleasures of Reading | JOSEPH EPSTEIN — 281

Copyrights and Credits — 303

Notes on Contributors — 307

Preface

RONALD KOURY

Around thirty years ago, the editors of the *Hudson Review* began to notice a new trend in literary criticism. Many of the best literary essayists and reviewers were sending us critical work written in a highly personal manner. They read like memoirs; in fact, some were clearly memoirs but literary criticism at the same time. This was in marked contrast to the theoretical, technocratic work that prevailed in many literary and academic venues, and in many places still does. We found these essay/memoirs refreshing. As time went on, the *Hudson Review* became a home for this kind of accessible, memoirist writing.

This collection features some of the best examples of this combination of personal impressions with literary criticism. The chapters—Awakening to Literature, Students and Teachers, Tributes, and Facing the Text—explore many facets of this theme. In the end, what unites these diverse contributions is the joy of appreciation, the pleasures of engaging with literature.

"Pleasure" is a loaded word in our culture; the very concept of it is, even today, suspect. The essays in this collection do not disappoint in that respect—all are lively and full of surprises, some, even subversive.

I owe an enormous debt to many people whose work was essential in the creation of this book. First and foremost to Paula Deitz, editor of the *Hudson Review*, who helped me every step of the way with invaluable advice and encouragement. Every day, I learn from her, her input with this book being a prime example. I have always looked up to longtime *Hudson Review* advisory editor William H. Pritchard, so I was honored when he agreed to write the introduction, which is a tribute to the collection. To my colleagues at the magazine, Zachary Wood, associate editor; Eileen Talone, assistant editor; and editorial interns William Grosholz Edwards, Jessica Lucia Pacitto, and Bates W. Crawford, I am extremely grateful for proofing and preparing the manuscript. Everyone at Syracuse University Press was a joy to work with: Deborah Manion, acquisitions editor; Lisa Renee Kuerbis, the marketing coordinator; Lynn P. Wilcox, design specialist, whose beautiful cover so enhances the book; Ann Youmans, copy editor; Kay Steinmetz, editorial and production manager; Kaitlin Busser, editorial assistant. Deepest appreciation to Michael A. Boyd and his generosity in supporting this anthology. Of course, the writers are what make the book—my enormous thanks to each of them.

Introduction

WILLIAM H. PRITCHARD

Among the memorable formulations in Wordsworth's great preface to *Lyrical Ballads*, 1798, one may serve to characterize a common spirit in the essays collected here. His formulation attempts to define and celebrate what the Poet is and does:

He is the rock of defense for human nature, an upholder and preserver, carrying everywhere with him relationship and love. In spite of difference of soil and climate, of language and manners, of laws and customs, in spite of things silently gone out of mind, and things violently destroyed, the poet binds together by passion and knowledge the vast empire of human society, as it is spread over the whole earth, and over all time.

Twenty-eight years old when he composed this preface, the young Wordsworth calls upon his resources of eloquence and inclusiveness to conjure up this vision of universal strength and sympathy that, he believes, informs his and Coleridge's collection of poems. Never before in English criticism had such claims been unapologetically put forth.

These essays by contributors to the *Hudson Review* are naturally pitched in a lower key, and their concerns are pointed in many directions with no obviously central theme uniting them. But although "theme" is too inclusive a word for what binds them together, there is a pervading spirit that, while not to be confused with Wordsworth's matchless evocation of the Poet, is nevertheless comparable to it. Calling the spirit "literary awakenings" invites questions, since immediately the sophisticated reader, perhaps a professor of English, asks to know what's gained by evoking "literary," an old-fashioned word that must earn its keep if it's to have reputable value.

In the final item of this book, the veteran writer of familiar essays, stories, and biographical evaluations, Joseph Epstein, coming to the end of his essential, if impossible, attempt to locate the pleasures of reading, suggests that wide reading over time would or ought to confer on one "the literary point of view." He puts it in quotes, as if to assure us that he knows how slippery a subject he's taken on, but proceeds to make perhaps the very least claim that can be made about the subject: that the literary point of view "teaches a worldly-wise skepticism, which comes through first in a distrust of general ideas." And he quotes with approval Ortega y Gasset: "As soon as one creates a concept, reality leaves the room." But Epstein doesn't merely endorse a healthy skepticism about general ideas as the final reward of wide reading; instead he has the temerity to insist that the literary point of view teaches us profoundly, and that what it teaches is "the richness, the complexity, the mystery of life." Such a claim invites further derision from the sophisticated: "mystery," "richness," "complexity"—what are these words but an admission that the product of wide reading is beyond words, beyond the resources of language altogether? Yet in a slightly different vocabulary, Wordsworth would have known and approved of what Epstein is advocating, and he would have sympathized with his essay's title, "The Pleasures of Reading," since for Wordsworth the production of pleasure was the first and last task of the poet's art: "It is a homage paid to the native and naked dignity of man, to the grand elementary principle of pleasure, by which he knows, and feels, and lives, and moves."

Many of the essays gathered here describe various, disparate awakenings to the pleasures of poetry, that is, of literature. In a poem that serves as the book's epigraph, Jeffrey Harrison takes us to his car on the way to the grocery store, which trip gets derailed by his absorption in a CD he's listening to of Virginia Woolf's *To the Lighthouse*. He overshoots the store, then sits with the car idling, "because now she is going over it all again / though differently this time, with new details,

/ or from inside the mind of someone else, / as if each person were a hive, with its own murmurs and stirrings." Visiting this "hive" for the first or maybe the tenth time produces something—"something we can take / with us as we fly back out into honeyed daylight."

Such visitations and discoveries are a recurrent experience in this collection. Perhaps the most explicit example of discovery, of and within a literary work, is Seamus Heaney's example of Wordsworth, whose great poem "Resolution and Independence" provides the most striking instance of a meeting where the poet "comes faces to face with something or someone in the outer world recognized as vital to the poet's inner creative life." Heaney's title, "Apt Admonishment," alludes to the climactic moment in the poem when Wordsworth (surely in no disguise), having thought of "mighty poets in their misery dead" and realized that "As high as we have mounted in delight / In our dejection do we sink as low," runs into an old leech gatherer on the lonely moor. A curious conversation with him ensues (no direct words from the man's lips are given), then a rather ordinary portrait of a poor man making do as best he can by gathering leeches is displaced in a stanza of visionary raptness:

> The old Man still stood talking by my side;
> But now his voice to me was like a stream
> Scarce heard; nor word from word could I divide;
> And the whole body of the Man did seem
> Like one whom I had met with in a dream;
> Or like a man from some far region sent,
> To give me human strength, by apt admonishment.

What Heaney calls, in a fine phrase, "the great unglamorous strength of Wordsworth's verse," saves the day for the despondent poet by leading him out of himself in an experience of "estrangement" that somehow returns him to life with renewed powers. But it is not, or should not be, the poet alone who is the beneficiary of this power and renewal; an active reader may also be taken to a place he hasn't quite been before. Not just the Man's effect on Wordsworth but the poem's effect on that reader provides something like apt admonishment, an aesthetic response that is also a moral and human one, which gives us entry for a time into the grand, elementary principle of pleasure.

Perhaps the most telling account in these essays of an awakening to literature that is also an estrangement from one's previous life is Antonio Muñoz Molina's description of his education as a writer and a citizen, consequent upon his youthful wide reading that took him into political spaces he hadn't been before. Growing up in Franco's Spain, he became a student radical essentially because it involved carrying around "prestigious books" as an antidote to the regime's totalitarian immunity to them. Ironically the regime encouraged his awakening to politics as well as to writing; the freedom he and others eventually won was something that "had to be learned the hard way by us Spaniards, because there were no teachers on hand." As the essay's title makes clear, it was a "double education" and one that could not have been achieved except through an estrangement from the mundane, from an ordinary world where both literature and political freedom were absent.

More than one person, I suspect, has begun their career of wide reading as an attractive alternative to other worldly duties and social responsibilities. When a teacher in elementary school, trying to interest us in poetry, assured us that we were not escaping from the world but rather engaging with it in praiseworthy moral terms, I probably assented, not foreseeing how often my preoccupation with literature was at least partly a way of dodging commonplace tasks like raking leaves or mowing the lawn, or, later, avoiding the social swing of things. That literature thought of as an escape still carries a weight of opprobrium seems unjustified when, as is the case with more than one of these essays about literary discovery, the struggle to "escape" is a struggle to build a more substantial identity. It is not simply a matter of receiving "apt admonishment" from works of genius, *King Lear* or *Paradise Lost*, but from more homely, even poorly regarded books and writers. Igor Webb's loving account of his romance with the Horatio Hornblower novels has everything to do with the fact that he discovered these books as a young Holocaust survivor, emigrating with his parents from Slovakia to Quito, Ecuador, then to an apartment at the northern tip of Manhattan where the youth made his discovery. Webb had missed out on having stories read to him as a child, and his parents seemed unable to introduce him to the "right" books. So, he tells us, when he came upon the first paragraph of *Lieutenant Hornblower* and met "a tall and rather gangling individual, with hollow cheeks and a melancholy cast of countenance," he found a soul brother or father. As a boy Webb was a neat dresser (his mother was a seamstress), and he took Hornblower—"whose uniform looked as if it had been put on in the dark and not readjusted since"—to heart, no longer feeling confined to his status as a well-dressed youth. He cites Jane Eyre, stuck in her constrained life and traveling through books into new realms of possibility. What Webb calls the desire for "guidance" enabled him as an "uncertain Slovak boy" to keep company with the upstanding Captain Hornblower who, like the child Webb with memories of wartime terrors, met his own terrors as well and triumphantly overcame them.

An even more intense, somewhat morbid awakening to literature is recounted by Joyce Zonana's history of her fixation on Dickens' famous character from *The Old Curiosity Shop*, Little Nell, whose death made thousands weep. Zonana encountered the book as a child of ten living in a two-bedroom apartment in Brooklyn and became possessed by the novel through "passionate, deep reading." To say the book and its character had constituted an escape from herself would be too mild a word for how she was taken possession of as a "child surrounded by fears, simultaneously frightened of and fascinated by a grotesquely menacing world." Later on, living in Philadelphia a few blocks from the statue of Dickens and Little Nell in Clark Park, she was scarcely aware that the book and its author had exerted such a formidable influence on her. Her story is about the book as refuge, and in identifying with its heroine—an activity professors like me warn students against—she can't imagine what her childhood would have been like had she not met Little Nell: "A witness, my alter ego, the self who existed in language and gave me a home there as well." The title of her essay says it all, succinctly, "Nell and I."

To those awakened readers who go on to become professional teachers of literature, there must always be some tension between what the profession encourages or demands from the aspirant and the aspirant's unease with the professorial burden. More than one writer in this collection is moved to meditate on the satisfaction or dissatisfaction with what they perceive to be treatments of "English" that maintain themselves at the expense of the human values and truths literature presumably serves. The poet and professor David Mason looks back upon his literary experience in college and is dissatisfied by what he remembers:

> When I read poetry in college I was taught to be impersonal, always impersonal, as if to avoid contaminating what I read. Now it seems to me that the force of personality is every bit as important as the mastery of craft. Reading and writing are an invitation to a great untidy conversation that spans generations and cultures.

Mason lays the "impersonal" idea to T. S. Eliot's influential essay, "Tradition and the Individual Talent," which calls poetry an escape from personality rather than an expression of that personality. It has more than once been pointed out how Eliot's own untidy personal life at the time was responsible in part for the impersonal demand or doctrine. Often forgotten however is the sentence in Eliot's essay that follows his assertion about poetry being an escape from emotion, from personality: "But, of course, only those who have personality and emotions know what it means to want to escape from those things." So the "escape" is really a recognition of how rich and troubling is the life that gave impulse to it. In his essay "Writer and Region," and using *Huckleberry Finn* as his key book, Wendell Berry worries that the striving to be "free" may involve an inability to imagine community life. (Huck wants to light out for the territory ahead of anything that would restrain him.) To neglect the moral imperative of community is insufficiently to recognize the tragic life "lighting out" attempts to escape. Literature has human, social responsibilities, which, in that early essay, Eliot neglected.

Often the writer, the teacher, discovers something or somebody that makes him call into question his previous academic training. It was so with the poet and critic Dana Gioia when, as a graduate student at Harvard, he found in Robert Fitzgerald's approach to poetry a simplicity and elegance for which he was both unprepared and deeply grateful. Studying the *Odyssey* with Fitzgerald, Gioia realized "how much my critical education had alienated me from my own experience of literature." Although he doesn't specify exactly just what that critical education consisted of, it evidently did not include the "unorthodox and often subjective remarks" his new professor made. Invariably, Gioia writes, the teacher and his students considered features of the poem that Fitzgerald found moving and memorable but that were neglected by the more orthodox, sometimes mechanical, approach Gioia had grown up with.

Unorthodoxy and subjectivity come in many forms, one of the most extreme being what George Watson found in the great critic Sir William Empson. Known to most through his formidable dealings with poems in his first book, *Seven Types of Ambiguity*, Empson, in Watson's eyes, was a very unacademic teacher whose early training in mathematics as a Cambridge undergraduate preceded his literary career. That training, Watson suggests, permitted him to enter literary studies as an amateur, "and he kept the freedom of the amateur to the end of his days." One of the ways in which Empson's critical operation differed from, even disdained, more conventional approaches to literature showed itself in an "unquenchable propensity to be flippant," a quality that, he sometimes feared, "might persuade the world that he did not mean what he said or that what he said might not be worth attending to." Very different from Robert Fitzgerald's urbane elegance, Empson's incorrigibly witty, sometimes disheveled manner was partly a way of holding off solemn, more "professional" critical behavior.

A literary education gains in satisfaction and complexity when the reader is prompted, in respect or annoyance, to talk back to the writer, to the book. Any teacher knows how difficult it is to provoke students to talk back to the poem or novel they're engaged with; somehow this smacks of irreverence, as if it were inappropriate for youth to question the presumed wisdom of their elders. And often it's preferable for the inexperienced reader to take it slow before venturing into colloquy with the experienced author. Of course the back talk needn't have been provoked by a single text or writer; it may stem from an idea or convention that seems to have taken hold, not necessarily to the reader's benefit. Such a convention is criticized in Clara Claiborne Park's "Talking Back to the Speaker," an original take on things academic-literary whose title anticipates the sharp and entertainingly useful piece to come.

Some decades ago, teaching a course in Great Books at a community college, Park was somewhat taken aback by a question from a not particularly bright student. The class had been reading Homer, Plato, Dante, and the student, concerned about their respective views of the afterlife, asked her, since each writer had a different view, which one of them was "true"? Today, she writes, she could tell them in her wisdom how Plato's Socrates is a fictional speaker invented to serve a particular artistic purpose, and that there is a difference between Dante the author and "Dante" the speaker in the poem. Such a sensible and sophisticated critical practice, Park claims, would have enlightened the student by raising "wall after glass wall between him and these vanished human voices he had come to think had something to say directly to him." At present this convenient wall of "the speaker" is part of any student's literary equipment; they know, or will quickly learn, that you say "the speaker" and not "Frost says": "That it's not Shakespeare who worries he's growing old, not Donne who's saying good-bye to his lover, not Keats who talks to a vase." Soon the "locution of detachment" will become second nature, and they will be ready to take on Ford's *The Good Soldier* and its untrustworthy narrator.

Park argues plausibly that increasing sophistication of critical theorizing about what a poem is—crudely, words on the page rather than the utterance of a poet—has amounted to the poem's dissolution: "Dissolved in the persona, his poem scattered under new rubrics like 'tone' and 'imagery,' the student is no longer in a position to ask questions about the attitudes and convictions of a single human being." She notes as well, tellingly, that there is inconsistency even within proponents of the speaker rather than the poet: such as Reuben Brower in *The Fields of Light* or the influential *Understanding Poetry* by Cleanth

Brooks and Robert Penn Warren. In the 1960 edition of that textbook, Park notes, "Brooks and Warren did not completely banish the poet; though Keats was speakerized, Marvell and Yeats were left alone." Overall she finds a gain in subtlety to be a loss in human community for those naïve community college students "eager to take literature into their own lives." Yet it's interesting to realize that Park's own subtlety as teacher and theorist vivifies her subject, making it not merely a matter of technical mechanics but a useful inquiry into its human consequences.

In a *TLS* review of a book about literary life in England since the first world war, the reviewer, Kate McLoughlin, concludes with a salute to reading she calls *joie de lire*. What does this joy consist of, she asks, and answers by invoking "literature's unique ability to fire the imagination, extend mental worlds, dazzle with the use of language and convey one's human ideas and experiences to others across time and space." This seemed to me a good twenty-first-century attempt to find further terms for the grand elementary principle of pleasure that Wordsworth championed more than two hundred years ago. In a few of the essays collected here, their very title suggests an overbalance of pleasure, as in Judith Pascoe's tribute to *Clarissa*: "Before I Read *Clarissa* I Was Nobody: Aspirational Reading and Samuel Richardson's Great Novel." Her title aspires to inspire, as she accounts for her aspirational reading of the novel in various lively ways, including confessing toward the essay's close that one of the reasons she likes *Clarissa* so much is "for the same petty reason that I like *The Princess Casamassima*—because I've read it and not everyone has." Petty enough, but in its perhaps ignoble reason for loving a book, it stays with us.

Pascoe teaches the novel to students at the University of Iowa, but her real interest is not in furthering *Clarissa* scholarship by adding another item to its bibliography. Her motives are more cagey:

> These days, I read *Clarissa* so that I can teach the novel to undergraduates. I justify teaching a whole course on *Clarissa*, urging students through the novel at the rate of one hundred pages per week, by making grandiose pedagogical claims in my course

description. I say I will use the novel as a window onto eighteenth-century culture; I suggest its critical reception will allow me to delineate the major schools of twentieth-century literary theory. But that's just to impress the curriculum committee. The way I draw undergraduates in is by suggesting they will be initiated into the exclusive coterie of people who have read *Clarissa* in its entirety. You wouldn't think this kind of bald elitist appeal would play very well at a state university in Iowa.

The sheer mischievousness of this is itself a product of the literary education Pascoe has acquired through wide reading of books that among other things are filled with superb moments of ironic comedy—of the "worldly-wise skepticism" Joseph Epstein counts as one of the important results of wide reading.

Let us conclude this brief look-around at the essays with by all odds the book's shortest one, a mere five pages by Thomas M. Disch on Byron. It doesn't do much more than communicate Mr. Disch's enthusiasm for "My Roommate, Lord Byron," whose erotic exploits earn him the title of the "nineteenth century's most accomplished make-out artist." No one ever accused William Wordsworth of filling this bill. In fact Disch mentions Wordsworth in making his claim that Byron is "the most living of all the Dead White Males who wrote poetry. Keats will shiver your soul to a deeper depth, and Wordsworth elevate it to a higher altitude, but if you simply want to spend the night with your best friend, Byron's the man." For all the contrast in diction, Disch's reader (who is Disch himself in no disguise) is in search of that same principle of pleasure Wordsworth evoked so memorably. Disch concludes almost before he begins with a tribute to Byron's power—"he will open the door to his soul, and to yours too." But he qualifies that claim by admitting, in an appropriately witty way, that "with Byron it is sometimes hard to get a word in edgewise, but that's the problem of having a genius for a friend."

Literary Awakenings

Listening to Virginia

To the Lighthouse on CD

Driving around town doing errands,
I almost have to pull to the side of the road
because I can't go on another minute without
seeing the words of some gorgeous passage
in the paperback I keep on the passenger seat . . .
but I resist that impulse and keep listening
until it is almost Woolf herself sitting beside me
like some dear great aunt who happens to be a genius
telling me stories in a voice like sparkling waves
and following eddies of thought into the minds
of other people sitting around a dinner table
or strolling under the trees, pulling me along
in the current of her words like a twig riding a stream
around boulders and down foaming cascades,
getting drawn into a whirlpool of consciousness
and sucked under swirling into the thoughts of
someone else, swimming for a time among the reeds
and glinting minnows before breaking free
and popping back up to the surface only to discover
that in my engrossment I've overshot
the grocery store and have to turn around,
and even after I'm settled in the parking lot
I can't stop but sit there with the car idling
because now she is going over it all again
though differently this time, with new details
or from inside the mind of someone else,
as if each person were a hive, with its own
murmurs and stirrings, that we visit like bees,
haunting its dark compartments, but reaching
only so far, never to the very heart, the queen's
chamber where the deepest secrets are stored
(and only there to truly know another person),

though the vibrations and the dance of the worker bees
tell us something, give us something we can take
with us as we fly back out into honeyed daylight.

Jeffrey Harrison

PART ONE

Awakening to Literature

A Double Education

ANTONIO MUÑOZ MOLINA

While General Francisco Franco lay slowly dying in a hospital bed in Madrid in the late fall of 1975, I lay reading novels in a rented student's room more than three hundred miles to the south, in Granada. After a dictatorship of almost forty years, Franco's approaching demise cast a spell of uncertainty and hope over the whole country. It was a somber kind of hope because it depended solely on the grim progress of Death, not on any kind of military coup or popular uprising, like the one which had recently overthrown the even more ancient dictatorship in nearby Portugal. Throughout Spain, time seemed to have come to a standstill. Our lives dangled in a void, in a haunting no man's land, or rather no man's time, between the past that was about to end and a future postponed for yet another day every time we heard in the news that His Excellency, against all odds, was still breathing thanks to a new blood transfusion or yet another session of cruel and pointless surgery. No one could foresee what the future would bring; the past had lasted for so long that it seemed impossible to picture something substantially different from the dull political reality most of us had always known. When a dictatorship lasts for so long, people tend to take it for granted as a part of the natural order of things, like aging or decay.

Born in 1956, I had seen from the very first day I entered school Franco's pictures along with the crucifix presiding over our classrooms. Even for my parents' generation, life before the dictatorship was little more than a fading childhood memory mixed with the distant excitement of the war. Now, late in 1975, almost twenty years old, well into my third year at the university, I was kept awake at night by the confusing news updates about Franco's health on the radio, and by my passion for literature, the inexhaustible happiness of reading and the anguish of trying to write. In my mind's eye, I saw myself as both a writer and an anti-Franco activist. However, in the real world, I was neither. Frequently I did not even attend class.

Fear of being beaten up or arrested and then tortured by the political police prevented me from joining my more courageous friends who had become militants in the illegal Communist Party, or others who had drifted further left into the arcane but very active small Maoist or Trotskyite groups whose main concern seemed not to bring down the dictatorship but to denounce and "unmask" the common revisionist foe: the Communist Party, El Partido, as all of us used to say.

Franco was dying an appallingly slow death surrounded by doctors who tried to keep him more or less alive for as long as possible by way of gruesome operations and transfusions, but the ruthless repressive machine, so well-honed after four decades of practice, was still intact. It felt as if change was near, but only two months earlier, five presumed terrorists had been summarily shot after a mock military trial. Thousands of political dissidents spent long years in prison, and if a member of an illegal union or a left-wing activist were arrested, he would usually expect very harsh treatment. Plainclothes detectives, disguised as students in every classroom, kept their eyes and ears open, or so we thought at the time. Policemen in sullen grey uniforms—"Los grises," the grey ones—sometimes on horseback, patrolled the area around the university.

But you only had to step inside its courtyards to find yourself in an altogether different world, a kind of harbinger of the long-delayed future. Huge makeshift political posters covered the walls along the hallways, filled with handwritten statements about anything and everything: Communist, Maoist, Trotskyite manifestos; denunciations of police brutality or the complicity of the U.S. State Department with the dictatorships in Latin America; proposals to turn the university and the whole education system upside down, etc. A classroom discussion might develop spontaneously into a full-fledged political argument over the likelihood of the dictatorship of the proletariat, or over the convenience of abolishing capitalism in the same blow that would easily knock down Francoism if only we students joined forces with workers and peasants. With all those heated discussions and cigarette smoke shrouding everything, at times you felt as if you were inside a pressure cooker rather than in a classroom.

It seemed that Franco would never really die and things would forever remain unchanged. Nevertheless a different country was already coming to life in fits and starts around us; in classrooms and on campuses, on newsstands where daring political headlines and half-naked young women lured our attention; in bookstores that prominently displayed in their windows books about Third World revolutions, and thick Marxist tracts, including *Das Kapital* and Lenin's *State and Revolution*, not to mention the hallowed works of Foucault, Althusser, Mao Zedong, Antonio Gramsci, you name it. Attendance at a political rally might land you in a cell at a police station or even in prison, and the so-called Political-Social Brigade still upheld its frightening record of beatings and torture, but you could merely walk into a bookstore to steep yourself in Marxism-Leninism.

Some international films were famously banned, mainly on the grounds of their sexual explicitness, but for a young voracious reader no obstacles other than poverty prevented you from laying your hands and eyes on any book you might care for. Francoism was a most illiterate regime. By the early seventies, those in power paid so little attention to books that they probably didn't imagine that any kind of threat might come from them.

Conversely, for us radical students, carrying a book in your armpit or deep in the pockets of your winter coat was, in itself, an act of defiance, like growing a beard or wearing work boots, or smoking rough black tobacco instead of sweet-smelling imperialist American filtered cigarettes. There was a name for those who visibly carried around prestigious books, "sobacos ilustrados," "enlightened armpits." The most daring among us were already moving further ahead, reading

Wilhelm Reich instead of Lenin and smoking pot or hashish rather than attending seminars on the basic concept of historical materialism. But drugs would take a little longer to become part of the scene, and the much talked about upcoming sexual revolution seemed as far out of reach as the political one.

I have one more personal reason to remember those days. In the fall of 1975, while the whole country held its breath every time an unexpected news report was announced on the radio, I had the chance, for the first time in my life, to indulge my unlimited hunger for books: not just reading them, but buying them as well. After two years of squalor, surviving on a very meager income, on the cheapest food and in the shabbiest student lodgings, I had finally won a generous scholarship that allowed me to rent a decent room and start the school year in what seemed to me comparative splendor. Franco lay dying in Madrid, but down south in Granada, on a mid-November morning, after being paid the first installment of my scholarship, I stumbled out of the savings bank like a drunkard, feeling in my pocket an envelope swollen with green one thousand peseta bills. The first thing I did upon leaving the bank was to walk into a café-bar and sit on a stool, clearing my throat before ordering a meal fit for my new wealth: a glass of foamy blond cold Spanish beer and a beefsteak sandwich. But it sounds yummier in Spanish: *pepito de ternera*. Giddy, thanks to the beer, my belly full, exhaling the smoke from a Marlboro, as befit a potentate, I went on to my next stop on that shopping spree: the finest bookstore in town. Many times I had stared with envy into its large windows at the books I longed for but could not afford. Even now I remember the one I bought myself that morning, after painful deliberation, a victim of an acute embarrassment of riches, like a child left alone in a toy store. I bought, and still treasure, the two gorgeous volumes of George Painter's biography of Marcel Proust.

I took a bus for the long ride to the very distant working-class neighborhood where my rented room was located. I had not yet accomplished very much as an aspiring writer or as an ardent anti-Francoist militant, but I could succeed in the far more pleasant endeavor of becoming an insatiable reader. And succeed I did, beyond my wildest expectations. I read Proust, and I read about Proust; I read Faulkner, I read Mario Vargas Llosa, Borges, Onetti; I read Raymond Chandler, Julio Cortázar, Flaubert, Stendhal. Long after midnight, I turned off the light, so excited by my reading that sleep would not come.

I would leave my room to buy more books and return reading all the way on the bus. Half the time, for one reason or another, because of the national days of mourning after Franco's death or the holidays when the new king was sworn in, the university was closed, which suited me all right. Some other times, the non-tenured professors repeatedly went on strike, or some groups of students would declare themselves in permanent assembly as an act of protest against police repression. It was exciting to experience the thrill of a collective upheaval not unlike those in Paris or Berkeley that we had read so much about, but for me, however, it was even better to stay home and lie in bed reading for hours on end, even into the night, surrounded by the books that kept piling up all over my small room. I was divided between conflicting loyalties. I considered myself a Marxist, but I couldn't overcome my boredom the moment I dutifully tried to understand the arcane concepts of historical materialism or, even worse, dialectical materialism. I wanted to take part in the upcoming revolution, but at the same time the fear of being arrested and therefore losing my scholarship kept me away from any real involvement in radical politics. Proust mattered to me far more than Lenin. A fellow student caught me reading *Swann's Way* in the middle of an antiestablishment rally and looked at me sideways while hurling at me one of the worst insults: You are a revisionist, aren't you? I felt myself in the thick of things and at the same time far away. Only much later would I learn that seeing things both from close up and with a degree of detachment is a quite useful attitude for a novelist. Marching among placards and red flags felt great, but the solitude of my room and my books appealed to me with a far more intimate attraction.

Nothing can compare to the sudden awareness of the limitless treasures that literature offers to a young open reader. Halfway into a wonderful book you find another one that looks even more promising. You jump into a new world the moment you drop off the one you had been living in up to then. I read Vargas Llosa's *La casa verde* and got lost for days in the Peruvian Amazon rain forest. Then I'd switch to Faulkner's *Absalom, Absalom!*, and a huge vibrant new universe would open up in front of me, one that was as crowded with people as the real world, remote yet surprisingly familiar, with that ghostly civil war that loomed so large over the present.

Reading works best by infection. I had started reading Faulkner because Juan Carlos Onetti mentioned him as his master and hero. Thanks to Borges I came across Chesterton and allowed myself to indulge in crime fiction and detective stories. But when it came to crime fiction nothing surpassed the romantic cynicism of Raymond Chandler's Philip Marlowe. Reading *Madame Bovary* I grimly accepted that writing a masterpiece might take at least five years of solitary toil and suffering. But then I read *The Charterhouse of Parma* and learned, with puzzlement and some relief, that another masterpiece might be cheerfully completed in fifty-four days. I lay in bed, read novels, and smoked my expensive American cigarettes, trying to put aside a gnawing remorse for squandering my scholarship on books, for missing my classes and many of the political rallies at the university. I wanted to do my bit in the struggle for a vaguely communist future, but I also wanted to read all those books. Out of them some spark might eventually fire my imagination and overwhelm me with the gift of a story, even of a novel. All I had to do was stay long enough in that room, awake, if necessary, till the early hours of the morning, and then leave the pleasant idleness of reading for the upright discipline of writing: sitting in front of the typewriter, staring at a blank sheet of paper, the way real writers did.

My room was sunny and small and had a view of a tiny garden with very thin young trees, and beyond that of rooftops with clotheslines and TV antennae and of the stunning white peaks of the Sierra Nevada, which turned to a delicate pink at sunset, reminding me of a line from one of Lorca's poems: "Granada was a pink doe over the weather vanes." I read Lorca because very soon after George Painter's Proust and after the whole set of *À la recherche*, I had treated myself to the very expensive gift of a leather-bound edition of García Lorca's complete works. Almost forty years earlier, in Granada, García Lorca had been murdered by a Fascist death squad. And yet, in Granada, his presence, or his absence, could still be felt very strongly, when you passed the well-known house where he had gone into hiding after fleeing his family's estate, or when you took a bus to the nearby village of Fuente Vaqueros, where he had been born. There you asked around and someone pointed out his birthplace—the front of a whitewashed house with no plaque in his memory.

Less than a year later, in June 1976, seven months after Franco's death, I returned to Fuente Vaqueros not as a lonely and frightened visitor but among a crowd of thousands of people who flooded the huge central square carrying placards with García Lorca's portrait, our clenched fists raised, while we rhythmically sang the syllables of his name, in commemoration of his birthday, and of the fortieth anniversary of his murder. I, too, hammered my raised fist and shouted so loud that my throat went sore and my right arm ached. For the first time since 1936, a caravan of buses and cars had traveled the little more than ten miles between Granada and Fuente Vaqueros under the merciless June sun to cry freedom and celebrate the memory of Lorca; but along with the excitement of being part of such an overwhelming tide of people came the ever-present fear, the awareness of danger. Civil Guards wearing black helmets and holding rifles and submachine guns stood all along the road and could be spotted on the roofs of the buildings surrounding Fuente Vaqueros square, where the podium with the microphones and a large photo of Lorca had been erected. Promise and threat gripped your heart with a physical immediacy. The taste of freedom was even more tantalizing because at any moment it might be snatched away from us, throwing us back into the still so recent darkness of oppression. That first legal democratic rally many of us attended had been granted permission only on condition that it would last exactly sixty minutes and that no political banners or symbols other than Lorca's portrait and name would wave over the heads in the crowd. "After forty years of silence, they give us an hour," said the first speaker on the podium. We shouted our heads off and then turned our gazes to the clock in the church tower and then to the heavily armed guards who looked down on us from the rooftops. For the first time in our lives, we dared to stand up to them, but only for an hour. But what an hour it was. It had felt great to stay by myself in a room of one's own, but it was even better to stand in the middle of a crowd sharing its strength and its fear, experiencing the civic joy, the uplifting strength of a collective purpose.

Freedom and writing, those two thrilling gifts, had something in common: both had to be learned, and they had to be learned the hard way by us Spaniards, because there were no teachers on hand. It was both the predicament and the privilege of my generation that we had to learn them at once, with nobody to turn to for advice, no near example to use as a template for the future.

During one school year, life around us would change so fast that quite often one lost one's grip on reality. Everything that had been delayed for so many years seemed to turn up at once after Franco's death. New political parties and new magazines and new daily newspapers and new bold radio stations and new theater companies kept popping up all over the place. Time didn't run as a straight arrow from the past into the future. There was no clear watershed date to put your finger on and claim it was the starting point of a new era, no July 4th or July 14th or April 25th. There were days when the dark forces from the recent past loomed so large before us that they seemed about to return with a vengeance. But there were also days when we felt in our hearts that we had shaken off and left behind the stultifying atmosphere of dictatorship and isolation. On a sleepy Easter Saturday in April 1977 the news broke that the Communist Party had been legalized, and the empty holiday streets suddenly filled with an uproar of honking cars and cheerful crowds fearlessly waving red flags with the yellow sickle and hammer. On another unremarkable day, word went out among horny male students that a girlie magazine openly showing female pubic hair had just hit the newsstands, pornography being one of the unfailing by-products of the arrival of democracy, along with hard drugs. A free election, the first one since 1936, was held barely a year and a half after Franco's death, on June 15, 1977. Millions of Spaniards strolled peacefully to the polling stations to support with their votes the more moderate choices, wiping out in a single stroke the far-flung visionaries on the Right and the Left. I was bitterly disappointed by the outcome of that election, of course, like many of my fellow radical students. If the moderate Left and the mildly conservative center right took most of the seats in Parliament, what hopes did we have of overthrowing the capitalist system by electoral means?

But another kind of revolution was sending its seismic waves through the whole country. Without asking permission or following any clear political cues, people were changing their lives, cheerfully and courageously getting rid of the past, going their own way. Contraceptives became far easier to come by, and young liberated women sometimes made a point of openly boasting that they were on the pill. Men and women of my parents' generation, who had had to leave school when they were children at the outset of war, and who had worked so hard to make a living in the worst years of postwar squalor, signed up for night school, eager to catch up on a long denied and now available education. Workers, women, the unemployed marched proudly for their rights at a time of recession and bleak economic prospects because the country had been hard hit by the oil crisis and unchecked inflation. All of a sudden, two decades of banned international films appeared in movie theaters, even in provincial Granada. With the same eagerness with which I read books in my tiny rented room, I began to see those movies. They had as powerful an effect on my aesthetic education and narrative voice as did the novels. In the darkness of a movie theater images sent a lightning bolt down your spine, and I don't mean only an intellectual one. I watched with mesmerized attention *A Clockwork Orange*, *In the Realm of the Senses*, *Last Tango in Paris*, *Death in Venice*, *Amarcord*, *The Conformist*. But also wonderful Spanish films that dared to challenge the threat of censorship: *The Spirit of the Beehive*, *Poachers*, *Cousin Angelica*. The movies shattered my whole self down to my very roots. They came to an end, and the lights went on, and you left the movie theater blinking at the daylight, trying to imagine a way of living up to the expectations awakened by these films, feverishly searching for a style of writing that would match the power of their images.

New night spots with loud exciting music and shadowy depths were also popping up all over the city, and pretty soon one became acquainted with the sweetish reek of pot and hashish, mixed with the lethargic long winding melodies of symphonic rock. Those of us from the hardcore left frowned on these decadent novelties. Wasn't it shameful to indulge in artificial paradises instead of keeping up the struggle for a classless society?

One warm spring night, in the very heart of Catholic Granada, I witnessed a cheerful parade of young men with heavily rouged lips and made-up faces, wearing floating white linen jackets and pants and purple silk scarves. They crossed the street and instantly traffic came to a halt even though the light had not yet turned green. They carried a banner decorated with unknown initials: F.H.A.R. It took me some time to learn what those initials stood for: Homosexual Front for Revolutionary Action. In the very city where Lorca had been murdered forty years before because, among other things, of the way he didn't conceal his gay sexual identity, a gay parade was now stopping traffic.

You had to learn, and you had to learn fast. Your hands were full, and your mind had to work at a maddening speed. But what an opportunity to learn for an aspiring writer: what a need to make some sense of what keeps rushing around you and at the same time to take stock of the long suppressed past and to try to peek into the fast approaching future. Old Republican exiles were returning, and they brought with them the living memory of a period of history erased from the record for more than forty years but never truly lost. The fast pace of change turned obsolete overnight convictions and dogmas held sacred for too long. The present was neither as good as many had wished for nor as bad as many more had predicted—its flow and its whirlwinds impossible to grasp. "To see what is in front of one's nose needs a constant struggle," said George Orwell. Even now, more than thirty years later, it is difficult for me to come to terms with those days, to realize the full extent of our uncertainty as I try to rid myself of the benefits of hindsight.

We should be careful not to fall into the temptation of foretelling the past. A stable democracy was by no means the unavoidable outcome of those years of hope and turmoil in Spain. By 1977, the economy seemed on the brink of collapse. Basque terrorists and extreme left-wing terrorists and fascist terrorists were kidnapping and murdering people almost on a daily basis, and a weak government seemed unable to put an end to the bloodshed, send the terrorists to jail, and even to bring the still overwhelmingly Francoist army under effective civilian control. A plague of heroin was raging among the young in working-class neighborhoods all over the country.

As for me, I continue to wonder at the number of strokes of luck that had to pile up so that I could end up not only having my writing published but making a living out of it as well. Almost every day, throughout all those promising and confusing years, I tried my hand at writing, always unsuccessfully. After reading Vargas Llosa or Faulkner, I would lay out the ambitious plot for a novel; the scope of the attempt meant that it was bound to fail even before the first line was written. But failure was equally close at hand if I gave up on large formats and settled for the more modest accomplishment of short fiction, trying to follow the beloved example of Borges, who had said that instead of exhausting oneself writing an actual novel, one might as well write a short story about an imaginary long book.

Perhaps I was too young, read far too much, saw too many movies, so wrapped up in fiction in that little room of mine that I didn't pay enough attention to the real world outside the window, to the real people I came across but barely noticed. Literature can blur your vision as effectively, and as inadvertently, as the dogmas of ideology. One of the few things that can be effectively taught about the craft of writing is this: you need to set aside the tools of your trade, your books and notebooks and laptops and literary magazines or blogs, and humbly train yourself to look at things and people with your eyes wide open, to prick up your ears to learn good stories and hear the flow of living speech. You need daring, and you need patience, pride and humility, foolish ambition and down-to-earth sense.

I didn't accomplish anything in those years of feverish reading and political turmoil, but the seed of the story that would eventually develop into my first novel was planted back then, and it had a lot to do with the novels I loved and with the peculiar challenges my generation was forced to tackle: how to honor and retrieve the past without losing sight of the pressing demands of the present moment; how to make sense of our lives torn apart between the old world and the new, between our emotional allegiance to those who fought so hard to bring us up and our need to break free from them and embrace our own calling.

Learning to be a writer was as hard as learning to be a citizen. In both cases you engage yourself in a process with no clear end in sight. Even more so in those years I am trying to bring back to you here. We—young writers, newborn citizens—had to make it up as we went along, in the midst of daunting circumstances. Freedom must be learned, not in dreams but through hard practice. Regardless of how many books you may have read, the only way to learn how to write is to face life head on. Democracy too is an acquired taste that only the practice of democracy can breed. The subtle skills of tolerance, public discourse, free dissent take long to sink in, especially when a society has been deprived of them for two generations. Very few among us Spaniards, either on the Left or the Right, held serious democratic convictions around 1977. We didn't look forward to democracy. We stumbled on it.

And yet, all things considered, we didn't do that badly. For the first time in its history, Spain has had a stable and working democracy for more than thirty years. Not a perfect one, not one fully capable of uprooting corruption, or to come to terms with the past or to dispel the darkening economic prospect of the future. But a democracy all the same, with universal health care and universal education, without the death penalty or imprisonment for life, with equal rights for women, with gay marriage. One always needs to bear in mind where we started from in order to grasp fully how far we have come. This is perhaps the reason I am so fond of recalling the young man locked up in the room full of books, now and then opening, with enduring disbelief and remorse, the drawer where he kept his fast dwindling treasure of large green crackling bank notes.

And at the end of the day, what I have learned as a writer over all these years overlaps with some of the convictions I hold as a citizen. Nothing is ever granted to us, neither the books yet unwritten nor the future of our democracy; and the moment you take something for granted, be it inspiration or the rule of law, you are already losing it, because you neglect to care for it as much as you should; our personal lives and the narratives we spin out of them are always played out against the backdrop of public events that we cannot control and are seldom if ever fully aware of; the past lies shallowly hidden beneath the thin crust of the present and may come back to life at any moment; and it seems almost impossible to find a reasonable way of enjoying freedom without losing sight of how fragile it is, how easily it can be lost, or forsaken, or stolen, or given away. Somehow or other, be it in articles, in novels, or in this memoir, I keep coming back and poring over these few themes which encompass my life as a writer and a citizen.

"Apt Admonishment"
Wordsworth as an Example

SEAMUS HEANEY

The history of poetry contains many accounts of what might be called poetic recognition scenes, meetings where the poet comes face to face with something or someone in the outer world recognized as vital to the poet's inner creative life, and accounts of these meetings represent some of the highest achievements in the art. When a practitioner describes an encounter with a living or dead master, or an equivalent moment of epiphany, something fundamental is usually at stake, often having to do with poetic vocation itself. At the level of autobiography, such scenes record crucial events in the growth or reorientation of the poet's mind; at the mythic level, on the other hand, they can be read as evidence of a close encounter between the poet and the muse.

One way of describing the function of myth is to say that it puts us in touch with the eternal. If, for example, you are a Viking warrior going into battle wearing an amulet of Thor's hammer round your neck, then you become all the Viking warriors who have ever been; all the strength and warrior valor the god stands for are in you and with you. You have been brought beyond your uncertain individual self and turned into something fortified and potentially invincible.

This essay is based on a lecture delivered at the Morgan Library and Museum, June 8, 2006.

The warrior, needless to say, won't be conscious of things in this way and, if questioned, would be very unlikely to employ such lofty terms. For him, wearing an amulet of Thor's hammer is just another practice that comes with his culture, something so habitual he may not even register its supernatural implications. And yet, if the practice is in itself unremarkable, it nevertheless occurs in an uncommon perspective. The casual action has its origin in arcane mystery, an aura of the sacred glimmers in the background, and while the person involved may entertain no particular awareness of it, his actions are still deeply implicated in a solemn order of reality.

What I want to write about here are moments when poets are reminded that theirs too is a solemn calling and are made newly conscious of the powers they serve. And that is why I make mention at the very beginning of "the muse." Poets in the twenty-first century are unlikely to invoke her the way Homer invoked her; probably the last one to call upon her in any serious way was John Milton, for although by then the invocation had become thoroughly conventional, in Milton's case the convention was animated and in effect sanctified by his identification of the muse with the Holy Spirit of his three-person Christian God. And yet, in spite of the archaic nature of the muse phenomenon, the several encounters between the poet and the other which I'll be discussing still flicker with gleams of mythic light—a light which emanates from an original source in the opening lines of Hesiod's *Theogony*.

Hesiod's dates are as uncertain as Homer's (probably sometime in the late eighth or early seventh century BC), although there is firm enough evidence that he was a farmer from the countryside in Boeotia, a man whose life was changed when the Muses, the daughters of memory, appeared at the head of his field and called him to a new task—which task would in turn confer upon him a new authority. A recent prose translation gives Hesiod's account of how he was chosen from among the other "field-dwelling shepherds" on Mount Helicon, those "mere bellies" unworthy of the laurel and the gift of inspiration:

> Let us begin to sing from the Heliconian Muses, who possess
> the great and holy mountain of Helicon and dance on their soft feet

around the violet-dark fountain and the altar of Cronus' mighty son. And after they have washed their tender skin in Permessus or Hippocrene or holy Olmeius, they perform choral dances on highest Helicon, beautiful, lovely ones, and move nimbly with their feet. Starting out from there, shrouded in thick invisibility, by night they walk, sending forth their very beautiful voice . . .

One time, they taught Hesiod beautiful song while he was pasturing lambs under holy Helicon. And this speech the goddesses spoke first of all to me, the Olympian Muses, the daughters of aegis-holding Zeus: "Field-dwelling shepherds, ignoble disgraces, mere bellies: we know how to say many false things similar to genuine ones, but we know, when we wish, how to proclaim true things." So spoke great Zeus' ready-speaking daughters, and they plucked a staff, a branch of luxuriant laurel, a marvel, and gave it to me, and they breathed a divine voice into me, so that I might glorify what will be and what was before, and they commanded me to sing of the blessed ones who always are, but always to sing of themselves first and last.

So, with Hesiod's foundational story in mind, let me repeat what I said at the start: poetic recognition scenes can be read at one level as significant biographical moments—"crucial events in the growth or reorientation of the poet's mind; at the mythic level, on the other hand, they can be read as evidence of a close encounter between the poet and the muse." And yet these moments of realization do not always or necessarily involve a face-to-face encounter with some great poetic forebear. In the modern era, the sense of visitation and rededication will often derive from meetings and occasions which are far less exalted but which are nevertheless bathed in an uncanny light, occasions when the poet has been, as it were, unhomed, has experienced the *unheimlich*.

Even in the modern period, however, the poet typically comes away from such encounters with a renewed sense of election, surer in his or her vocation. What is being enacted or recalled is usually an experience of confirmation, of the spirit coming into its own, a door being opened or a path being entered upon. Usually also the experience is unexpected and out of the ordinary, in spite of the fact that it occurs in the normal course of events, in the everyday world. A strange thing happens. A spot of time becomes a spot of the timeless, becomes, in effect, one of "the hiding places of [the poet's] power."

In the first canto of *The Divine Comedy*, for example, when Dante meets the shade of Virgil, he is not immediately aware that heaven has intervened to send the Latin poet to be his guide, yet a high sense of mystery and destiny does nevertheless prevail; and when, in "Little Gidding," T. S. Eliot meets a familiar ghost in the dawn light after an air raid in wartime London—a ghost whom Eliot thought of as an emanation of the recently dead William Butler Yeats—there is a similar feeling of mystery and destiny in surroundings that are entirely matter of fact. In both cases, the sense of rare occasion is present in the way the language goes a little bit beyond its usual operations: Dante meets Virgil "*là dove 'l sol tace*"—"where the sun is silent"—and his appearance "*per lungo silenzio parea fioco*"—"seemed faint through long silence"; and in a passage which directly imitates and pays homage to the art of Dante, Eliot says of the stranger he meets "in the uncertain hour before the morning" that he had

> the sudden look of some dead master
> Whom I had known, forgotten, half recalled
> Both one and many; in the brown baked features
> The eyes of a familiar compound ghost
> Both intimate and unidentifiable.

Dante and Eliot, of course, are highly self-conscious artificers, and the contexts in which they situate these encounters are unapologetically literary. Your response to what's happening in each case will be enhanced if you happen to know and have a feel for the history of poets and poetry. Neither of them resorts to the ancient invocation of the Muses, but both signal the elevated nature of their experience by recourse to idioms and allusions drawn from the world of high culture. In each case, we are immediately aware that what is at stake is Vocation with a capital V.

Yet direct literary allusion and the appearance of great literary forebears are not the only ways in which poets situate themselves spiritually and artistically. In the age of Freud, there was a far more fluid awareness of the sources of inspiration, a much greater readiness to locate the radiance of the gift in those very areas of the psyche that have been the most repressed. D. H. Lawrence's snake, for example, in the poem of that name, is surely a messenger from the hiding place of his own gift, a gift whose operations, Lawrence believed, were obstructed and deformed by the conventional processes of education and socialization. The snake emerges from a fissure in the earth-wall and trails his slack body down to the water-trough, drinks from it and is then about to withdraw.

At which point, Lawrence tells us, he picked up a clumsy log and threw it at the water-trough with a clatter, scaring the snake so that the "part of him that was left behind convulsed in undignified haste. / Writhed like lightning and was gone." "And immediately," the poet goes on, "I regretted it. / . . . I despised myself and the voices of my accursed human education." Which is to say that he realized instinctively that he had sinned against his gift, broken his covenant with the powers in the hiding place, and, as he says in the last lines of the poem, had "something to expiate, / A pettiness."

It is Lawrence's sixth sense that tells him he has something to expiate, and unless a poet continues to follow this sixth sense, he or she is never going to be entirely sure of the creative ground. And the reason for this is fairly obvious and fairly simple and was stated with characteristic directness by the late Ted Hughes. A poet's first duty, Hughes wrote, is to his gift, and yet, as he also wrote,

> Many considerations assault [the poet's] faith in the finality, wisdom and sufficiency of his gift. Its operation is not only shadowy and indefinable. It is intermittent. It has none of the obvious attachment to publicly exciting and seemingly important affairs . . . in which his intelligent contemporaries have such confidence, and so it receives no immediate encouragement.

And Hughes goes on:

Certain memories, images, sounds, feelings, thoughts, and the relationships between these, have for some reason become luminous at the core of his mind: it is in his attempt to bring them out, without impairment, into a comparatively dark world, that he makes his poems.

For a dedicated poet, in other words, the achievement of a true poem is a way of establishing self-worth in a world that does not necessarily regard poetry as being of any great worth in itself. Let me therefore proceed to consider a poem which had just such resolving effect on the poet who wrote it, a poem by Wordsworth now known canonically as "Resolution and Independence," but originally referred to by the poet and his circle as "The Leech Gatherer." The incident upon which the poem is based was recorded by the poet's sister in her Grasmere journal.

"We met an old man almost double," Dorothy Wordsworth writes on October 3, 1800. "He had on a coat thrown over his shoulders.... Under this he carried a bundle and had an apron on and a night cap. His face was interesting. He had dark eyes and a long nose ... He was of Scotch parents but had been born in the army. He had had a wife, 'a good woman, and it pleased God to bless us with ten children.' All these were dead but one, [a sailor] of whom he had not heard for many years.... His trade was to gather leeches, but now leeches are scarce and he had not the strength for it. He lived by begging and was making his way to Carlisle, where he would buy a few godly books to sell. He said leeches were very scarce partly owing to this dry season, but many years they have been scarce ... Leeches were formerly 2/6 [per] 100; they are now 30/. He had been hurt in driving a cart, his leg broke his body driven over, his skull fractured."

Even in the Wordsworths' time, the occupation of leech gathering was dying out, and the character in William's poem, who is recognizably the one described here and who presumably sold leeches to members of the medical profession, is now facing a drastic economic crisis. But when William comes to write about him, his concern is not primarily with the old man's economic prospects. What the poet is engaged on, after all, is dream work, not documentary. What absorbs him, what awakens his imagination and his powers of incantation is the equanimity with which the old man faces his crisis:

> Himself he propped, his body, limbs and face,
> Upon a long grey shaft of shaven wood,
> And still as I drew near with gentle pace
> Beside the little pond or moorish flood,
> Motionless as a cloud the old man stood
> That heareth not the loud winds when they call,
> And moveth altogether, if it move at all.
>
> At length, himself unsettling, he the pond
> Stirred with his staff, and fixedly did look
> Upon the muddy water, which he conned
> As if he had been reading in a book;
> And now such freedom as I could I took,
> And drawing to his side, to him did say,
> "This morning gives us promise of a glorious day."
>
> A gentle answer did the old man make,
> In courteous speech which forth he slowly drew,
> And him with further words I thus bespake,
> "What kind of work is that which you pursue?
> This is a lonely place for one like you."
> He answered me with pleasure and surprise,
> And there was while he spake a fire about his eyes.
> . . . .
> He told me that he to this pond had come
> To gather leeches, being old and poor—
> Employment hazardous and wearisome!
> And he had many hardships to endure;
> From pond to pond he roamed, from moor to moor,
> Housing, with God's good help, by choice or chance,
> And in this way he gained an honest maintenance.

> The old man still stood talking at my side,
> But now his voice to me was like a stream
> Scarce heard, nor word from word could I divide;
> And the whole body of the man did seem
> Like one whom I had met with in a dream,
> Or like a man from some far region sent
> To give me human strength by apt admonishment.

Here, as in the case of Hesiod, of Dante, of Eliot, of Lawrence, and, one might add, of Elizabeth Bishop who, when she looked through the window of her bus, saw into the big othering eyes of a moose that had come out of the *selva oscura* of the Maine woods—here, as in all those cases, the admonishing agent is one who appears in a haunted, dreamy light, like a messenger "from some far region sent." We participate in an experience of absorption in another life: in each case, the poet arrives on the scene either abstracted or disoriented and is then brought more fully alive to his or her obligations and capacities—is helped, in fact, to get back in touch with his or her proper poetic gifts. The writing has a mesmeric effect, and one senses that the composition of the poem must have had a similar self-mesmerizing effect upon the poet: "Certain memories, images, sounds and feelings, and the relationship between these, have [indeed] become . . . luminous at the core of [each] poet's mind," and the encounter serves to remind him or her of the priority of those memories and images and the poetic obligation he or she owes to them—the obligation, that is, to bring these personally vital bits of psychic life out "without impairment, into a comparatively dark world."

Ted Hughes was right to stress what he called the luminous aspect of such memories and images and to insist that they are not one-off, chance occurrences but belong together in a web of relationships and are interrelated as part of an overall system of gravitation and association. The leech gatherer, for example, was connected subliminally in Wordsworth's mind with several other solitary figures who had appeared to him in the ordinary course of his life, and who all attained a visionary dimension in his poetry subsequently. In William's reimagining of their meeting, of course, the old man is singularly isolated, a figure who looms up against a vast moorland background, but as we can see from Dorothy's journal, when the Wordsworths actually encountered him, they were all walking on the public road; and in fact it is instructive to compare Dorothy's typically swift, alert, on-the-spot annotation of their encounter with the poet's later re-envisaging of it.

The two accounts represent not only two kinds of writing but two orders of achievement, and as such they provide a way of commenting upon the exemplary nature of William Wordsworth's art. The two orders might be characterized as the observational in the case of the journal entry and the imaginative in the case of "Resolution and Independence." Both writings are about meeting a person at once destitute and dignified, but one is a little dossier of information about the leech gatherer as an individual broken and bent by circumstance, whilst the other is a presentation of the same man not just an individual case but, in a manner of speaking, as the very measure of man.

Dorothy is, as ever, vividly in sympathy with the figure in front of her, but the figure is still, we might say, drawn from the model. He is the focus of the writer's daytime understanding, a life study, so to speak, but not a double, no way an inhabitant of the mythic or the oneiric world. On the other hand, what distinguishes the figure of the leech gatherer as he appears in "Resolution and Independence" is precisely this aura of strangeness, this sense that the figure is not a sociological specimen being observed and presented as a symptom of an ill-divided society, but rather somebody who has entered the poet's consciousness as a dream presence, an emanation or, to employ Wordsworth's own word again, an "admonition":

> The old man still stood talking at my side:
> But now his voice to me was like a stream
> Scarce heard; nor word from word could I divide;
> And the whole body of the man did seem
> Like one whom I had met with in a dream:
> Or like a man from some far region sent,
> To give me human strength by apt admonishment.

Wordsworth finished the first draft of "The Leech Gatherer" on May 9, 1802,[1] but even in this one stanza there is enough to remind us of this poet's extraordinary gift of sympathy and the great unglamorous strength of his verse. Here again we are listening to poetry that vindicates the claims Wordsworth would make in his preface to the eighteenth edition of *Lyrical Ballads*. In that document, in words which have become familiar but are never stale, he declared:

> The principal object, then, which I proposed to myself in these poems was to choose incidents and situations from common life and to relate or describe them, throughout, as far as was possible, in a selection of language really used by men; and, at the same time, to throw over them a certain coloring of imagination, whereby ordinary things would be presented to the mind in an unusual way; and, further, and above all, to make these incidents and situations interesting by tracing in them, truly though not ostentatiously, the primary laws of our nature.

It's a wonderful manifesto, and it describes accurately the appeal and exemplary quality of Wordsworth's poetry, particularly in passages like the ones I've just cited. In such instances, the poet does precisely what he promises to do: he traces primary laws rather than dictates them, the law in this case being the one that says human beings, given the right conditions, have an immense and heartbreaking capacity for dignified endurance; and furthermore, to witness such endurance helps the rest of us also to endure. Yet Wordsworth does not force this conclusion; instead he divines and feels his way towards it. The coloring of imagination, as he calls it, means that a remembered incident is helped to develop into a poem in the language—all in good time and yet ahead of its time. Before Freud comes along to define the uncanny, before Joyce fixes upon his notion of the epiphany, before Lawrence puts his trust in the promptings of his creatureliness rather

---

1. Mary Moorman, *William Wordsworth: A Biography: The Early Years, 1770–1803* (Oxford: Oxford University Press, 1957), 544.

than the voices of his education, Wordsworth finds a way to bridge the gap between the quotidian and the visionary worlds, between a world where the conventions of social exchange issue in words like "This morning gives us promise of a glorious day" and one where human words are heard within a new and haunting acoustic and human presence is backlit with gleams from a world of enduring forms.

Much, much more could be said and should be said about "Resolution and Independence," but at this point I want to pass on, in conclusion, to a poem of my own which was written thirty-six years ago, during the Easter holidays of 1970. It is called "The Tollund Man," and it could carry as its epigraph the lines, "And the whole body of the man did seem / Like one whom I had met with in a dream." And yet the whole body of the man who inspired my poem had appeared to me only in photographs. In fact, by the time the poem got written, all that remained of the body in question was a head, preserved nowadays in a display case in a small museum in Jutland, at Silkeborg, not far from the city of Aarhus in Denmark. But those photographs had an effect on me comparable to the effect of the leech gatherer on Wordsworth. It was as if the Tollund Man and I had come from far away to a predestined meeting: a meeting where there was something familiar between us yet something that was also estranging and luminous.

The figure in question had been known to the world in general since the evening in May 1950 when he was dug up out of a bog at Tollund by two old brothers cutting peat for their kitchen range. I first met the Tollund Man, however, in a book published in 1969, a translation of a work by the Danish archaeologist P. V. Glob, entitled in English *The Bog People*, but the effect of the meeting was instantaneous. Opening Glob's book was like opening a gate, crossing a line into a new field where the air was headier, the ground more mysteriously ancestral, the sense of scope altogether more ample. I was entranced first and foremost by the image of the old Dane's head and face, seen in black and white, in almost life-size close-up. The man had been strangled, and around what remained of his neck there was a coil of rope, yet the features were beautifully in repose. The look of serenity may have been produced by the pressure of the bog over the course of fifteen or twenty centuries, although there was speculation that the resigned expression came from the fact that the man had been a willing participant in a fertility rite. This, Glob suggested, could have involved his being betrothed to the goddess of the earth, being paraded on a wagon as her bridegroom, and being bedded down with her in the bog—so that spring should return and the cycle of nature be renewed.

For whatever reason, however, there was indeed a rare vulnerability about the wrinkles of the man's brow, his demure mouth, his slightly bristled upper lip, and the faint glisten of the skin on his closed eyelids. I knew from the scientific evidence that this was the head and face of a northern European countryman of the Iron Age, preserved in the peat for the best part of two millennia, yet he felt as close to me as a contemporary, as familiar as my Great Uncle Hughie, who had a similar bristle on his long upper lip and a similar weathered look that suggested both stoicism and a capacity for survival. At the same time, the head had the stillness and focus of a votive object. It did not appear like human remains. It invited contemplation, seemed capable of putting one in touch with the timeless. And yet if it could have spoken, it looked as if it might have said the kind of thing that my country elders had once been in the habit of saying. "Aye, times are hard, young Heaney," it might have remarked, "but then, aren't we hard too?"

By Easter 1970 times were indeed hard in Northern Ireland, and becoming steadily harder. Two years before, in the city of Derry, a Civil Rights march had been baton-charged by the Royal Ulster Constabulary, and that clash started off a chain of events which drove the inhabitants of the place back into the fierce, frozen, ineffectual political and sectarian attitudes that for a little while in the mid-sixties had shown some signs of thaw. Now, however, the local Unionist administration had so mishandled the Nationalist minority's protests and demands for a new dispensation that the IRA had re-formed as the Provisional IRA. The Provisionals straightway resumed their armed struggle against what they regarded as the British occupation of Northern Ireland, the British Army arrived to take them on, and as I wrote at the time, we were all of a sudden "hug[ging] our little destiny again."

That phrase occurred in the dedicatory verse to my third collection, *Wintering Out* (1972), but the poem in the book which really took the measure of the times was "The Tollund Man." Although it rehearses different images of death and atrocity committed in the course of twentieth-century Irish wars of independence and attrition, the main focus of the poem is on the iconic head, a head which had the same kind of brown baked features as Eliot's familiar compound ghost, and which possesses to this day the same look of being "forgotten, half-recalled, both one and many." And just as Eliot fixed what he called "a pointed scrutiny" on the face of his dawn walker, so I gazed with complete entrancement at my familiar ghost, as if he were indeed "a man from some far region sent / To give me human strength by apt admonishment." This, then, is the poem:

I
Some day I will go to Aarhus
To see his peat-brown head,
The mild pods of his eye-lids,
His pointed skin cap.

In the flat country nearby
Where they dug him out,
His last gruel of winter seeds
Caked in his stomach,

Naked except for
The cap, noose and girdle,
I will stand a long time.
Bridegroom to the goddess,

She tightened her torc on him
And opened her fen,
Those dark juices working
Him to a saint's kept body,

Trove of the turfcutters'
Honeycombed workings.

Now his stained face
Reposes at Aarhus.

II
I could risk blasphemy,
Consecrate the cauldron bog
Our holy ground, and pray him
To make germinate

The scattered, ambushed
Flesh of labourers,
Stockinged corpses
Laid out in the farmyards,

Tell-tale skin and teeth
Flecking the sleepers
Of four young brothers,
Trailed for miles along the lines.

III
Something of his sad freedom
As he rode the tumbril
Should come to me, driving,
Saying the names

Tollund, Grauballe, Nebelgard,
Watching the pointing hands
Of country people,
Not knowing their tongue.

Out there in Jutland
In the old mankilling parishes
I will feel lost,
Unhappy and at home.

 Two years after the publication of *Wintering Out*, I gave a lecture in London to members of the Royal Society of Literature. In it I said, "When I wrote ['The Tollund Man'] I had a completely new sensation, one of fear. It was a vow to go on pilgrimage and [as it came to me] I felt . . . that unless I was deeply in earnest about what I was saying, I was simply invoking dangers for myself."

This may have been a somewhat melodramatic declaration, but the minute I wrote the lines, "Some day I will go to Aarhus / To see his peat-brown head / the mild pods of his eye-lids / His pointed skin cap," I found myself in a new field of force. It emanated from an aura that surrounded the head, an aura supplied no doubt by stories I used to hear in my Catholic childhood about the undecayed flesh of a dead body being a sign of sainthood in the living person, emanating also, perhaps, from the image of the face of Christ on Veronica's napkin—the napkin with which she was supposed to have wiped his bleeding features as he made his way to Calvary. But here in a twentieth-century museum were the actual features of a sacrificial victim, a man of sorrows, a man who could have been my neighbor, one whose outer looks seemed to be an inviolable image of the inner state I and others shared silently in those days, "lost, unhappy and at home."

And yet the contemplation of the face and the writing of the poem had a pacifying effect. The spirit felt less alone. Not consoled but stayed, in the words of Robert Frost, "against confusion." And here I would go back once more to Wordsworth and notice that he begins his poem about the leech gatherer in a mood which he calls "despondency," a mood haunted by thoughts which he calls "untoward," and further notice that he ends absolved of these feelings, in a frame of mind that is now full of a new resolution and independence: from now on, as a result of his meeting with the old man but also of his having written the poem, Wordsworth will be inhabited, in a manner of speaking, by his inner leech gatherer and will re-enter the usual life in a spirit that is better prepared and better disposed. When the old man has ended his discourse, which, says Wordsworth, was "cheerfully uttered, with demeanour kind," the poet declares,

> I could have laughed myself to scorn to find
> In that decrepit man so firm a mind.

"God," said I, "be my help and stay secure.
I'll think of the leech gatherer on the lonely moor."

This is an example of what the writing of a poem can do: it can lead the writer out of himself or herself, provide an experience of estrangement, and then resituate him or her in the usual life, bemused, as it were, as if for a moment the gift for uttering truth had been possessed, as if from a laurel tree luxuriantly in bloom the Muses broke a branch and gave it for a staff and breathed a sacred voice into the mouth. Or to make the case more autobiographically, with reference to "The Tollund Man": here was a poem written at a time when the literary scene in Northern Ireland was buzzing with debate about how the poets should be responding to the crisis in their society, a time when symposia were sizzling with the contributions of intelligent contemporaries and the ideologues were full of intensity about these exciting public events. And in that confusing Babel, my total immersion in the element of the bog man was a reminder of the necessary extra dimension and the truly credible order of poetry itself.

Needless to say, when I was writing "The Tollund Man" (the first draft came swiftly), I was not thinking of Wordsworth or Hesiod or Eliot or the Muses. When I call Wordsworth an example, I just mean to cite his poem "Resolution and Independence" as an instance of something constant in the poetic life, something indeed that is indispensable to it. Call it apt admonishment, call it contact with the hiding places, call it inspiration, call it the staying power of lyric, call it the bringing of memories that are luminous into the relatively dark world, call it what you like, but be sure it is what a poet's inner faith and freedom depends upon. And the myth of his own meaningfulness among those intelligent contemporaries depends upon it also.

The Poem and the Path

ANDREW MOTION

Edward Thomas

Edward Thomas was the first poet I fell in love with; I was sixteen, from a country background in which books and writing played no significant part, and felt he was speaking to me about things I knew. Hedges, fields, woods, the sky at evening, aspen trees, elm trees, sedge warblers, paths. Paths especially, and paths of all kinds. Little flint-studded tracks, hill roads wet with rain, winding routes into the dark heart of forests, straight foot-beaten ways across the tops of bare downs. Even to someone like my teenage self, who had no confidence as a reader of poems, it was clear that everything Thomas wrote was in one way or another to do with traveling—with being on the move and noticing as he moved, with fleeing the self and tracking the self, with journeying through life. And, moreover, with traveling through a landscape which, however grand and large its symbolic values might be, was always exactly detailed and local. That is why I took to him so strongly: he made me feel I had walked up to the largest and most abstract things in my head, but that when I looked down at my shoes, they were covered in real raindrops, real grass flecks, real dust.

In the forty years since I first read Thomas, my love for his writing has deepened continuously: he is one of the handful of poets I find

First presented as a series of talks on BBC Radio 3's *The Essay*, January 4–8, 2010.

absolutely necessary. By now, of course, I know a lot more about him than I did back in my A level classroom. I know, among other things, that his path poetry forms part of a great tradition of writing about walking; I also know how it reflects the likings and loyalties of his own life. He was a restless man whose wanderlust was confined largely to the South Country of England (with occasional excursions into Wales, where he felt an ancestral allegiance). And this restlessness was the expression of a paradox which has never lost its power to engross and move me. That is to say, Thomas simultaneously felt himself to be "an old inhabitant of earth"—someone who had the most profound sense of belonging to his country and knew the names and natures of its landscape very intimately—and at the same time someone who felt modern industrialized life had uprooted him: he referred to himself as "a superfluous man."

For all these reasons, it feels right to look on the paths in Thomas' poems as things which give very mixed messages. They are places of respite as well as travail, of delight as well as anxiety, of certainty as well as uncertainty, of beginning as well as ending. Because he was writing poetry in the early years of World War I, his paths all lead to France. Because he was writing in the eye of eternity, they all lead to "the unfathomable deep / Forest where all must lose / Their way." On the other hand, because he was writing as a countryman, his paths also lead to certain consolations: they present us with emblems of human endurance and durability, despite their inevitable destinations.

We will find other poets reaching similar conclusions in all the other poems I am writing about in this series—though admittedly not always in the context of the English countryside. Saying this means confronting something recurrent in human behavior, and also something stable in the way that paths have been treated in poems down the generations. I want to have a quick look at this before coming back to Thomas.

Poetry and paths have been natural partners. We hear the rhythm of human feet in the movement of feet in a line; we see the journey in poetry as abiding proof of human curiosity, adventure, and identity-making. It is there in the track of Homer's journeys, in the war-treks of

Beowulf, in the strange travels of the Green Knight, in the pilgrimage of Chaucer's society-in-miniature, and in the displacements of Shakespeare's lovers and soldiers and statesmen. I sketch all this because there is a tendency for us to think of the link between poetry and traveling (and especially of poetry and walking) as a marriage that was made during the Enlightenment. But it is not the brand-new thing that implies. The link between poetry and paths is a very ancient thing, as ancient as the hills. It was not established during the Enlightenment; it was revitalized by the Enlightenment—by Rousseau (who says in his *Confessions*: "I can only meditate when I am walking. When I stop, I cease to think, my mind only works with my legs"), and later by Wordsworth. By the time he and the other Romantic poets began to have their say, they were conscious of inheriting a long, complex, and invigorating tradition and of having adapted it to manifest a new kind of certainty. The certainty that the individual mattered, that democracy mattered. To walk was to assert the primacy of the self. Paths were the lifelines the self used to gather and ratify its importance.

Having said that Wordsworth was not the first person to understand this, I immediately need to say he understood it more deeply than most people who had lived before him. It has been estimated that he walked about 180,000 miles in the course of his long life, and the effect, implications, and opportunities of walking feed virtually all the poems he wrote. Walking is, indeed, precisely the means by which he wrote—striding up and down, composing aloud (he called it "bumming"). It gives vital structure and impetus to the language and philosophy of masterpieces like "Tintern Abbey," "The Leech Gatherer," and the whole of *The Prelude*. Everywhere you look in his poems, you see the footprint of a walking man and some sort of tribute to the paths, tracks, and roads he has passed along. "I love a public road," he says:

> I love a public road: few sights there are
> That please me more; such object hath had the power
> O'er my imagination since the dawn
> Of childhood, when its disappearing line,

Seen daily afar off, on one bare steep
Beyond the limits which my feet had trod
Was like a guide into eternity,
At least to things unknown and without bound.

The opening phrase of this passage ("I love a public road") is one to which Edward Thomas pays homage in his own very beautiful and sinuous lyric "Roads": "I love roads," it begins: "The goddesses that dwell / Far along invisible / Are my favourite gods." This kind of reference is typical Thomas. His poems seem and sound completely natural, completely un-literary, and yet in truth are little echo chambers, containing acts of homage to Romantic poets and other writers whose own enthusiasms confirmed his preoccupation with walking and the means of walking. As well as Wordsworth, we see the footprint of Hazlitt, Coleridge, De Quincey, Thoreau and Emerson, Richard Jefferies, and his contemporary countrymen such as W. H. Hudson. Thomas' poems, in other words, score their success as hymns to and accounts of walking by allowing themselves to be walked through by sympathetic others. The weight of a welcome ancestry helps press them into shape.[1]

Part of that ancestry, and in a way that is unique in English poetry, is self-engendered. That is to say, many of the quotations that appear in Thomas' poems come from the prose books he wrote in the earlier part of his life before turning to poems in the last two-and-a-bit years before he was killed in 1917. This is certainly and valuably the case with the poem I am writing about here—a poem called "Old Man," which was only the third poem Thomas wrote, on December 6, 1914. I recorded it for the BBC last summer when I went to visit the house in which it was written, in the village of Steep in Hampshire. Afterwards, I walked up the beech hangar behind the house to stand by the memorial stone on the part of the hill known as the Shoulder of

---

1. I am indebted to *Wanderlust: A History of Walking* by Rebecca Solnit (London: Verso, 2006) for much of the historical context provided in these essays.

Mutton. The July breeze came through the trees like an express train, while cloud shadows blobbed and melted across the fields below.

Old Man

Old Man, or Lad's-love,—in the name there's nothing
To one that knows not Lad's-love, or Old Man,
The hoar-green feathery herb, almost a tree,
Growing with rosemary and lavender.
Even to one that knows it well, the names
Half decorate, half perplex, the thing it is:
At least, what that is clings not to the names
In spite of time. And yet I like the names.

The herb itself I like not, but for certain
I love it, as some day the child will love it
Who plucks a feather from the door-side bush
Whenever she goes in or out of the house.
Often she waits there, snipping the tips and shrivelling
The shreds at last on to the path, perhaps
Thinking, perhaps of nothing, till she sniffs
Her fingers and runs off. The bush is still
But half as tall as she, though it is as old;
So well she clips it. Not a word she says;
And I can only wonder how much hereafter
She will remember, with that bitter scent,
Of garden rows, and ancient damson-trees
Topping a hedge, a bent path to a door,
A low thick bush beside the door, and me
Forbidding her to pick.

                      As for myself,
Where first I met the bitter scent is lost.
I, too, often shrivel the grey shreds,
Sniff them and think and sniff again and try
Once more to think what it is I am remembering,
Always in vain. I cannot like the scent,

> Yet I would rather give up others more sweet,
> With no meaning, than this bitter one.
>
> I have mislaid the key. I sniff the spray
> And think of nothing; I see and I hear nothing;
> Yet seem, too, to be listening, lying in wait
> For what I should, yet never can, remember:
> No garden appears, no path, no hoar-green bush
> Of Lad's-love, or Old Man, no child beside,
> Neither father nor mother, nor any playmate;
> Only an avenue, dark, nameless, without end.

The first trace of what became the poem "Old Man" appears in a fragment of autobiography, *The Childhood of Edward Thomas*, in which Thomas writes of an early memory: "As I stood with my back to the house among the tall blossoming bushes I had no sense of any end to the garden between its brown fences: there remains in my mind a greenness, at once lowly and endless." Subsequently, only a year or so before the poem, Thomas produced another passage, in his topographical book *The South Country*, in which he speaks about having "much drowsy pleasure in the mere act of memory" and describes the way certain scenes and plants (including Lad's-love) trigger sensations poised between happiness and unhappiness, and in which the figure of a little girl appears. When we turn to the poem, all these shadowy details are given a shape which is both recognizably clear and appropriately nebulous, by Thomas' decision to arrange them round a path. Memory may be the subject of the poem—its tantalizations, its elusiveness, its way of combining past, present and future—but the path is the track to the subject. It is so much so, in fact, it becomes a part of the subject and the stimulus for its final great image.

Let us have a closer look and see how this happens. In the opening lines of the poem, we are most definitely introduced to certain kinds of uncertainty. This starts with the names—"Old Man, or Lad's-love" (the genus of this English plant is *Artemisia*—the name showing the honor in which it was once held and establishing its association with Diana, the Healer; the bitterness of the herb, to which Thomas soon refers, is registered in another of its names: wormwood). These names of the herb are at once paradoxical and contradictory: they simultaneously fix the plant as a recognizable thing and confuse the speaker of the poem by half decorating and half perplexing "the thing it is." These doubts immediately deepen: the herb looks both old and young (it is "hoar-green"); it is indeed an herb, but it is "almost a tree." And so on. Given all this, it is not surprising to find the speaker saying that while he likes the names, he "likes not" the herb—only to confound this by saying across the ambiguity-haunted stretch of a line break, "but for certain / I love it." You might say that this accumulation of uncertainties points to a wonderful richness of response—an uncanny ability to see all sides of everything—and so in a sense it does. As we read the poem, we feel that we are watching a mind at full stretch as it struggles to make necessary reconciliations and to do justice to experience by calibrating it very finely. But at the same time the many-mindedness suggests the risk of a kind of paralysis. (It is worth remembering here that Thomas' friend Robert Frost wrote "The Road Not Taken" for Thomas.)

This is where the path plays its vital role. We first see it as we glimpse the child, who is waiting outside the door, snipping tips off the bush "and shrivelling / The shreds at last on to the path, perhaps / Thinking, perhaps of nothing." Even though the uncertainties of the poem are still potent here (everything is still half decorating, half perplexing the speaker's sense of what is reliable), they are suddenly bolstered by a swift description of actualities—by the scent of the garden rows, and the damson trees topping the hedge—which give the path its local habitation. To put this another way: at this stage in the poem, the path is introduced as a kind of platform, a stretch of steady ground on which the speaker can stand and ask questions about how the mind might be full or empty, about how speech might or might not help in the operation of memory, about what parts of experience might stay with us and what evaporate, and about the relative values of happy and unhappy ("bitter") memories.

There is no clear answer to any of these questions, but that is the point. Uncertainty and indecision: these are the foundation stones of

Thomas' truthful response to experience. He may be a different sort of formalist than T. S. Eliot, and he may use a very different range of images, but he has a lot in common with J. Alfred Prufrock, who is an altogether more urban kind of pedestrian. And in the next stanza Thomas confirms his doubtfulness by turning his gaze away from path and child to the interior of his own self. That is to say, he gives his own personal evidence of how memories escape, and yet of how he feels that bitterness contributes more to his sense of himself than other memories "more sweet." What he is describing here is the fundamental Romantic perception—that the self is defined by knowledge of suffering and hardship, and that a degree of bafflement is essential to the acquisition of wisdom.

Up to this point in the poem, Thomas has been placing himself by the door into the cottage, where the bush grows and the path begins or ends—depending on which direction he looks. As the poem enters its very beautiful last verse, his mind moves from doors to keys. "I have mislaid the key," he says. The transition is from local to symbolic, but the word has a sense of actual weight which allows the experience to stay vivid in our minds as readers. In exactly the same sort of way, the path also becomes transmogrified while yet continuing to be the thing it is. It is changed from being the simple "bent" track that runs to and from the house door and becomes instead an "avenue, dark, nameless, without end." It is a wonderfully rich idea, which depends on our thinking of the path as a thing which is at once real and figurative, and in either case as the place where the speaker can witness the final show of opposites. He is unable to re-enter the past, yet endlessly waiting to do just that. He is confronting the blankness of memory, yet filled with a sense of its palpable completion. The coloration, the mood, the world of the last line is like the negative of a photograph.

When we spell out the facts of loss and frustration encompassed in the last stanza of "Old Man," we register a mood of regret—the sense of a very subtle mind being baulked by the hard facts of human limitation. Whichever way we look down the path, we find a bleak prospect. If we look behind us into the past, we see a memory bank that has been eradicated, and if we look forward into the future, we see death—the deathliness of one of Thomas' last poems, "Lights Out," where he tells us, "Many a road and track / That, since the dawn's first crack, / Up to the forest brink, / Deceived the travellers, / Suddenly now blurs, / And in they sink."

Yet at the same time as we feel the truth of these things, in life and in the poem, we also experience something else—something lighter and more affirmative. The steady walking pace of "Old Man," its evenly emphatic tone, and the bewitching intimacy of its cadence all pull us towards life. So do the facts of the poem that are set in real time—a real garden, a real child, and a real path. It is, in other words, the final ambiguity of this profoundly ambiguous poem to make us feel a degree of resignation and even acceptance. The path is the place where the speaker of the poem is tested and found to be resilient. As it says on the memorial stone on the Shoulder of Mutton hill, "I rose up, and knew that I was tired, and continued my journey."

As I stated earlier, the way Wordsworth in the late eighteenth and early nineteenth centuries transformed how people thought about walking—making it seem a bolder, more attractive, and more democratic activity—exerted a powerful influence. Although Thomas seldom writes poems in which Wordsworthianly long hikes play much of a role (his semi-symbolic early poem "The Other" is an exception proving the rule), he nevertheless very often writes poems about walking which, like Wordsworth's, offer a means of encountering other citizens of the highway (retired soldiers, beggars, tramps, etc.). He also very often structures poems around walks which have no specific beginning or termination. Because we as readers are uncertain about their precise length, we are inclined to read them as epitomes of the journey of life itself. Our ignorance about their duration confirms the many other kinds of two-mindedness which give Thomas' poems their particular mood and subject. He is the master of indecision, and his paths are the stages on which his intimate dramas are played out.

Norman MacCaig

Norman MacCaig was born thirty-two years after Thomas, in Edinburgh, in 1910. Although their styles differ in important respects

(MacCaig is more playful with his language, and more open to humor in his tone), they share some important characteristics. They are both comparatively soft- and level-speakers, they both have exceptionally sharp eyes, and they both tend to leave their large ideas embedded in their local observations—preferring not to tell their readers what to think while encouraging them to work it out for themselves. There is an important connection between their abiding themes, too. Even though their culture and geography are very different (Thomas southern English, MacCaig north of the border), they both have a sense of internal division—which manifests itself in many poems as a sense of simultaneous close connection with, and exclusion from, the scene they are passing through.

In the case of Thomas, this conflict is generally set within or against the backcloth of the South Country or on the fringes of London (where he was born); with MacCaig, it takes place in his native Edinburgh, or Assynt, in the Scottish Highlands, where he spent a part of most years of his life (he died in 1996). Even when he was in full-time employment (initially as a teacher in primary schools, then as Fellow in Creative Writing in Edinburgh in the mid-1960s, then as Reader in Poetry at Sterling), he spent his summers in Achmelvich, and Inverkirkaig, near Lochinver.

The poem by MacCaig that I am going to discuss gives no clue as to its precise setting—though it's reasonable to guess that it remembers one of these summer retreats.

The Shore Road

The sea pursued
Its beastlike amours, rolling in its sweat
And beautiful under the moon; and a leaf was
A lively architecture in the light.

The space between
Was full, to splitting point, of presences
So oilily adjustable a walking man
Pushed through and trailed behind no turbulence.

> The walking man
> With octaves in his guts was quartertone
> In octaves of octaves that climbed up and down
> Beyond his hearing, to back parts of the moon.
>
> As though things were
> Perpetual chronologies of themselves,
> He sounded his small history, to make complete
> The interval of leaves and rutting waves.
>
> Or so he thought,
> And heard his hard shoes scrunching in the grit,
> Smelt salt and iodine in the wind and knew
> The door was near, the supper, the small lamplight.

Before I look more closely at the motors and motives of the poem, I want to think for a minute about the context it creates for itself regardless of particular geography. The playful leaps of its language, which moves very freely between different concepts and kinds of perception (blunt one minute, cultured the next), might remind us of the American poet Wallace Stevens—it has something of his clever, compressed, allusive and aesthetic manner. Yet a much more certain light is shed by the walking poets and philosophers I began to mention earlier. By Rousseau—who habitually describes walking as a way to enhance a contemplative mood while assenting to the virtues of simplicity and self-sufficiency; and by Wordsworth, who liberated walkers from parks and gardens and set them along public roads, or over crag and torrent, where they could discover the magnificence of ordinary lives and hear the poetry of ordinary speech.

Even though the freshness of the Wordsworthian vision—its absolutely un-pedestrian view of what it meant to be a pedestrian—altered somewhat during the later nineteenth century, it is fair to say that he pioneered a change in attitudes to walking which has been widely cherished ever since. Victorian walkers may have been prone to stopping en route to moralize or sentimentalize about the value of their activity. The growth of towns, the spread of public transport, and the compromising of the old town/country relationship by the expansion of suburbs: all these things might have affected the Wordsworthian verities. But even before the environmental movement of our own time, there were still powerful voices speaking in their support: John Muir in the United States, Richard Jefferies in England. Like their more recent counterparts, these tramper-writers wanted to assert the democratic rights that walking embodies, to prove their concern for environmental issues, and also to confirm the value of a connection with the ordinary. Or rather, to prove that what has a reputation for being ordinary is in fact extraordinary. Solnit reminds us that Gary Snyder, the American poet, spoke for them all (in his own inimitable way) when he took Jack Kerouac, author of *On the Road*, for an overnight hike to the sea and back across Mount Tamalpais, across the bay from San Francisco, in 1956. En route, he told Kerouac, "The closer you get to real matter, rock air fire and wood, boy, the more spiritual the world is."

In Norman MacCaig's poem "The Shore Road," all sorts of inheritances from the large literature of walking have been digested and absorbed. Yet there is no doubt in my mind that MacCaig is feeding off them, whether his poem admits it or not. Like all pieces of writing, the poem exists in a slipstream of influences, of imaginative opportunities which have been won and handed on down the generations. (The same principle applies to even the most startlingly "original" writers.) MacCaig's poem is shaped in a particularly decisive way by the influence of walking poetry which sanctions pathways as lines that combine a sense of certainty, purpose, progression, and self-definition with an equally strong and opposite sense of uncertainty, indecision, bafflement, and self-doubt. We saw this drama played out in Edward Thomas' "Old Man." In MacCaig's poem, the tensions affect one another differently and produce a different outcome.

Initially, MacCaig invites us to concentrate on the uncertainty of things. A shore road, after all, is a very uncertain thing because a shore is the place where two elements meet and tussle and compromise one another: sea washes away the land; land has the capacity to re-form elsewhere. A person taking such a road enters an in-between place—one is neither quite here nor there. Given this, it is not surprising to find the "man" of the poem (if it is MacCaig, he has removed himself from himself and become the third person) feeling that he is part of a world where the constituent elements are not on terms with one another. On the one hand there is the creaturely sea—predatory (it is in the act of "pursuing"), sexually untamed (it is engaged in "beastlike amours"), alarming (it is "rolling in its sweat"), and yet still "beautiful." On the other hand there is a wind-tousled leaf—"a lively architecture in the light." The difference between the beastly sea and the delicate leaf could hardly be clearer—especially when we consider that the word "architecture" carries connotations of ingenious design, of planned-ness, whereas the sea appears to be an expression of crude instinct.

All this is conveyed in the first four lines—which, like the remaining four verses, partly assonate or half-rhyme in the second and fourth lines, so as to create the sound of meeting and parting, of likeness and unlikeness. Which is the acoustic expression of ideas the poem has already started to explore. It is only at the beginning of the second verse that we see the person who has himself seen all this—the "walking man." Or rather "a walking man": the difference is important because the indefinite article makes us realize that it could be anyone—could be you or me. What has been seen turns out to be a set of provocations to think about separations of one kind or another ("the space between"). Separations, that is, between the thing the sea is and the thing a leaf is—and, arising from that, separations between object and perception, between animate and inanimate, between instinct and design, between the word for a thing and the thing itself, between the self and the thing a self observes. The questions are so multiple, we are immediately told this "space" is in fact not really a space at all, certainly not an empty one, but actually "full, to splitting point, of presences."

This triggers another rush of questions in our mind. What kind of presences does the poem mean? Are they other kinds of natural element? Are they human beings who have walked this way before, pondering the same or similar questions? Are they ideas of cohesion and belonging? We are not told at this stage. We are only advised that they are so "oilily adjustable" that a walking man meets a minimal resistance as he engages with them and leaves no trace of his contact. On the face of it, this seems a good thing, a kind of acceptance. But "oilily" is disgusting—as rank in its own way as "beastlike amours"—and to leave no trace . . . well, that repudiates a fundamental human instinct. If we pass through existence and leave no mark, we are bound to wonder why we exist at all.

The third verse begins by seeming to confirm that "the walking man" (now at least dignified by that definite article) is a part of "the space between" things—one of the adjustable, evanescent presences. He is described as "a quartertone," which is a space of a kind. But what do we make of the musical reference here and elsewhere in the verse? (The man has "octaves in his guts"; he is "a quartertone / In octaves of octaves that climbed up and down / Beyond his hearing.") It seems to come out of nowhere, yet belongs with "architecture" in being man-made, and also because like architecture it appeals to our sense of order and ingenuity. In other words, music is a stay against merely empty "space" and a way of organizing it. It is a confirmation of human existence and of how existence may be considered to have a purpose. All the more so because the music within the walking man, even if he is not completely aware of it (he cannot hear it all), is a means of conveying him to the "back parts of the moon"—an evidently extremely remote and inaccessible place.

The heart of the poem is beginning to come clear. Walking the uncertain shore road between instinct and imaginative (even spiritual) achievement, the man doubts his identity and purpose but begins to suspect that his efforts to reconcile divergent things in nature (that is, in his own nature and in the surrounding world) can be the making of him. And the fourth verse seems to corroborate this slight increase of confidence. It is the walking man's life as some kind of musician, as an artist (someone with "octaves in his guts") that gives him an imaginative connection with his world. At the same time as it grants this, it also establishes in him a sense of history ("As though things were / Perpetual chronologies of themselves" as distinct from being just "oilily adjustable") and a way of dealing with the sense of fragmentation ("to make complete / The interval of leaf and rutting waves").

That is how things stand at the end of the penultimate verse. But the last verse begins with a note of caution: "Or so he thought." Does that mean everything he has said so far is a delusion? That the consolations of the shore road are shifting sand? The poem refuses to give a definite answer. What it does instead is to move away from the comparatively abstract or symbolic language of the three central verses and return to the physical and actual that we found at the beginning. Here, though, the references are more specifically local and domestic: "hard shoes scrunching on the grit," "salt and iodine in the wind," a door "near," and inside that door "the supper, the small lamplight." It is difficult not to connect these homely images with the "beastlike amours" of the first verse and wonder whether the final off-page reconciliations of opposites and filling of space is to be a sexual one. Perhaps even a violently sexual one as "beastlike" seems to imply. But the ordinariness of the closing details and the parsimony of "small" seem to check this, just as the reference to "salt and iodine" seems to indicate a process of healing and purifying, though admittedly one that will sting.

I would say that what we have in the final verse, with troubling undertones, is an image of homecoming that is predominantly welcome. It allows us to read the phrase "Or so he thought" as an expression of trust in the power and authority of thought, while also permitting the sense of delusion to linger. But even as I say this, I want to insist that it would be a mistake to settle comfortably for one way of reading the poem, and one way alone. Nothing that "the walking man" decides to think about his experience in "The Shore Road" is in fact sure. The road is an in-between place; his ability to leave a mark is in doubt; the likelihood of him establishing a particular identity is also questionable. But in spite of this, his human imagining and thinking do offer a consolation. They lead him to the far side of the moon, on a self-justifying, self-fulfilling journey of enormous extent and excitement. And at the same time they remind him of the value—and provide a means of connecting with—the marvelous ordinary: the nearby door, "the supper, the small lamplight."

Elizabeth Bishop

When the American poet Elizabeth Bishop died in 1979, the press in Great Britain paid very little attention. Admittedly the *Times* was on strike and could not have published her obituary even if it had wanted to—but none of the other broadsheets paid any attention either. It was negligent but hardly surprising. During her lifetime, on both sides of the Atlantic, she was the least celebrated of her gifted generation. Robert Lowell, John Berryman (along with Sylvia Plath, Anne Sexton, and Theodore Roethke, who were also drawn into their glamorous and self-destructive orbit)—these were the poets who got the headlines and the readers. Bishop, by contrast, was too softly spoken, too preoccupied by detail, too reticent to seem important.

This was strange, since soft-spokenness etc. were the very qualities being most praised and prized in England at this time. The famous debate which had been kicked off by A. L. Alvarez in 1963, in his influential anthology *The New Poetry*, had been intended to favor a modernistic, freeform, red-in-tooth-and-claw poetry that Alvarez associated with Ted Hughes and to criticize and marginalize the more "genteel" poetry associated with Philip Larkin. But from the early sixties until the end of Larkin's life in 1985, it was Larkin's style of writing that dominated public interest and admiration—a style which preferred understatement, ironical deflation, modest straight-looking and formal elegance, and deprecated everything histrionic in rhetoric or extravagant in form. A style in which, as I say, Bishop excelled, and which concentrated on subjects that also seemed likely to appeal to the taste of British poetry readers.

Even though Bishop was born and died in America, a good deal of her life was spent traveling—in Europe, and especially in South America (she lived for many years in Brazil). Her poems return again and again to themes associated with this restless way of living. She is, as she says in "The Map," more interested in the mapmaker's than the historian's colors because these describe topographical truths which lie deeper than historical or political truths. To say this means asserting a notion of fundamental cohesion, which one might sensibly call her abiding theme, and from which arises her most arresting stylistic device: her tendency to find similarities between things. She has a genius for seeing what she calls "correspondences"—in "The Map," for instance, "These peninsulas [which] take the water between thumb and finger / like women feeling for the smoothness of yard-goods," and elsewhere fireflies "exactly like the bubbles in champagne," or seawater "the color of the gas flame turned down as low as possible." Certainly, when we come across such images, we experience a delight in exactitude for its own sake and a collector's relish for oddity and newness. But we also feel an argument being proved on our pulses, an argument about the unity of the phenomenal world and the human world which perceives it. Bishop may be a footloose poet, but her brilliant eye allows her to settle and live wherever she can see. The question that most preoccupies her is how she can see best. What kind of life allows it?

Both Thomas' "Old Man" and MacCaig's "The Shore Road" invoke the rich tradition of writing about travel, and the paths and roads on which travelers move, and both—from very different angles—focus on the complex relationship between physical movement and intellectual or emotional stability (or the lack of it). I would hesitate to say this was a peculiarly British theme (its roots, after all, lie in Enlightenment Europe, and its tentacles reach out to great American nature writers like Thoreau and Emerson). But I am confident to say it is a theme that seems to attract British writers especially strongly, and which therefore makes another link between them and Bishop. Like Robert Frost before her, for many philosophical and cultural reasons, as well as reasons to do with formal sympathies and resemblances, there are good reasons for thinking of her as a poet with whom British readers might feel they have a special relationship. Indeed, in the thirty years since her death, her reputation has risen steadily. Far from being the neglected one of her generation, she now is the acknowledged genius—someone whose style and interests are wonderfully tuned to the life of our times.

The poem by Bishop I want to discuss is called "Questions of Travel":

> There are too many waterfalls here; the crowded streams
> hurry too rapidly down to the sea,
> and the pressure of so many clouds on the mountaintops
> makes them spill over the sides in soft slow-motion,
> turning to waterfalls under our very eyes.
> —For if those streaks, those mile-long, shiny, tearstains,
> aren't waterfalls yet,
> in a quick age or so, as ages go here,
> they probably will be.
> But if the streams and clouds keep travelling, travelling,
> the mountains look like the hulls of capsized ships,
> slime-hung and barnacled.
>
> Think of the long trip home.
> Should we have stayed at home and thought of here?
> Where should we be today?
> Is it right to be watching strangers in a play
> in this strangest of theatres?
> What childishness is it that while there's a breath of life
> in our bodies, we are determined to rush
> to see the sun the other way around?
> The tiniest green hummingbird in the world?
> To stare at some inexplicable old stonework,
> inexplicable and impenetrable,
> at any view,
> instantly seen and always, always delightful?
> Oh, must we dream our dreams
> and have them, too?
> And have we room
> for one more folded sunset, still quite warm?

But surely it would have been a pity
not to have seen the trees along this road,
really exaggerated in their beauty,
not to have seen them gesturing
like noble pantomimists, robed in pink.
—Not to have had to stop for gas and heard
the sad, two-noted, wooden tune
of disparate wooden clogs
carelessly clacking over
a grease-stained filling-station floor.
(In another country the clogs would all be tested.
Each pair there would have identical pitch.)
—A pity not to have heard
the other, less primitive music of the fat brown bird
who sings above the broken gasoline pump
in a bamboo church of Jesuit baroque:
three towers, five silver crosses.
—Yes, a pity not to have pondered,
blurr'dly and inconclusively,
on what connection can exist for centuries
between the crudest wooden footwear
and, careful and finicky,
the whittled fantasies of wooden footwear
and, careful and finicky,
the whittled fantasies of wooden cages.
—Never to have studied history in
the weak calligraphy of songbirds' cages.
—And never to have had to listen to rain
so much like politicians' speeches:
two hours of unrelenting oratory
and then a sudden golden silence
in which the traveller takes a notebook, writes:

"Is it lack of imagination that makes us come
to imagined places, not just stay at home?

*Or could Pascal have been not entirely right
about just sitting quietly in one's room?*

*Continent, city, country, society:
the choice is never wide and never free.
And here, or there . . . No. Should we have stayed at home,
wherever that may be?"*

Unlike other poems in this series, "Questions of Travel" is not a poem which features paths or roads or tracks of any definite kind. It is, as it says, a poem about travel in general—a poem which raises and ventilates the questions for which all paths and roads provide a locus. It was originally collected in a volume of the same name, published in 1965, where it opens the first section entitled "Brazil." So it is fair to assume the country she is talking about in the poem is indeed Brazil—though the first thing I want to say is that we are never explicitly told that, we are told it is simply "here." which allows us to think we might in fact be anywhere. But what sort of "here" is it, and what kind of reaction does it provoke? We understand in the first stanza that there are reasons to dislike the place—the waterfalls are "too many," the streams are "crowded" and hurry "too rapidly to the sea," the clouds exert a strange dreamy "pressure," which means they "spill" wastefully over the sides of the mountains.

There are consolations—though admittedly of an implicit rather than an acknowledged kind. The first derives from the sound of the poem. Even though the lines report feelings of dislike or disappointment, they are nevertheless delivered in a mood of something like relaxation. Although we experience a little suspense as we come round the line endings, this anxiety is sublimated by a sense of drowsiness (a falling asleep, which the lines imitate with their own soft conversational fall), a lotus-eating kind of mood (the atmosphere somewhat resembles the atmosphere of Tennyson's poem "The Lotos-Eaters") in which any feelings of vulnerability are held in check. And not just held in check by the music of the poem, but also by the operations of the eye. However un-likeable the "too many waterfalls" and so on might be, the eagerness with which "our very eyes" see them and translate them into human terms, is overwhelming. And nowhere more so than in the last three lines of this opening section, where Bishop says, "But if the streams and clouds keep travelling, travelling, / the mountains look like the hulls of capsized ships, / slime-hung and barnacled." The point here, as I understand it, is that even if the water-world teaches a hard lesson about transience and certain sorts of disappointment, and even if the mountains look wrecked (they are "capsized") and pretty disgusting ("slime-hung and barnacled"), the pleasure derived from converting them into such an ingenious image is still a reward. An overwhelming reward, in fact—almost a colonizing reward—which establishes the supremacy and comfort of being human.

This opening stanza is like a statement of themes in a symphony. In the next section of the poem, its assertions are examined and tested by a set of questions. I do not have space to unpack the implications of each—there are eight of them—but their themes, bolstered and deepened by associated questions about broad human and precisely cultural isolation, funnel towards a cry-like climax: "Oh, must we dream our dreams / and have them too?" Or to put it prosaically, can we not trust our imaginations in isolation to do the work of our senses on the ground? Are our invented worlds not damaged by contact with the actual world? It is hard to frame a more fundamental question. In essence, Bishop is asking, what is the point of experience, and what is the difference between imaginary experience and felt experience? Looked at from one point of view, it allows the apparent conclusion to the first part of the poem to remain intact: the inward human life can be a sufficient reward, even without any commitment to or involvement in the wide world. Looked at from another point of view, it implies a weariness with the world and a retreat into the self which can hardly avoid seeming like a diminution of the self. At this point, the poem seems to invoke Tennyson's "Lady of Shalott" more than his "Lotos-Eaters."

In the third long stanza, Bishop alters her tone to admit more of that trademark naturalism which borders on the faux-naïve. It allows her an innocence of expression which encourages an innocence of

The Poem and the Path   55

looking—an unhindered, unprejudiced, childlike wide-eyed-ness. "But surely it would have been a pity," she says (and then repeats the word "pity" twice in the next twenty lines), "not to have seen" various sites-on-the-ground that the imagination ("dreams") would not have provided had it been left to its own devices. Importantly, the sites she then gives us are chosen either for their excess (the trees "really exaggerated in their beauty . . . gesturing / like noble pantomimists") or for their beautiful ordinariness ("the two-noted" tune of the clogs, the oily floor, the "fat brown bird" (which, significantly, she cannot identify), or for their enchanting juxtapositions (the bird and the bamboo church, the clogs and "the whittled fantasies of wooden cages"). She seems to be saying, among other things, that the exaggerated and the ordinary are two ends of a spectrum of perception, and that when left un-stimulated by experience, the imagination is unlikely to see their value. That seems to be a point for traveling and not staying at home.

Although the tone of the poem encourages us to think that these observations are being made artlessly, they are in fact highly organized, as I have just indicated. They are catalogued to back up the argument that Bishop has already made with one part of her mind—that the imagination cannot do everything. That it depends for its future life on the continual collection of material. That things in themselves, even the most easily overlooked things, have a fascination which is proof of life. And that there is a correspondence between things that validate human beings even as they include them. At the end of the stanza, Bishop confirms this by reverting to the language of "The Map." History, she says, exists not in grand deeds but "in / the weak calligraphy of songbirds' cages." And when human pleasure is baulked (as it is by "two hours of unrelenting" rain falling "like politicians' speeches"), it finds its reward not in public action but in "silence" and the self-communion which permits reflection.

The reflection comes in the final eight lines of the poem, all italicized, and written as quatrains rhyming aaba, aaba. The sudden tightening of form seems to suggest an equally sudden mood of decisiveness—a resolution. In fact, and characteristically, Bishop keeps questioning, not answering:

> *"Is it lack of imagination that makes us come*
> *to imagined places, not just stay at home?*
> *Or could Pascal have been not entirely right*
> *about just sitting quietly in one's room?*
>
> *Continent, city, country, society:*
> *the choice is never wide and never free.*
> *And here, or there . . . No. Should we have stayed at home,*
> *wherever that may be?"*

The first verse here revisits the earlier question of "must we dream our dreams / and have them, too?" It is more like a recapitulation than a progression and invites us to leave the poem feeling that it has in fact traveled nowhere. But the second verse nudges things on. "[T]he choice [of places to visit] is never wide and never free" it says, with a strange flat authority, before suddenly becoming less certain again. The phrase "And here, or there" seems likely to conclude that there might not be very much essential difference between places, however various they seem to be—but as things turn out, it does not reach that conclusion. Or any conclusion. The phrase peters out into dot dot dot—which is then checked against a stern-looking "No." What does this "No" mean? That whether we are here or there really does make no difference? Or that being either here or there makes all the difference in the world? One could argue it either way.

The ambiguity of this single word is addressed in the final phrase of the poem, which is where it reaches a conclusion by referring back to the main body of the poem and finding a correspondence with what has gone before. Here it is again: "Should we have stayed at home, / wherever that may be?" This is the second time we have heard the word "home" in six lines, and the third time we have heard it in the poem. The first time was at the beginning of the second stanza—"Think of the long trip home"—where home was posited as a more nearly definite place. Now it is more nearly abstract—an individual mental state, not a political state bounded by history and process. A state which has the rewards of inventiveness, self-definition, and various kinds of security, but which needs the world of experience to engender and bolster those things. Which needs more travel, more paths, more roads, in order to feel the value of questioning their purpose—and in some degree even their reality.

Waterloo, the Story of an Obsession

LOUIS SIMPSON

I wrote away to England for *Vanity Fair*, enclosing a postal money order. There wasn't a copy at school: the library didn't have one, and it wasn't on the shelves with mildewed books that had been set for examinations. There were copies of *Kenilworth* and *Virginibus Puerisque*, but no *Vanity Fair*.

In the holidays I had seen a movie with George Arliss as the Duke of Wellington, and there were glimpses of the Battle of Waterloo, far too brief for my liking. The Duke stood in the stirrups, waved his hat and shouted, "Up, Guards, and at 'em!," whereupon the English soldiers charged and the French ran away. I wanted more of it, and when I came across a reference to Thackeray, saying that in *Vanity Fair* he wrote about the Waterloo campaign, I sent for the book.

It took weeks for my letter to travel by boat to London, and the book to make the voyage back, but it came at last and was delivered to me during evening Prep when we got our mail. I unwrapped the package with an excitement I wish I could recapture. In the days that followed I would take *Vanity Fair* out to the willows and, lying on my elbows, read carefully, aware that this was a classic. I was an avid reader, but for fun—this was the first book I read in the consciousness of the act.

I came to the Duchess of Richmond's ball. I came to the Battle of Waterloo and . . . it wasn't there! I felt a disappointment that, happily, I cannot recapture.

Perhaps the author was meaning to put it in later . . . sometimes they did that . . . in a later chapter one of the characters would look back and remember. But the hope was immediately extinguished. The author had warned, as my heart sank, that he did not "rank among the military novelists." Worse . . . when the decks were cleared for action he would go below "and wait meekly." Now he was saying that for Englishmen and Frenchmen in years to come to continue murdering each other would be carrying out a "Devil's code of honour." There would be no battles in *Vanity Fair*—he disapproved of battles—apparently his middle name, Makepeace, stood for something. I found the point of view incomprehensible. None of the boys at school would have agreed with it, nor the masters who urged us on the football field to play up for the name of the house. How could anyone not enjoy French cavalry charges and British squares wreathed in smoke?

I read on—I had paid for the book out of my pocket money—and as I read I forgot the purpose I had set out with and discovered literature. When I finished *Vanity Fair,* I wanted more by the same author—I had fallen under the enchantment of his voice.

It would have to wait till the holidays when I was in Kingston. I would be able to borrow his books at the public library or perhaps find one on King Street. There was a store that sold cheap editions. Cheap? They were beautiful to me with their red or blue or green jackets and drawings on the inside.

But I didn't have to go to the Kingston library or spend my pocket money. I had a friend named Dennis Anderson. He was my friend during the holidays—there were friends you had at school and friends you saw in the holidays. We went to the same school, in the mountains a hundred miles to the west of Kingston, but I was two years older so that during the term we hardly set eyes on each other. Once at the beginning of term, when we had just got back to school, I was walking on the barbecue with another boy in Form 4A when we encountered Dennis. He spoke to me as though we were still back home. The boy who was with me laughed incredulously—it was unheard-of for a boy in 3A to speak to a 4A boy in this manner. I didn't answer, and Dennis looked abashed as we walked by. But when the holidays started we went swimming together and played Ping-Pong on his veranda. His house was practically next door—there was only an empty lot between.

Beside these holiday activities we had something else in common: we each had a stepmother. I was fond of mine but never quite at ease—I was afraid of doing something that might offend her. I think that Dennis felt the same. Once when we were playing Ping-Pong his stepmother spoke to him about something he had done wrong or failed to do. When she went away I saw two tears running down his cheeks.

Our fathers had divorced and remarried . . . they had new wives and had moved to new houses. This was at Bournemouth, to the east of Kingston, an area that was being developed. It was outside the town proper, and I think that my father moved there because he was an outsider. It was not unusual for a married man in Jamaica to have a mistress, but divorce was something else—it was not as respectable in the thirties as it is today.

When he was married to my mother he had a busy social life—they did a lot of entertaining at home. But very few people came to the house at Bournemouth . . . ones he had business with. The "lawn tennis" parties he and my mother gave at "Volyn"—named after the province in Russia she came from—were a thing of the past. By letting his private life be made public, he had fallen into disgrace . . . at least for a while. But I can imagine what he would have said if anyone had suggested this. He was a lawyer with a reputation for speaking harshly.

One afternoon I was playing Ping-Pong with Dennis on his veranda and he was beating me by a point or two as he always did. In swimming too his hand would touch the wall a second before mine. His stepmother Arlene was sitting on the glider doing her toenails. She was an American and dressed like one, wearing shorts around the house. She asked if we'd like some lemonade. I said "No thanks" the first time she asked, as we were taught to do, and "Yes thanks" when she asked again. She went inside to make it.

In a few minutes she called to us. On my way through the drawing room I went over to look at the books. There was a row in green leather with gold lettering. They were all by Thackeray. I couldn't believe my eyes. I had seen them before but not noticed the name. Then it had meant nothing to me.

Arlene saw me gazing. I asked if I could look at one. She said yes, and I took down one of the volumes. The leather was smooth, the paper thick, and the type clear. There were pictures, but not the simple line drawings of the novels with red, blue, or green jackets. Those showed people doing something . . . a woman sitting on a chair and a man leaning over to speak to her. A cuirassier on his horse slashing with his saber at a Scotsman in kilts who was reaching up with his bayonet to impale the cuirassier. These pictures were of streets and drawing rooms, marvelously detailed. Of a cathedral. A meadow with cows. There was a sheet of tissue paper over each picture that you lifted to see what lay beneath.

"Would you like to borrow it?" she said.

∽

No one reads Thackeray today—his ideas have not worn well. They were those of an English clubman, far more intelligent than most, but one who has spent his life in one of the professions, and seen much of the world, and has come to the conclusion that all is vanity. After which he orders dinner and smokes a cigar. "Vanity of vanities, saith the Preacher . . . all is vanity. What profit hath a man of all his labour which he taketh under the sun?" Perhaps so, but it is not a thought to sustain you when you have to labor, not for vanity and profit but in order to live.

The world that used to argue over which was the greater writer, Dickens or Thackeray, has opted for Dickens, especially at Christmas. But Thackeray seems to be telling the truth, while Dickens exaggerates. Dickens' humor is laid on with a shovel, and his plots are melodramatic. He does beat Thackeray hands down for sheer entertainment. There's Mr. Micawber and Scrooge, and Magwitch jumping up behind a tombstone to give you a scare. There's Oliver asking for more, and Bill Sikes clubbing Nancy to death and being chased over the rooftops and falling to his death, swinging from a rope. You can't miss the moral in Dickens, while Thackeray may not seem to have one. But Thackeray could tell a story you could believe, and there was something else he could do: evoke the tears of things. Not our tears—you can leave that to Dickens—but the tears of things because we are leaving them behind and only we can speak for them.

But no one reads Thackeray, not even in the university. I said as much to Gordon Ray. I was visiting from California and would be in New York for a few days, and he wanted us to have lunch to discuss some business having to do with Guggenheim fellowships. He was in charge of the program. He was also the biographer of Thackeray, and as soon as I could I brought the conversation around to *Vanity Fair* and an idea I had. I would try it out on Gordon . . . it would be like hearing from Thackeray himself.

I said, "Becky Sharp was Jewish."

Gordon stared, and I hastened to explain. *Vanity Fair* was published in 1848. Three years later Thackeray published "Rebecca and Rowena," a burlesque as he called it, of Walter Scott's *Ivanhoe*. "Rebecca and Rowena" tells what happened to Ivanhoe and Rowena after their marriage. The flaxen-haired, blue-eyed, Anglo-Saxon heroine, Rowena, has turned into a pious shrew. Ivanhoe is miserable and yearns for the tender, compassionate Jewess, Rebecca.

Rowena in "Rebecca and Rowena" corresponds to Amelia in *Vanity Fair*. They are both the vapid, butter-wouldn't-melt-in-her-mouth heroine of standard Victorian fiction. By the end of *Vanity Fair*, Dobbin, whose love she has exploited throughout, is already quite disillusioned with Amelia—Who, the showman asks, having his desire is satisfied? In a few years Amelia will have turned into Rowena of "Rebecca and Rowena." And Becky Sharp, whose life runs parallel to Amelia's, and crosses it and diverges, corresponds to Rebecca of "Rebecca and Rowena." As Rebecca is Jewish, so must Becky be.

Of course their characters are entirely different. Becky is "sharp," pushy, on the make, and beyond the pale, as Jews are said to be at the club. All the more seductive because she is beyond the pale. Devilish fun, doncher know, but you wouldn't want to tie up with one, not on your life.

A few hundred years ago the English believed that Jews poisoned wells and cut up Christian children in Satanic rituals. By the end of *Vanity Fair*, Becky has become positively witch-like. She has Jos Sedley in thrall. When Dobbin urges him to break off the connection and come away, Jos beseeches him not to say anything about their conversation to Becky: "she'd kill me if she knew it. You don't know what a terrible woman she is." And when Jos dies shortly after, there is a strong suggestion that she has indeed killed him in order to get at the money from the insurance policy he made out in her name. I think that Thackeray is appalled by the life in his puppet, the creation of his own forbidden desires, and is making her repellent so that he can break off his own unfortunate attachment.

What did Gordon make of my idea? I don't know . . . he didn't say, and we went back to discussing Guggenheim business. Scholars have ways of knowing if a man is "sound," whether or not he is a bona fide scholar, and I don't think Gordon thought I was.

Many years later I wrote a letter to the *Times* (London) *Literary Supplement*. They had published an article that said that Thackeray did not write about Jews. I wrote in to say that Becky Sharp was Jewish, pointing out that she anticipated Rebecca in his burlesque of *Ivanhoe*. The editor replied, thanking me for my letter and regretting that they could not publish it.

Kingston had been transformed. The walls were peeling and the roofs were patched with sheets of tin. Houses and gardens had been swallowed up by the town, and people stood on the corners and stared at you as you drove by. Those who could afford to do so had retreated into the hills where they lived behind barred doors and windows.

One evening Miriam and I had dinner with Dennis Anderson and his wife Maura. They lived in one of the safer neighborhoods, but when we drove through the gate two Dobermans rose to their feet, rattling their chains. A watchman told them to be quiet, it was okay, and we proceeded to the house.

Dennis was at the door to greet us. It took me a while to make out, in the face of the confident, socially adept man, the features of the sensitive boy I had known. He had taken over his father's export business and expanded it. Maura was an artist . . . the paintings in the drawing room were hers.

He talked about boys we had been to school with and what had become of them. The school bully, Weller, was dead. The big, brawling fellow, Henriquez, who used to box with my brother, had gone brawling once too often and had his nose bitten off. Jim Dolan was a contractor . . . he built a big stadium but got in over his head financially and had to leave the island. He was living in Miami. Others had done well. Phillips had migrated to Canada and made a name for himself in the social sciences. He wrote books. He had tried reading one, Dennis said, but he couldn't . . . it was too technical.

Had I been to see the house at Bournemouth where I used to live? Yes, I said, and had been surprised . . . it was bigger than I remembered, which was not what people said about going back. Squatters had taken it over. What I found most surprising was that a factory had been built in the empty lot between our houses and had gone through a cycle of life . . . people had worked there, and now it was abandoned and falling apart, with cracks in the walls. It was as though I had closed my eyes for a moment and opened them again, and a lifetime had gone by.

It wasn't a factory, he said, but a garage. Anyway our houses, his father's and mine, were going to be torn down. There were plans to drive a highway along the shore, connecting with the road to the airport.

He mentioned people I must know. Did I know So-and-So? No, I said, I didn't. Well, I must know Such-and-Such? I didn't know him either.

He showed me a room with shelves filled with trophies. He had won them by his swimming, and he had taken a swimming team on a world tour. So racing against each other in the pool at Bournemouth had paid off.

His father, Kenneth, had been murdered. One day a man walked into the store on Harbour Street and shot him dead. Kenneth kept a revolver close by, but this time he was taken by surprise. He had a mistress, and it was said that her husband paid to have it done, but nothing was ever proved. Did I remember his stepmother Arlene? Of course, how could I forget her? I remembered her legs as she sat painting her toenails, and how she let me borrow *The Newcomes*. And *Henry Esmond*, but I bogged down in *Pendennis*. She went back to the States after Kenneth was murdered and married an architect. She was living in Denver . . . he had a card from her at Christmas.

∽

Like Thackeray I'm at a bit of a loss to know what it adds up to, fact and fiction, things that have happened and things I've read about or seen in movies. Becky Sharp and Amelia and some women I've known . . . a character in Dickens and brawling Henriquez who had his nose bitten off . . . When time has gone by they leave the same impression.

So what is fact and what is fiction? Some people worry a great deal about this. I've known some who threw up their hands in despair and said that nothing was real, only what was in their heads and what they said or wrote. They thought this was real.

Why do you have to choose? Why not just think that everything is real? I've no doubt about the Battle of Waterloo—it happened, thousands were there, and for many years afterward people were talking about it, and some would show you their wounds. Hundreds of books have been written . . . I can recommend *Napoleon and Waterloo*, by Major A. F. Becke, R.F.A. (Retired), Hon. M.A. (Oxon.). I wouldn't recommend the French; after all they lost the battle. The biggest whopper is by Victor Hugo: he has a "hollow road" into which their cavalry plunged—that was why they lost. And Stendhal has a description that's a movie by Robbe-Grillet—there are no people, just a landscape and a few figures moving in the distance.

The Battle of Waterloo is taking place on June 18, 1815, ten miles southeast of Brussels. It began at 11:30 and is now in the second phase, the attempt to break the British squares with cavalry. Sheer madness!

It begins with a distant rumbling. A line appears on the crest. It thickens and becomes a moving mass. There are lines of horsemen, flashes of helmets and breastplates. The guns in front of the squares fire and the gunners come running back. The ranks open to receive them and close again.

The horsemen are thirty yards away when the order comes to fire. When the smoke clears they are riding between the squares. One will pull his horse's head around and gallop towards a square, but the horse stops . . . it won't do it. The rider brandishes his saber and yells and is shot out of the saddle. The ground is littered with men in cuirasses lying on their backs like turtles. Others are scuttling away.

There are hurrahs. But they stop . . . To the front, on the crest of the slope, guns are arriving and being unlimbered. There's the double sound of a gun, and the ball buries itself in the mud. Other guns join in . . . the air is full of whistlings and the thud of iron hitting flesh. Something flies by . . . an arm or a leg?

No, just a shadow. I'm lying on my elbows beneath the willows, reading Erckmann-Chatrian. The sound isn't cannon but the *plock* of a bat. The cheers are for our side—they must be piling on runs.

Writer and Region

WENDELL BERRY

I first read *Huckleberry Finn* when I was a young boy. My great-grandmother's copy was in the bookcase in my grandparents' living room in Port Royal, Kentucky. It was the Webster edition, with E. W. Kemble's illustrations. My mother may have told me that it was a classic, but I did not *know* that it was, for I had no understanding of that category, and I did not read books because they were classics. I don't remember starting to read *Huckleberry Finn*, or how many times I read it; I can only testify that it is a book that is, to me, literally familiar: involved in my family life.

I can say too that I "got a lot out of it." From early in my childhood I was not what was known as a good boy. My badness was that I was headstrong and did not respond positively to institutions. School and Sunday school and church were prisons to me. I loved being out of them, and I did not behave well in them. *Huckleberry Finn* gave me a comforting sense of precedent, and it refined my awareness of the open, outdoor world that my "badness" tended toward.

That is to say that *Huckleberry Finn* made my boyhood imaginable to me in a way that it otherwise would not have been. And, later, it helped to make my grandfather's boyhood in Port Royal imaginable to me. Still later, when I had come to some knowledge of literature and history, I saw that that old green book had, fairly early, made imaginable to me my family's life as inhabitants of the great river system to which we, like Mark Twain, belonged. The world my grandfather had grown up in, in the eighties and nineties, was not greatly changed from the world of Mark Twain's boyhood in the thirties and forties. And the vestiges of that world had not entirely passed away by my own boyhood in the thirties and forties of the next century.

My point is that *Huckleberry Finn* is about a world I know, or knew, which it both taught me about and taught me to imagine. That it did this before I could have known that it was doing it, and certainly before anybody told me to expect it to do it, suggests its greatness to me more forcibly than any critical assessment that I have ever read. It is called a great American book; I think of it, because I have so experienced it, as a transfiguring regional book.

As a boy resentful of enclosures, I think I felt immediately the great beauty, the great liberation, at first so fearful to him, of the passage in Chapter 1, when Huck, in a movement that happens over and over in his book, escapes the strictures of the evangelical Miss Watson and, before he even leaves the house, comes into the presence of the country:

> By-and-by they fetched the niggers in and had prayers, and then everybody was off to bed. I went up to my room with a piece of candle and put it on the table. Then I set down in a chair by the window and tried to think of something cheerful, but it warn't no use. I felt so lonesome I most wished I was dead. The stars was shining, and the leaves rustled in the woods ever so mournful; and I heard an owl, away off, who-whooing about somebody that was dead, and a whippoorwill and a dog crying about somebody that was going to die; and the wind was trying to whisper something to me and I couldn't make out what it was, and so it made the cold shivers run over me.

It is a fearful liberation because the country, so recently settled by white people, is already both haunted and threatened. But the liberation is nevertheless authentic, both for Huck and for the place and the people he speaks for. In the building and summoning rhythm of his catalogue of the night sounds, in the sudden realization (his and ours) of the equality of his voice to his subject, we feel a young intelligence breaking the confines of convention and expectation to confront the world itself: the night, the woods, and eventually the river and all it would lead to.

By now we can see the kinship, in this respect, between Huck's voice and earlier ones to the east. We feel the same sort of outbreak as we read:

> When I wrote the following pages, or rather the bulk of them, I lived alone, in the woods, a mile from any neighbor, in a house which I had built myself, on the shore of Walden Pond, in Concord, Massachusetts, and earned my living by the work of my hands only.

That was thirty years before *Huckleberry Finn*. The voice is certainly more cultivated, more adult, more reticent, but the compulsion to get *out* is the same.

And a year after that we hear:

> I loafe and invite my soul,
> I lean and loafe at my ease . . . observing a spear of summer grass.

And we literally *see* the outbreak here as Whitman's line grows long and prehensile to include the objects and acts of a country's life that had not been included in verse before.

But Huck's voice is both fresher and historically more improbable than those. There is something miraculous about it. It is not Mark Twain's voice. It is the voice, we can only say, of a great genius named Huckleberry Finn, who inhabited a somewhat lesser genius named Mark Twain, who inhabited a frustrated businessman named Samuel Clemens. And Huck speaks of and for and as his place, the gathering place of the continent's inland waters. His is a voice governed always by the need to flow, to move outward.

It seems miraculous also that this voice should have risen suddenly out of the practice of "comic journalism," a genre amusing enough sometimes, but extremely limited, now hard to read and impossible to need. It was this way of writing that gave us what I understand as regional*ism*: work that is ostentatiously provincial, condescending, and exploitive. That *Huckleberry Finn* starts from there is evident from its first paragraph. The wonder is that within three pages the genius of the book is fully revealed, and it is a regional genius that for 220 pages (in the Library of America edition) remains untainted by regionalism. The voice is sublimely confident of its own adequacy to its own necessities, its eloquence. Throughout those pages the book never condescends to its characters or its subject; it never glances over its shoulder at literary opinion; it never fears for its reputation in any "center of culture"; it reposes, like Eliot's Chinese jar, moving and still, at the center of its own occasion.

I should add too that the outbreak or upwelling of this voice, impulsive and freedom-bent as it is, is not disorderly. The freeing of Huck's voice is not a feat of power. The voice is enabled by an economy and a sense of pace that are infallible, and innately formal.

That the book fails toward the end—in the 67 pages, to be exact, that follow the reappearance of Tom Sawyer—is pretty generally acknowledged. It does not fail exactly into the vice that is called regionalism, though its failure may have influenced or licensed the regionalism that followed; it fails into a curious frivolity. It has been all along a story of escape. A runaway slave is an escaper, and Huck is deeply implicated, finally by his deliberate choice, in Jim's escape; but he is making his own escape, as well, from Miss Watson's indoor piety. After Tom reenters the story, these authentic escapes culminate in a bogus one: the freeing of a slave who, as Tom knows, has already been freed. It is as though Mark Twain has recovered authorship of the book from Huck Finn at this point—only to discover that he does not know how to write it.

Then occurs the wounding and recovery of Tom and the surprising entrance of his Aunt Polly who, true to her character, clears things up in no time—a delightful scene; there is wonderful writing in the book right through to the end.

But Mark Twain is not yet done with his theme of escape. The book ends with Huck's determination to "light out for the Territory" to escape being adopted and "sivilized" by Tom's Aunt Sally. And here, I think, we are left face to face with a flaw in Mark Twain's character that is also a flaw in our national character, a flaw in our history, and a flaw in much of our literature.

As I have said, Huck's point about Miss Watson is well taken and well made. There is an extremity, an enclosure, of conventional piety and propriety that needs to be escaped. A part of the business of young people is to escape it. But this point, having been made once, does not need to be made again. In the last sentence, Huck is made to suggest a virtual identity between Miss Watson and Aunt Sally. But the two women are not at all alike. Aunt Sally is a sweet, motherly, entirely affectionate woman, from whom there is little need to escape because she has no aptitude for confinement. The only time that she succeeds in confining Huck, she does so by *trusting* him. And so when the book says, "Aunt Sally she's going to adopt me and sivilize me and I can't stand it. I been there before," one can only conclude that it is not Huck talking about Aunt Sally, but Mark Twain talking, still, about the oppressive female piety of Miss Watson.

Something is badly awry here. At the end of this great book we are asked to believe, or to believe that Huck believes, that there are no choices between the "civilization" represented by pious slave-owners such as Miss Watson or lethal "gentlemen" such as Col. Sherburn, and lighting out for the Territory. This hopeless polarity marks the exit of Mark Twain's highest imagination from his work. Afterwards, we get *Pudd'nhead Wilson*, a fine book, but inferior to *Huckleberry Finn*, and then the inconsolable grief, bitterness, and despair of the last years.

It is arguable, I think, that our country's culture is still suspended as if at the end of *Huckleberry Finn*, assuming that its only choices are either a deadly "civilization" of piety and violence or an escape into some "Territory" where we may remain free of adulthood and community obligation. We want to be free; we want to have rights; we want to have power; we do not yet want much to do with responsibility. We have imagined the great and estimable freedom of boyhood, of which Huck Finn remains the finest spokesman. We have imagined the bachelorhoods of nature and genius and power: the contemplative, the artist, the hunter, the cowboy, the general, the president—lives dedicated and solitary in the Territory of individual adventure or responsibility. But boyhood and bachelorhood have remained our norms of "liberation," for women as well as men. We have hardly begun to imagine the coming to responsibility that is the meaning, and the liberation, of growing up. We have hardly begun to imagine community life and the tragedy that is at the heart of community life.

Mark Twain's avowed preference for boyhood, as the time of truthfulness, is well known. Beyond boyhood, he glimpsed the possibility of bachelorhood, an escape to "the Territory," where individual freedom and integrity might be maintained—and so, perhaps, he imagined Pudd'nhead Wilson, a solitary genius devoted to truth and justice, standing apart in the preserve of cynical honesty.

He also imagined Aunt Polly and Aunt Sally. They, I think, are the true grown-ups of the Mississippi novels. They have their faults, of course, which are the faults of their time and place, but mainly they are decent people, responsible members of the community, faithful to duties, capable of love, trust, and long-suffering, willing to care for orphan children. The characters of both women are affectionately drawn; Mark Twain evidently was moved by them. And yet he made no acknowledgment of their worth. He insists upon regarding them as dampeners of youthful high spirits, and in the end he refuses to distinguish them at all from the objectionable Miss Watson.

There is, then, something stunted in *Huckleberry Finn*. I have hated to think so, for a long time I tried consciously *not* to think so, but it is so. What is stunted is the growth of Huck's character. When Mark Twain replaces Huck as author, he does so apparently to make sure that Huck remains a boy. Huck's growing up, which through the crisis of his fidelity to Jim ("All right, then, I'll *go* to hell") has been central to the drama of the book, is suddenly thwarted first by the Tom-foolery of Jim's "evasion," and then by Huck's planned escape to the "Territory." The real "evasion" of the last chapters is Huck's, or Mark Twain's, evasion of the community responsibility which would have been a natural and expectable next step after his declaration of loyalty to his friend. Mark Twain's failure or inability to imagine this possibility was a disaster for his finest character, Huck, whom we next see not as a grown man but as a partner in another boyish evasion, a fantastical balloon-excursion to the Pyramids.

I am supposing, then, that *Huckleberry Finn* fails in failing to imagine a responsible, adult community life. And I am supposing further that this is the failure of Mark Twain's life, and of our life, so far, as a society.

Community life, as I suggested earlier, is tragic, and it is so because it involves unremittingly the need to survive mortality, partiality, and evil. Because they so clung to boyhood, and to the boy's vision of free bachelorhood, neither Huck Finn nor Mark Twain could enter community life as I am attempting to understand it. A boy can experience grief and horror, but he cannot experience that fulfillment and catharsis of grief, fear, and pity that we call tragedy, and remain a boy. Nor can he experience tragedy in solitude or as a stranger, for it is only experienceable in the context of a beloved community. The fulfillment and catharsis that Aristotle described as the communal result of tragic drama is an artificial enactment of the way a mature community survives tragedy in fact. The community wisdom of tragic drama is in the implicit understanding that no community can survive that cannot survive the worst. Tragic drama attests to the community's need to survive the worst that it knows or imagines can happen.

In his own life Mark Twain experienced deep grief over the deaths of loved ones, and also severe financial losses. But these experiences seem to have had the effect of isolating him, rather than binding him to a community. The experience of great personal loss, moreover, is not much dealt with in those Mississippi books that are most native to his imagination: *Tom Sawyer*, *Huckleberry Finn*, and *Life on the Mississippi*. The only such experience that I remember in those books is the story, in *Life on the Mississippi*, of his brother Henry's death after an explosion on the steamboat *Pennsylvania*. Twain's account of this is extremely moving, but it is peculiar in that he represents himself— though his mother, a brother, and a sister still lived—as Henry's *only* mourner. No other family member is mentioned.

What is wanting, apparently, is the tragic imagination that, through communal form or ceremony, permits great loss to be recognized, suffered, and borne, and that makes possible some sort of consolation and renewal. What is wanting is the return to the beloved community, or to the possibility of one. That would return us to a renewed and corrected awareness of our partiality and mortality, but also to healing and to joy in a renewed awareness of our love and hope for one another. Without that return we may know innocence and horror and grief, but not tragedy and joy. Not consolation or forgiveness or redemption. There is grief and horror in Mark Twain's life and work, but not the tragic imagination or the imagined tragedy that finally delivers from grief and horror.

He seems rather to have gone deeper and deeper into grief and horror as his losses accumulated, and deeper into outrage as he continued to meditate on the injustices and cruelties of history. At the same time he withdraws farther and farther from community and the imagining of community, until at last his Hadleyburg—such a village as he had earlier written about critically enough, but with sympathy and good humor too—becomes merely a target. It receives an anonymous and indiscriminate retribution for its greed and self-righteousness—evils that community life has always had to oppose, correct, ignore, indulge, or forgive in order to survive. All observers of communities have been aware of such evils, Huck Finn having been one of the acutest of them, but now it is as if Huck has been replaced by Colonel Sherburn. "The Man That Corrupted Hadleyburg" is based on the devastating assumption that people are no better than their faults. In old age, Mark Twain had become obsessed with "the damned human race" and the malevolence of God—ideas that were severely isolating and, ultimately, self-indulgent. He was finally incapable of that magnanimity that is the most difficult and the most necessary: forgiveness of human nature and human circumstance. Given human nature and human circumstance, our only relief is in this forgiveness, which then restores us to community and its ancient cycle of loss and grief, hope and joy.

And so it seems to me that Mark Twain's example remains crucial for us, both for its virtues and its faults. He taught American writers to be writers by teaching them to be *regional* writers. The great gift of *Huckleberry Finn*, in itself and to us, is its ability to be regional without being provincial. Provincialism is always self-conscious. It is the conscious sentimentalization of or condescension to or apology for a province. In its most acute phase, it is the fear of provinciality. It is what I earlier called "regionalism." There is, as I said, none of that in the first thirty-two chapters of *Huckleberry Finn*. (In the final eleven chapters it is there in the person of Tom Sawyer, who is a self-made provincial.) Mark Twain apparently knew, or he had the grace to trust Huck to know, that *every* writer is a regional writer, even if he or she writes about a fashionable region such as New York City. The value of this insight, embodied as it is in a great voice and a great tale, is simply unreckonable. If he had done nothing else, that would have made him indispensable to us.

But his faults are our own, just as much as his virtues. There are two chief faults, and they are related: the yen to escape to the Territory, and retribution against the life that one has escaped or wishes to escape. Mark Twain was new, for his place, in his virtue. In his faults he was old, a spokesman for tendencies already long-established in our history. That these tendencies remain well-established among us ought to be clear enough. Wallace Stegner had them in mind when he wrote, in *The Sound of Mountain Water*,

> For many, the whole process of intellectual and literary growth is a movement, not through or beyond, but away from the people and society they know best, the faiths they still at bottom accept, the little raw provincial world for which they keep an apologetic affection.

Mr. Stegner's "away from" indicates, of course, an escape to the Territory. And there are many kinds of Territory to escape to. The Territory that hinterland writers have escaped to has almost always been first of all that of some metropolis or "center of culture." This is not necessarily dangerous because it is not necessarily an escape. Great cities are probably necessary to the life of the arts, and all of us who have gone to them have benefitted.

But once one has reached the city, other Territories open up, and some of these *are* dangerous. There is, first, the Territory of condescension and retribution toward one's origins. In our country, this is not just a Territory but virtually a literary genre. From the sophisticated, cosmopolitan city, one's old home begins to look like a "little raw provincial world." One begins to deplore "small town gossip" and "the suffocating proprieties of small town life"—forgetting that gossip occurs only among people who know each other, and that propriety is a dead issue only among strangers. The danger is not just in the falsification, the false generalization, that necessarily attends a *distant* scorn or anger, but also in the loss of the subject or the vision of community life, and in the very questionable exemption that scorners and avengers customarily issue to themselves.

And so there is the Territory of self-righteousness. It is easy to assume that we do not participate in what we are not in the presence of. But if we are members of a society, we participate, willy-nilly, in its evils. Not to know this is obviously to be in error, but it is also to neglect some of the most necessary and the most interesting work. How do we reduce our dependency on what is wrong? The answer to that question will necessarily be practical and will be correctable by practice and by practical standards. Another name for self-righteousness is economic and political unconsciousness.

There is also the Territory of historical self-righteousness: if *we* had lived south of the Ohio in 1830, *we* would not have owned slaves; if *we* had lived on the frontier, *we* would have killed no Indians, violated no treaties, stolen no land. But the probability is overwhelming that if we had belonged to the generations we deplore, we would have behaved deplorably. The probability is overwhelming that we *belong* to a generation that will be found by its successors to have behaved deplorably. Not to know that is, again, to be in error and to neglect essential work, and some of this work, as before, is work of the imagination. How can we imagine our situation or our history if we think we are superior to it?

There is the Territory of despair, where it is assumed that what is objectionable is "inevitable," and so there too the essential work is neglected. How can we have something better if we do not imagine it? How can we imagine it if we do not hope for it? How can we hope for it if we do not attempt it?

There is the Territory of the national or the global point of view, in which one does not pay attention to anything in particular. Akin to that is the Territory of abstraction, a regionalism of the mind. This territory originally belonged to philosophers, mathematicians, economists, tank thinkers, and the like, but now some claims are being staked out in it for literature. At a meeting in honor of the *Southern Review*, held in the fall of 1985 at Baton Rouge, one of the needs identified, according to an article in the *New York Times Book Review*,[1] was "to redefine Southernness without resort to geography." If the participants all agreed on any one thing, the article concluded,

> it is perhaps that accepted definitions of regionalism have been unnecessarily self-limiting up to now. The gradual disappearance of the traditional, material South does not mean that Southernness is disappearing, any more than blackness is threatened by integration, or sacredness by secularization. If anything, these metaregions . . . , based as they are upon values, achieve distinction in direct proportion to the homogenization of the physical world. By coming to terms with a concept of regionalism that is no longer based on geographical or material considerations, *The Southern Review* is sidestepping those forces that would organize the world around an unnatural consensus.

Parts of that statement are not comprehensible. Blackness, I would think, *would* be threatened by integration, and sacredness by secularization; dilution at least is certainly implied in both instances. We might as well say that fire is a state of mind and thus is not threatened by water. And how might blackness and sacredness, which have never

---

1. Mark K. Stengel, "Modernism on the Mississippi: *The Southern Review* 1935-85," *New York Times Book Review*, November 24, 1985, 3 and 35.

been regions, be "metaregions"? And is the natural world subject to limitless homogenization? There are, after all, Southern species of plants and animals that will not thrive in the North, and vice versa.

This "metaregion," at any rate, this region "without resort to geography," is a map without a territory, which is to say a map impossible to correct, a map subject to become fantastical and silly like that Southern chivalry-of-the-mind that Mark Twain so properly condemned. How this "metaregion" could resist homogenization and "unnatural consensus" is not clear. At any rate, it abandons the real region to the homogenizers: You just homogenize all you want to, and we will sit here being Southern in our minds.

And akin to that, in turn, is the Territory of artistic primacy or autonomy, in which it is assumed that no value is inherent in subjects, but that value is conferred upon subjects by the art and the attention of the artist. The subjects of the world are only "raw material." As William Matthews writes in a recent article,[2] "A poet beginning to make something needs raw material, something to transform." For Marianne Moore, he says,

> subject matter is not in itself important, except that it gives her the opportunity to speak about something that engages her passions. What is important instead is what she can discover to say.

And he concludes:

> It is not, of course, the subject that is or isn't dull, but the quality of attention we do or do not pay to it, and the strength of our will to transform. Dull subjects are those we have failed.

This apparently assumes that for the animals and humans who are not fine artists, who have discovered nothing to say, the world is dull, which of course is not true. It assumes also that attention is of interest in itself, which is not true either.

---

2. William Matthews, "Dull Subjects," *New England Review and Bread Loaf Quarterly* (Winter 1985): 142–52.

In fact, attention is of value only insofar as it is paid in the proper discharge of an obligation. To pay attention is to come into the presence of a subject. In one of its root senses, it is to "stretch toward" a subject, in a kind of aspiration. We speak of "paying attention" because of a correct perception that attention is *owed*—that, without our attention and our attending, our subjects, including ourselves, are endangered.

Mr. Matthews' trivializing of subjects in the interest of poetry industrializes the art. He is talking about an art oriented exclusively to production, like coal mining. Like an industrial entrepreneur, he regards the places and creatures and experiences of the world as "raw material," valueless until exploited.

The test of imagination, ultimately, is not the territory of art or the territory of the mind, but the territory underfoot. That is not to say that there is no territory of art or of the mind, but only that it is not a separate territory. It is not exempt either from the principles above it or from the country below it. It is a territory, then, that is subject to correction—by, among other things, paying attention. To remove it from the possibility of correction is finally to destroy art and thought, and the territory underfoot as well.

Memory, for instance, must be a pattern upon the actual country, not a cluster of relics in a museum or a written history. What Barry Lopez, following Yi-Fu Tuan, calls "the invisible landscape" of communal association and usage must serve the visible as a guide and as a protector; the visible landscape must verify and correct the invisible. The invisible landscape, alone, becomes false, sentimental, and useless, just as the visible landscape, alone, becomes a strange land, threatening to humans and vulnerable to human abuse.

To assume that the context of literature is "the literary world" is, I believe, simply wrong. That its real habitat is the household and the community—that it can and does affect, and in practical ways, the life of a place—may not be recognized by most theorists and critics for a while yet. But they will finally come to it, because finally they will have to. And when they do, they will renew the study of literature and restore it to importance.

Emerson, in "The American Scholar," worrying about the increasing specialization of human enterprises, thought that the individual, to be whole, "must sometimes return from his own labor to embrace all the other laborers"—a solution that he acknowledged to be impossible. The result, he saw, was that "Man is thus metamorphosed into a thing, into many things." The solution that he apparently did think possible was a return out of specialization and separateness to the human definition, so that a thinker or scholar would not be a "mere thinker," a thinking specialist, but "Man Thinking." But this return is not meant to be a retreat into abstraction, for Emerson understood "Man Thinking" as a thinker committed to action: "Action is with the scholar subordinate, but it is essential. Without it, he is not yet man."

And action, of course, implies place and community. There can be disembodied thought but not disembodied action. Action, embodied thought, requires local and communal reference. To act, in short, is to live. Living "is a total act. Thinking is a partial act." And one does not live alone. Living is a communal act, whether or not its communality is acknowledged. And so Emerson writes,

> I grasp the hands of those next me, and take my place in the ring to suffer and to work, taught by an instinct, that so shall the dumb abyss be vocal with speech.

Emerson's spiritual heroism can sometimes be questionable or tiresome, but he can also write splendidly accurate, exacting sentences, and that is one of them. We see how it legislates against what we now call "groupiness"; neighborhood is a given condition, not a contrived one; he is not talking about a "planned community" or a "network," but about the necessary interdependence of those who are "next" to each other. We see how it invokes dance, acting in concert, as a metaphor of almost limitless reference. We see how the phrase "to suffer and to work" refuses sentimentalization. We see how common work, common suffering, and a common willingness to join and belong are understood as the conditions upon which speech is possible in "the dumb abyss" in which we are divided.

This leads us, probably, to as good a definition of the beloved community as we can hope for: common experience and common effort on a common ground to which one willingly belongs. The life of such a community has been very little regarded in American literature. Our writers have been much concerned with the individual who is misunderstood or mistreated by a community that is in no sense beloved, as in *The Scarlet Letter*. From Thoreau to Hemingway and his successors, a great deal of sympathy and interest has been given to the individual as pariah or gadfly or exile. In Faulkner, a community is the subject, but it is a community disintegrating as it was doomed to do by the original sins of land greed, violent honor, and slavery. There are in Faulkner some characters who keep alive the hope of community, or at least the fundamental decencies on which community depends, and in Faulkner, as in Mark Twain, these are chiefly women: Dilsey, Lena Grove, the properly outraged Mrs. Littlejohn.

The one American book, that I know, that is about a beloved community—a settled, established white American community with a sustaining common culture, and mostly beneficent toward both its members and its place—is Sarah Orne Jewett's *The Country of the Pointed Firs*. The community that the book describes, the coastal village of Dunnet, Maine, and the neighboring islands and back country, is an endangered species on the book's own evidence: a lot of its characters are old and childless, without heirs or successors—and with the twentieth century ahead of it, it could not last. But though we see it in its last days, we see it whole.

We see it whole, I think, because we see it both in its time and in its timelessness. The centerpiece of the book, the Bowden family reunion, is described in the particularity of a present act, but it is perceived also, as such an event must be, as a reenactment; to see is to remember:

> There was a wide path mowed for us across the field, and, as we moved along, the birds flew up out of the thick second crop of clover, and the bees hummed as if it still were June. There was a flashing of white gulls over the water where the fleet of boats rode

> the low waves together in the cove, swaying their small masts as if they kept time to our steps. The plash of the water could be heard faintly, yet still be heard; we might have been a company of ancient Greeks . . .

Thus, though it precisely renders its place and time, the book never subsides into the flimsy contemporaneity of "local color."

The narrator of the book is one who departs and returns, and her returns are homecomings—to herself as well as to the place:

> . . . the first salt wind from the east, the first sight of a lighthouse set boldly on its outer rock, the flash of a gull, the waiting procession of seaward-bound firs on an island, made me feel solid and definite again, instead of a poor incoherent being. Life was resumed, and anxious living blew away as if it had not been. I could not breathe deep enough or long enough. It was a return to happiness.

Anyone acquainted with the sentimentalities of American regionalism will look on that word "happiness" with suspicion. But here it is not sentimental, for the work and suffering of the community are fully faced and acknowledged. The narrator's return is not to an idyll of the boondocks; it is a re-entrance into Emerson's "ring." The community is happy in that it has survived its remembered tragedies, has reshaped itself coherently around its known losses, has included kindly its eccentrics, invalids, oddities, and even its one would-be exile. The wonderful heroine of the book, and its emblem, Mrs. Elmira Todd, a childless widow, who in her youth "had loved one who was far above her," is a healer—a grower, gatherer, and dispenser of medicinal herbs.

She is also a dispenser of intelligent talk about her kinfolk and neighbors. More than any book I know, this one makes its way by conversation, engrossing exchanges of talk in which Mrs. Todd and many others reveal to the narrator their life and history and geography. And perhaps the great cultural insight of the book is stated by Mrs. Todd:

> Conversation's got to have some root in the past, or else you've got to explain every remark you make, an' it wears a person out.

The conversation wells up out of memory, and in a sense *is* the community, the presence of its past and its hope, speaking in the dumb abyss.

The Poetry of Life
and the Life of Poetry

DAVID MASON

> It's like a book, I think, this bloomin' world. . . .
> —*Rudyard Kipling*

1. Forms of Memory

I owe my existence to the Japanese Imperial Army. Not in the way you might be guessing—the incident I am about to relate happened a decade before I was born, and my mother was safely tucked away in a California college for women.

It happened to my father at twenty-four, a red-haired Naval Lieutenant on the bridge of a destroyer, the USS *Terry*, patrolling the waters off Iwo Jima. You know about the famous battle there, five weeks of the bloodiest conflict imaginable—unimaginable, in fact, the stories numbing a listener, the storytellers so physically or psychologically wounded that sometimes they can hardly bear their own survival. Compared to the Marines on the island, who often fought hand-to-hand against the Japanese, my father's position at sea was, I suppose, relatively safe. He never spoke of this when I was growing up. Now in his seventies, he tells the story as if it can't be suppressed any longer, as if he too can't believe he survived.

In daytime the destroyers usually lay off the southeast shore of Iwo Jima, bombarding targets radioed to them by Marine spotters.

On this particular night they were sent to protect supply ships moving away from the island. The crew, at battle stations all night, had evaded a torpedo dropped from one of the Japanese planes that scouted them. As dawn came, the destroyers were ordered back to their daytime stations. While the Captain and crew tried to sleep, my father, Officer of the Deck, took the ship down the northeast side of the island several miles from shore.

He couldn't have known the enemy had hidden heavy artillery in caves on the island. These were British coastal guns captured at Singapore, mounted on rails so they could be wheeled out, fired, and wheeled back into their caves before invaders detected their location. Years later I listened to my father converse with a man who had been an artillery officer in the Canadian Army. This friend described the noise made by these big British guns, and my father said, "I know that noise. I've been shot at by them."

The first shells fired from the island at the *Terry* exploded in a huge geyser just off the bow. My father ordered a zigzag course away from the island and wakened the Captain, who then took charge as my father ran to his post on the gun-director turret. He had hardly reached it when they were hit—WHAM—smack in the middle of the ship. All electrical circuits went out at once, and the five-inch guns were left to fire at the shore as best they could.

"Blood all over the place," my father said. He was okay, but he felt stunned and helpless. Everywhere there were young boys killed or missing body parts. As if God had made a fist and brought it down amidships. A lot of boys had been alive, and suddenly they were in pieces. The dying or seriously wounded were more than the doctor and the one uninjured corpsman could handle. The engine rooms were flooded, and the *Terry* lay dead in the water until other ships came to take her in tow.

The memory of dead and wounded boys has never left my father; it may have contributed to his decision after the war to become a doctor. He could not talk about it for years. He mistrusted the words or the impact they might have on him or us if he tried to describe it all, especially his own questions about whether he had set the ship on the best course that morning. But the truth is that nobody had known about the hidden guns.

For the *Terry* the battle of Iwo Jima had ended. They were going home, which meant they would miss the dreaded invasion of Japan. Not all of them made it, however. My father's Gunnery Officer friend received a transfer to another destroyer headed for Okinawa. He remembers the young man's grief at the news; as his eyes filled with tears he had said, "I know I'll never see my wife again."

Whenever I hear that part of the story I think of the movies. You know what will happen next. The guy who takes out the photo of his wife or girlfriend is always the guy who gets killed in the next battle. We've watched it happen so often that we can hardly believe it any more. But life is sometimes full of clichés. You don't have to believe in fate to say that so-and-so was fated to die in such and such a way. Even as I write this I wonder: Am I telling you the story or merely transcribing a version of some war story that has happened many times over? Do I give form to the tale, or do I uncover a form that is already there? Fated or not, this young officer was killed instantly by a *kamikaze* when it crashed into the bridge of his new ship.

My father and the *Terry* were spared the *kamikazes*. They limped home to the United States for a period of recovery. At a dance near San Francisco my father and mother met—so you can see how I owe my existence to the Japanese Imperial Army. If they had not captured the British guns at Singapore and shipped them to Iwo Jima with its ant farm of caves and opened fire on the USS *Terry*, my brothers and I would never have been born.

This story, it often seems to me, has an inherent form; the teller only uncovers it. We say that life is full of ironies, which we discover by looking back, even looking back only a moment or two. But do we live the plots of stories already told? Do the seasons and planets rhyme? Perhaps these are idle questions. Everyone knows that life is formless and that art is not. Even the most chaotic painting has a frame around it, but who are we to say that birth and death are the frame around our lives? We assume that life is chaos. Our usual metaphors are a wilderness, a wind-tossed sea, a jungle with or without sidewalks. And so it seems. We see through a glass, darkly. We call art, as Robert Frost called poetry, "a momentary stay against confusion."

But to say that we do not always perceive a form is not proof that no form exists. Our greatest pleasures often derive from form—the feeling of connection, completion, touch. It seems that the mind naturally rejects formlessness. As John Frederick Nims has written, "The word *form* has a variety of meanings, some of them antipodal. For the philosophers *forma* can mean *soul*, the informing principle that animates whatever is alive and organizes whatever is not. But for most writers *form* is more likely to mean *body* than *soul*. . . ." Whether we create form or merely perceive its immanence in nature, or both, I cannot say. But I can at least explore some of those moments when life seems to have a shape, when it seems poetic, and compare them to the life of poetry, the routine devotion to its pleasures.

I have sometimes felt that I was part of a story, and that I had a sacred duty to transcribe as much of it as I could. My story has something to do with my father's war. In 1974 I unloaded fishing boats for six months in Dutch Harbor, Alaska, which, as it happens, had been bombed by the Japanese in World War II. Dutch Harbor was still a little-known outpost not quite halfway out the Aleutian chain. When I lived there it was an empty place, ghostly, its weather usually dreary like a sodden blanket. The hills were utterly bare, like Hebridean moors, and one could see spent volcanos on the island of Unalaska. Everywhere there were empty buildings: Quonset huts and old wooden barracks weathered silver. There were broken concrete bunkers, rusty trucks half-buried on the beaches, miles of oxidized copper wire running through the weedy tundra. These were the ruins of a World War II military base. I have known several men who served there during the war. They shudder when they recall the horizontal rain, the steady boredom, the horror of Attu—a smaller Iwo Jima— and not one of them has ever expressed to me a desire to return to that place.

My own memories are not so hellish, and with good reason. In 1974 we had finished our latest war and had only Watergate to worry about. But I do remember the ruins: the old prison camp, the officers' quarters. Dutch Harbor was a sort of garbage dump of World War II, a scavenger's paradise. I thought of it as my essential landscape—the desolate home of all literal and figurative war babies, the off-center eye of history's storm.

Derek Walcott, who grew up on another isolated island far to the south, has said that "The sigh of history rises over ruins, not over landscapes. . . ." That is not entirely true. Sometimes the landscape is the ruined temple. Sometimes it is the battlefield. In South Dakota, for example, you can still see the shallow ravine at Wounded Knee where the Seventh Cavalry slaughtered three hundred Sioux. There is a wooden sign on which the word "Battle" has been replaced by the word "Massacre." There is a graveyard with a small monument. But the landscape is haunted too. The story lives in the grass and the lay of the land.

I felt that way about Dutch Harbor. Walking far from the ghost town of old barracks, I still felt the presence of history like some aboriginal songline. Unalaska's Church of the Holy Ascension attests to the Russian conquerors and their God, but so does the distant, snowy volcano with its Russian name. It wasn't only the buildings that told these stories. It was the hills, and the cold inhumanity, the luster and boredom of the sea.

2. The Old Philosophers

Theorists who hold life and art completely separate are killing the thing they supposedly love. The word "text" as it is used by many critics now fills me with anger, because it so often reduces history or literature to a system of arbitrary codes, interpretations rather than events. By contrast, even a philosophical poet like Wallace Stevens was clearly concerned with being in the world, noticing oranges and coffee as much as the poem about oranges and coffee. Yes, the poem about the orange is not the orange, but it influences our awareness of the orange. The sermon about death is not death, but the dead body is a fact beyond interpretation. In Plato's *Phaedo*, Socrates waxes wise about the life after death, adding that "no reasonable man ought to insist that the facts are exactly as I have described them." Then he drinks the hemlock and dies slowly from the feet up. We may be aware that accounts of the death are open to interpretation, just as the dialogues of Plato subvert their own assertions by offering more than one voice. But the body is a fact beyond interpretation. History may be composed of texts, but it is also composed of dead and living bodies. Our interpretation of events is not the events themselves, and truth matters even when we doubt our ability to know it.

For Stevens, who successfully navigated the world of business yet enjoyed meditative walks or quiet moments alone in a New York cathedral, human existence was a symbiosis of the real and the imagined. In his beautiful lecture "The Noble Rider and the Sound of Words," delivered at Princeton in wartime, he speaks of "the pressure of reality," by which he particularly means the sort of catastrophic global events anyone could read about in the daily papers. The pressure was indeed great, as German, Italian, and Japanese nationalists advanced on all fronts. Stevens felt that, in our society, the imagination was also losing ground to this "pressure of reality." The world of facts which he inhabited every day had little use for an imagined nobility.

Nobility, Stevens said, was a force, and imaginative activities like poetry were needed to keep it alive in the world:

> It is not an artifice that the mind has added to human nature. The mind has added nothing to human nature. It is a violence from within that protects us from the violence without. It is the imagination pressing back against the pressure of reality. It seems, in the last analysis, to have something to do with our self-preservation; and that, no doubt, is why the expression of it, the sound of its words, helps us live our lives.

This most reticent and philosophical of poets actually declared that poetry helps us live our lives! It is more than a closed system of interpretations. It speaks to us and in us. Sometimes it even ennobles us. It is a way of being in the world.

Of course, poetry is only one of the arts and only one kind of imaginative organization. But these activities have indeed been helpful, preserving some part of us even as we preserve them. The classical scholar Bernard Knox recalls a moment in World War II when poetry and life intersected for him. A member of the OSS who saw plenty of action, he found himself in 1944 fighting the Germans alongside Italian partisans in the mountains south of Modena. At one point, huddled in a ruined house under fire from a German machine gun, he picked up a copy of Virgil in the debris, "one of a series of classical texts issued by the Royal Italian Academy to celebrate the greatness of ancient (and modern) Rome; the title page bore the improbable heading, in Latin, IUSSU BENEDICTI MUSSOLINI—'By Order of Benito Mussolini.'" Knox tells this story in the introduction to his *Essays Ancient and Modern* by way of explaining his subsequent career as a scholar. Recalling that Virgil's poems had once been thought prophetic, he opened the book to a passage from the first Georgic, which he translates as follows:

> Here right and wrong are reversed; so many wars in the world, so many faces of evil. The plow is despised and rejected; the farmers marched off, the field untended. The curving sickles are beaten straight to make swords. On one side the East moves to war, on the other, Germany. Neighboring cities tear up their treaties and take to arms; the vicious war god rages the world over.

Knox's meditation on these words and the moment of finding them strikes me as a beautiful example of the poetry of life and the life of poetry:

> These lines, written thirty years before the birth of Christ, expressed, more directly and passionately than any modern statement I know of, the reality of the world I was living in: the shell-pocked, mine-infested fields, the shattered cities and the starving population of that Italy Virgil so loved, the misery of the whole world at war. And there was in fact a sort of prophecy in it. "On one side the East moves to war." I did not know it yet, but the unit in which I served was to be selected for a role in the main Japanese landing, which was already in the planning stage. In this case, luckily for all of us, the Virgilian oracle was wrong.

> It was time to move up. I tried to get the book into one of my pockets, but it was too big and I threw it down. But as we ran and crawled through the rubble I thought to myself: "If I ever get out of this, I'm going back to the classics and study them seriously."

This full-time avocation, literature, has much to do with life as we live it, searching for our place in the narrative of humankind.

It may be that I am telling too many war stories here—especially for someone who, thankfully, has no experience of warfare. But these tales of extremity only confirm what I also feel about so-called ordinary life: that the world we imagine and the world we inhabit with our bodies are deeply related.

Now I recall the case of Patrick Leigh Fermor, the great English travel writer who lives in southern Greece. For a time I was his neighbor, my one-room hut sharing an Edenic bay with his more spacious villa. I remember sitting in my doorway on a summer night while Fermor's opera recordings drifted to me over the olives and cypresses. The breeze off the mountains cooled me; the grating cicadas quit their racket when the sun went down. I had no electricity in that little house, so I read his books by lamplight, devouring everything he had written to impress him with my knowledge of it when we met. His prose was so rich that it made me hungry, and I actually had to eat bread and cheese while reading. His words increased my appetite for language and experience.

I was twenty-five years old; to me Fermor represented a literary ideal, the intellectual and physical life melded in one Byronic personality. Years later, while I plodded through graduate school, I frequently envied Fermor's alternative to a college education—in the early 1930s he had walked from the Hook of Holland to Constantinople (even the use of that name is fraught with historical significance). He was also legendary for his involvement with the Cretan resistance during World War II, having masterminded their kidnapping of Major-General Heinrich Kreipe, the commander of the German garrison. Fermor has never told the full story of these events, choosing instead to translate a Greek version by George Psychoundakis. But in *A Time of Gifts*, the first volume of his masterful travel memoir, Fermor relates a story not unlike that of Bernard Knox:

> The hazards of war landed me among the crags of occupied Crete with a band of Cretan guerillas and a captive German general whom we had waylaid and carried off into the mountains three days before. The German garrison of the island were in hot, but luckily temporarily misdirected, chase. It was a time of anxiety and danger; and for our captive, of hardship and distress. During a lull in the pursuit, we woke up among the rocks just as a brilliant dawn was breaking over the crest of Mount Ida. We had been toiling over it, through snow and then rain, for the last two days. Looking across the valley at this flashing mountain-crest, the general murmured to himself:
>
> > Vides ut alta stet nive candidum
> > Soracte . . .
>
> It was one of the ones I knew! I continued from where he had left off:
>
> > nec iam sustineant onus
> > Silvae laborantes, geluque
> > Flumina constiterint acuto,
>
> and so on, through the remaining five stanzas to the end. The general's blue eyes swivelled away from the mountain-top to mine— and when I'd finished, after a long silence, he said: "Ach so, Herr Major!" It was very strange. As though, for a long moment, the war had ceased to exist. We had both drunk at the same fountains long before; and things were different between us for the rest of our time together.

I remember arguing with a friend about this scene.[1] The friend thought it preposterous, declaring that a Hollywood cliché of noble aristocracy

---

1. Fermor quotes Horace's *Odes* (I. ix). Here is John Dryden's 1685 version of the stanza:

had found its way into Fermor's memory, and then into his book. But I had ample opportunity to observe Fermor's recall of verse in several languages. It was another aspect of his character I had admired and tried to imitate. I also knew that, despite the objections of cynics, people do remember poems or songs or key phrases at surprising moments in life, as if pressing back against the pressure of reality.

Another soldier, Field-Marshal A. P. Wavell, demonstrated his prodigious memory for verse by collecting a 400-page anthology from memory. *Other Men's Flowers*, published in 1944, comprised only poems that Wavell had by heart. He acknowledged that his choices would seem old-fashioned to some, but the anthology does have its treasures, like the Kipling I quote at the beginning of this essay. My point about Wavell is that he was a practical man, a soldier whose 1916 wound cost him the sight in one eye, a masterful strategist whose 1941 book, *Generals and Generalship*, was read and reread by Erwin Rommel, and finally, he was one of the last Viceroys of India. Yet this man needed poetry and knew that others needed it. *Other Men's Flowers* sold extremely well, and in his preface to the revised edition Wavell paid homage to one of his readers:

> A tribute which I greatly valued came in the form of an annotated copy which a friend sent me. The annotations had been made by a soldier who read *Other Men's Flowers* during the period of his final training for D-Day in Normandy. As he read each poem he put the date on which and sometimes the circumstances in which he had read it; and added his comments of enjoyment, indifference or dislike. He had finished the volume while crossing to Normandy and had fallen in the battle shortly afterwards. I often turn up that copy and read

---

    Behold yon mountain's hoary height,
        Made higher with new mounts of snow;
    Again, behold the winter's weight
        Oppress the laboring woods below;
    And streams with icy fetters bound
    Benumbed and cramped to solid ground.

the comments, which reveal a fine, somewhat puritan, character and shrewd judgment. I am proud that my selection should have helped him in those days, and that it was on the whole to his taste. I hope I may have helped and entertained many such others.

This poetry was not intended to be patriotic propaganda gearing the soldier's mind for war; it was intended to help and entertain. Though Wavell's choices would surely not meet the approval of most academic critics now, I find his anthology strangely moving because it was made by a man who believed in poetry's sustaining power. He knew that the best forms of expression are often those we want most to remember.

Life appears on occasion to have form, to borrow its form from poetry even as poetry borrows from life. I return to Wallace Stevens, this time his wartime poem, "Notes Toward a Supreme Fiction":

> Soldier, there is a war between the mind
> And Sky, between thought and day and night. It is
> For that the poet is always in the sun,
>
> Patches the moon together in his room
> To his Virgilian cadences, up down,
> Up down. It is a war that never ends.
>
> Yet it depends on yours. The two are one.
> They are a plural, a right and left, a pair,
> Two parallels that meet if only in
>
> The meeting of their shadows or that meet
> In a book in a barrack, a letter from Malay.

Poetry needn't always refer to the world in a straightforward manner, just as the world is frequently not straightforward with us. The spell of nonsense is as important as the elegy or prayer. We can hope poetry that matters is remembered, brought into our lives out of need or pleasure. The pleasure in a line may not be universal, the need may be weaker than our need for water, but poetry has proven tenacious in its survival.

3. The Impersonal Poet

When I read poetry in college, I was taught to be impersonal, always impersonal, as if to avoid contaminating what I read. Now it seems to me that the force of personality is every bit as important as the mastery of craft. Reading and writing are an invitation to a great untidy conversation that spans generations and cultures. The idea that we must be impersonal derives partly from T. S. Eliot, but did anyone ever really believe that Eliot was not present in his poems? That wan smile, the self so distanced from itself, that nearly Hindu monasticism and sly humor are all there. We have the *Waste Land* manuscript with Vivienne Eliot's "WONDERFUL" scrawled next to what seems a weirdly confessional passage. And we have the two volumes of Lyndall Gordon's critical biography, the fullest discussion yet of the interplay of life and art in Eliot's career.

Eliot's early denial of personality, especially in "Tradition and the Individual Talent," was rooted in his own psychological defenses, as well as in his talent for philosophical and religious abstraction. But this denial rapidly became doctrine, easily misinterpreted by droves of readers and writers. Eliot himself constantly revised his position on the matter, and his later work—especially *Four Quartets* and *The Family Reunion*—is decidedly confessional.

"Discoveries in art . . . ," wrote Marianne Moore, "are personal before they are general." There must be various levels of detachment in both life and art. The detachment of artists from their craft is a simple necessity, and Modernists were obsessed with craft, with remaking the forms of expression. When Eliot separates "the man who suffers and the mind which creates," he may well be neurotic, but it is the defining neurosis of art. His desire to direct criticism to the poem and not the poet is also extremely helpful, leading to the technique of "close reading" in the classroom and in most academic criticism. Nowadays close reading bores me; I long to attach discussions of poetry to discussions of everything else. But close, even impersonal reading remains an essential skill for students to master, and we should acknowledge the useful legacy of Eliot's ideas.

Once at a literary gathering a poet asked me whom I enjoyed reading—this was in about 1982. I harkened back to the early poems of Eliot, some of which I had memorized while in high school. When I mentioned this, the poet turned on one heel and marched away from me in righteous indignation. To admire Eliot was, in certain circles, tantamount to admiring an impersonal royalist snob. Worse, it was like admiring the desiccated corpse of the Western tradition. I can only say that most dismissals of Eliot appear to have been made by people who have not read the full range of his criticism. His arguments against a wholly secular society, for example, now seem prescient in some ways. He saw that the materialism of a consumer culture was insufficient to ensure our survival; in *The Idea of a Christian Society* his environmental position is nearly indistinguishable from that of the Sierra Club.

Eliot also modified his ideas about impersonality, especially in his 1940 essay on Yeats, where he explored "two forms of impersonality: that which is natural to the skilled craftsman, and that which is more and more achieved by the maturing artist." Yeats, he said, began as the former but became the latter. In other words, it is possible for a poet to be passionately local yet convey "a general truth." Universality is suspect in some quarters, I suppose, but I would submit that we cannot have great art without it. For better or worse, Eliot influenced writers all over the world: Montale, Seferis and Achebe come immediately to mind. Dante, Shakespeare, and Yeats have had similarly global influence, which suggests that the particularities of their art have not impeded their expressions of general truths. The argument against masterpieces of this magnitude is an argument for an exclusively local poetry, which would be severely limiting. Wallace Stevens' friend, George Santayana, wrote that "The sole advantage in possessing great works of literature lies in what they can help us to become." Perhaps this was what led Stevens to declare that poetry helps us live our lives. I do not think either man meant this simplistically. Poetry is not quite bread; it does not feed the refugees who feel the pressure of reality so intensely now. But it is an awareness, a verbal precision that offers flashes of lucidity.

One of the greatest modern commentators on the poetry of life and the life of poetry is W. H. Auden. Everyone remembers his declaration that "poetry makes nothing happen," but few recall his modification of it, his insistence on poetry's survival as "A way of happening, a mouth." No modern poet was more acutely aware of the distance between political or religious experiences and their expression in poetry. As he said in *New Year Letter*:

> Art in intention is mimesis
> But, realized, the resemblance ceases;
> Art is not life and cannot be
> A midwife to society,
> For art is a *fait accompli*.

Like Robert Frost, Auden called poetry a game and denied its practicality. But both poets understood its usefulness for our consciousness of being in the world. Like his literary godfather, Eliot, Auden spoke of impersonality in poetry, wrongly suggesting that his biography would reveal nothing of importance about his art. But *The Dyer's Hand* makes it clear that Auden did not believe absolutely in the separation of life and art:

> Speaking for myself, the questions which interest me most when reading a poem are two. The first is technical: "Here is a verbal contraption. How does it work?" The second is, in the broadest sense, moral: "What kind of a guy inhabits this poem? What is his notion of the good life or the good place? His notion of the Evil One? What does he conceal from the reader? What does he conceal even from himself?"

Auden believed that the social nature of language precluded any absolutely private or solipsistic writing. "There are other social animals who have signal codes," he wrote, " . . . but only man has a language by means of which he can disclose himself to his neighbor, which he could not do and would not want to do if he did not first possess the capacity and need to disclose himself to himself."

We may feel isolated from each other, from God, from any meaning we have desired, but the language of poetry can't help being a kind of ceremony. It insists, sometimes against all reason, that we are not alone, that our most intimate or noble, trivial or terrible natures are already understood.

4. My Mother's Secret

For a poet one possible ambition is to write something so beautiful, so precise, so true, that another person, preferably many people, would choose to remember it. We may never agree on some ultimate canon of literature, but the belief in masterpieces, in great books, is essential to cultural survival.

When I was in college I read Yeats. I did not understand him, even when I had read Richard Ellmann's clarifications of his life and work, but I was besotted by the poetry. After college I refused to read Yeats for six years, fearing that his personality would completely overwhelm my own.

Language entered me through the ear; my mind lagged far behind in its development. When I was sixteen, I read the Benjy section of William Faulkner's *The Sound and the Fury* while driving a pea combine in the Skagit Valley. The combines were gigantic shucking cylinders hauled behind diesel tractors. We drove slowly in the summer heat, the dust and chaff flying thick about us. In a forty-acre field I could get a page or two read while inching down a single row of swathed pea vines. I did not understand a word I was reading, but the poetry of Faulkner's voice entered and became part of my life. Benjy's sad vulnerability and hyper-awareness of the natural world got under my skin. Later, Eugene O'Neill's wretched family became mine, though it turns out that I was far luckier than O'Neill. Eliot's "Preludes" made perfect sense, but only as mood, as tone—I had never seen gaslights or cab horses and knew nothing of his philosophy. I was moved by his vision of vulnerable people, and my teenage cynicism found confirmation in the poem's abrupt closure: "The worlds revolve like ancient women / Gathering fuel in vacant lots."

In college I extolled difficult literature that I did not understand. I remember sitting at the family dinner table one vacation when my older brother insisted that I explain why Faulkner was a great writer. I could not, because I did not understand what my ear had taken in. My brother mocked me, and I left the table in tears.

Something else happened to me on one of those vacations. I attempted to write the following anecdote into a short story, which I showed to my favorite professor; he told me that the story was full of inaccuracies. People just didn't behave the way I had them behave. "People don't walk around quoting poetry," he said. About most of the story he was surely right, but not that last remark. People do quote poetry, or refer to it—some do, anyway—and they connect it to their lives.

My parents had been divorced for years when this happened. I won't go into the gory details, except to say that in hindsight their divorce has the inevitability of art. It too was set in motion by the war, or events long before the war. My mother had raised my brothers and me through hard times. Both of my parents endured hard times, but I am particularly concerned here with my mother. She was dating a man who had taught me to play chess years before, and who took an active interest in my love of reading. On one of my trips home from college I had brought my selected Yeats, and after dinner I sat in the living room with this man and my mother, talking about the Irish poet.

My mother was a psychology professor, and, though our house was full of books, I had never thought of her as someone who read poetry. She surprised me by saying there was a poem of Yeats she especially liked and asked to borrow my book. While she leafed through it, looking for the poem, I tried to show off my knowledge to her indulgent friend.

At last she found the poem. She did not read it aloud, but passed the book to me so I could see what she had indicated. Here is the poem I read silently that night:

> Others because you did not keep
> That deep-sworn vow have been friends of mine;

> Yet always when I look death in the face,
> When I clamber to the heights of sleep,
> Or when I grow excited with wine,
> Suddenly I meet your face.

Of course I did not understand it at the time. She was talking to me through Yeats, using the poem to explain her life to me. She wanted me to know that she still loved my father, despite all the hell they put each other through. Yeats's voice speaks across time. It is specific to his life, his loves and prejudices. Yet it becomes one of our voices too, the imagination pressing back against the pressure of reality. The poetry of life and the life of poetry mean that reality alone is no place to live.

PART TWO

Students and Teachers

Talking Back to the Speaker

CLARA CLAIBORNE PARK

Let's suppose I have something to say. And I fool around with it, and write it again, and try it another way, and another, because even though it's saying what I want it to, it's not saying it right. And suppose it finally comes to me that the trouble (part of the trouble) is the *voice*: that I'm writing it for the *Hudson Review* when it should be for *PMLA*. Or vice versa. So I rewrite it one more time and send it in. If it's published, and if (just suppose) it's talked about, its thesis, its illustrations, its attitudes, its arguments, will not be attributed to a speaker. They will be attributed to me.

I have, of course, a number of voices. I want to juggle two of them here: one loose, a bit anecdotal, appropriate to personal history, the other appropriate to the chase through texts. The texts will show how small can be the beginnings of a major change in the conditions of literary perception, and how inconspicuously it can achieve authority. I'll use the other voice to insinuate what I think.

"It has become traditional," explains J. Paul Hunter in the poetry volume of *The Norton Introduction to Literature*,

> to distinguish between the person who wrote the poem and the person who speaks in a poem, for an author often chooses to speak through a character quite different from his or her real self.

Traditional: what everybody knows, without knowing how we know it; the universal practice which has come to seem right. Hunter, with his "often," is a pretty low-key expositor of the tradition, willingly conceding that "in many poems the speaker is very like the author, or [there's a catch] very like what the author wishes to think he or she is like," and that "between the speaker who is a fully distinct character and the author speaking honestly and directly, are many degrees of detachment." Written not for freshmen but for us, M. H. Abrams' *Glossary of Literary Terms* is considerably more categorical:

> In recent literary discussion "persona" is often applied to the first-person narrator, the "I," of a narrative poem or novel, or the lyric speaker whose voice we listen to in a lyric poem. Examples of personae are . . . the first-person narrator of Milton's *Paradise Lost* (who in the opening passages of various books discourses at some length about himself); the Gulliver who tells us about his misadventures in *Gulliver's Travels*; . . . the speaker who talks first to himself, then to his sister, in Wordsworth's "Tintern Abbey"; the speaker who utters Keats's "Ode to a Nightingale" . . . ; and the Duke who tells the emissary about his former wife in Browning's "My Last Duchess." By calling these speakers "personae" . . . we stress the fact that they are all part of the fiction, characters invented for a particular artistic purpose. That the "I" in each of these works is not the author as he exists in his everyday life is obvious enough in the case of Swift's Gulliver and Browning's Duke, less obvious in the case of Milton . . . , and does not seem obvious at all to an unsophisticated reader of the lyric poems of Wordsworth and Keats.

For "recent literary discussion" Hunter's "degrees of detachment" are only a function of the reader's naiveté. That every literary "I" is fictional is "a fact." "We stress" it. It takes only a single pronoun to embody a tradition.

Now an anecdote. I've told it elsewhere, so I'll keep it short:

It's twenty-five years ago. You can tell, because I'm teaching Great Books, and in a community college, and to pretty much everyone who comes in off the street. We're reading the *Inferno*; a student, not one of the smart ones, raises his hand. He hasn't spoken before, but today he has a question. "We've read what Homer says about the afterlife, and what Plato says, and now we're reading what Dante says, and they're all different, Mrs. Park. *Which of them is true?*"

The good students rustle and smirk; already they know (how?) that this isn't a question you ask in English class. A bit of irony will reinforce them and solace me; they're on my side, I need them, teaching isn't easy. Or I can drop irony for sympathetic explanation, summon I. A. Richards out of the air in which he is unquestionably hovering, and say something to the effect that "the statements which appear in the poetry are there for the sake of their effects upon feelings, not for their own sake," and that "to question whether they deserve serious attention as *statements claiming truth* is to mistake their function." I catch myself just in time. Who is closer to Plato and Dante, I and my little band of sophisticates or this earnest questioner? Which of us is reading as they expected to be read?

That happened long ago. Today we have a more elaborate armamentarium against the profound demands of naiveté. Today I could explain to my student that Plato told his myths of the afterlife through a speaker who though called Socrates was only a fiction invented for a particular artistic purpose. I could involve him in distinctions between Dante the narrator and Dante the poet. I could invoke spectres, an "implied author," a ghostly "authorial presence." I could raise wall after glass wall between him and these vanished human voices he had come to think had something to say directly to him. If I really worked at it, I could bring even such a student to believe what my smart students of a generation ago already suspected: that in English class, what's relevant is what's interesting, not what, if anything, is true.

Actually, I don't get many students like that anymore. I'm teaching in a different place, and time, too, alters curriculum and consumers. Great Books aren't being taught much these days: teachers have doubts about "the canon"; students' interests in literature seldom reach back past 1900. Not that they're not smart. Most of the students in my sections of Introduction to Literature don't need Hunter's explanation; some wouldn't even be surprised by Abrams'. The preppies and the kids from suburban high schools already know what you are supposed to do when you talk about a poem; the others will find out the first week that you say "the speaker" and not "Frost says," that it's not Shakespeare who's worried he's growing old, not Donne who's saying good-bye to his lover, not Keats who talks to a vase. Soon the locution of detachment will become second nature. A class on "Channel Firing" will clue in the laggards, since the others have already had "My Last Duchess." Next step *The Turn of the Screw*, or if that's too familiar, *The Good Soldier*. That'll learn 'em whom to trust.

The speaker. The narrator. I want here to trace something of the history of this innocent locution, since there was within living memory a time when it wasn't traditional, when the distinction between "the person who writes" and "the person who speaks" went unmade, except, of course, when poems like Browning's enforced it. Did reading feel different then? If language conditions experience—and certainly to think *that* has become traditional—so pervasive a change in the way we talk about poems and stories must matter, must affect as well as reflect the way they are taught and encountered—not to say written. Does critical and pedagogic practice enact an idea of progress, of gain uncompensated by loss? What should we conclude about a time when professors and critics were more unsophisticated than today's freshmen, when everybody said "the poet says," or "Milton," or "Keats" as if it was the most natural thing in the world? For memory informs me, and my coevals confirm, that it was possible as recently as the forties to take courses from the likes of Austin Warren and F. O. Matthiessen and emerge innocent of the distinction. Back then, when Yeats wrote that his heart was driven wild, we assumed that—masks or no masks—he meant it.

It happened that between the forties and the sixties I was out of the academic world, and when I got back into it, the tradition was in place. My colleagues taught "My Last Duchess" and "Channel Firing"; they said "the speaker"; they talked about voice and tone. One likes to do the done thing; soon I was doing it too. I do it to this day, off and on, at least when I'm teaching Introduction to Literature. But because I didn't grow up with it, because I encountered the ideas not as an exciting corrective but as a fact accomplished, I still view it as an outsider. It is as an outsider that I interrogate the nagging discomfort I feel when I hear the words, or read them, or say them. It's small, but in twenty-five years it hasn't gone away. It is out of that discomfort that I chase down the history of the phrase and ponder its implications.

If I can remember a time before the speaker, I can remember too how we read poetry in the olden days. By the time I was eighteen, I had read hundreds of poems, thousands of lines, hitting the high spots, sieving out phrases that fitted my sense of life, ignoring the rest; drunk on eloquence, sometimes merely on sound, on Abanah and Pharphar, on silken Samarcand and cedared Lebanon—reading like a child, if that conveys any meaning today when it's a rare child who grows up on poetry. We were still reading like that in college; the word "impressionistic" was made for us. We didn't know you *could* analyze a poem. I remember the exams—marvelous, expansive essay topics, tempered by "spot questions," previously unseen passages whose period and author we must identify merely by style, by the way the words went. We got quite good at this, so we must have learned something, but nevertheless it was a revelation to take Matthiessen's course and pay *attention* to poems, to watch meaning emerge from the scrutiny of syntax and symbol and structure. Imagine it, you could write a whole paper on one poem. Unbeknownst, we were being introduced to "close reading," to the New Criticism, as yet hardly christened. But not to "the speaker."

People had written about poetry (if we begin with Plato) for more than two millennia without feeling the need for such a phrase. Where should I start my chase? Not with Johnson; champion of the common reader, his sense of the poet's relation to his utterance would be as direct as Sidney's a century and a half before. Shelley wouldn't use it, nor Wordsworth, nor Arnold. Though Chambers' Victorian *Cyclopedia* recognized the "mysterious, misanthropic personage who tells the story of Tennyson's *Maud*," or the possibility that some of Shakespeare's sonnets were "written in a feigned character," there was no word of a speaker. Maybe Eliot? For our generation of readers, everything started with him.

How the years telescope our past! Revisited, Eliot sounded a lot closer to Arnold than to Cleanth Brooks; he didn't do close reading, found it "very tiring" when other people did, had, apparently, no need for "the speaker." I. A. Richards? That seemed more likely. He had given us poetry as pseudostatement, and one good distancing mechanism deserves another. I took out *Practical Criticism*.

Cambridge students in the twenties, apparently, read no better than our freshmen do today. (But how much better they wrote! How wide their vocabularies! How complex their sentence structure! How much they seemed to know about prosody, about literary history, even though it only seemed to get in their way!) They read, in fact, much as I had twenty years later, and Richards had found out what to do about it. By the simple but original expedient of presenting them with unattributed poems, he deprived them of their hard-learned stereotypes and, sentence by sentence, insisted that they attend to what the poet was saying. In 1943, I hadn't really thought that poems came in sentences, like prose; I'd thought they were a different kind of thing altogether.

Since Richards had literally eliminated the poet from his students' experience of reading, I was ready momentarily to encounter the poet's surrogate, the speaker. And so I did, first in a trivial example (quoted from a rather obtuse student who had evidently reached for the phrase lacking the poet's name), then used by Richards himself.

> Furthermore, the speaker . . . chooses or arranges his words differently as his audience varies. . . . Finally, apart from what he says (Sense), his attitude to what he is talking about (Feeling), and his attitude to his listener (Tone) there is the speaker's intention, his aim, . . . the effect he is endeavouring to promote.

Had I already located the ur-persona? Not so fast. The book was half over. Richards had considered thirteen poems without mentioning a speaker; he was now embarking on a general discussion, not of poetry, but of "human utterances," of speech itself. Naturally speech implied a speaker. This one, like most others, had aims and intentions, endeavored to promote effects; "We speak," Richards informed us, "to say something." His *we* was inclusive. Here was no mask, no "voice," no Duke of Ferrara, not even necessarily a writer. Richards' speaker was only ourselves talking. I kept on reading, but in 185 more pages the speaker did not reappear.

Might he show up in Richards' star pupil? William Empson's *Seven Types of Ambiguity* appeared in 1930, the year after *Practical Criticism*. It gave us a word we couldn't do without, and taught us, more than any other single book, how much could be teased out of a poem. (Eliot was later to refer to "the lemon-squeezer school of criticism.") But it did not distinguish poet and speaker. The single time Empson used the term was to make clear, in discussing Herbert's *The Sacrifice*, that "the speaker is Jesus." The phrase was available at need, but normal usage remained, to use Abrams' word, "unsophisticated." It did not occur to Empson to render anonymous that "speaker who talks first to himself, then to his sister" in "Tintern Abbey," or to attenuate Wordsworth's relation to what, in Empson's straightforward words, "he wants to make a statement about."

> Wordsworth seems to have believed in his own doctrines and wanted people to know what they were. It is reasonable, then, to try to extract from this passage definite opinions on the relations of God, man, and nature.
>
> Wordsworth may . . . have *felt a something far more deeply interfused* than the *presence* that *disturbed* him.
>
> He talks as if he owned a creed.

When Empson writes of Shelley's Skylark that "the poet is rapt into an ecstasy which purifies itself into nescience," it might be Matthew Arnold.

Five years later, in R. P. Blackmur's *The Double Agent*, the speaker's voice is still inaudible, even in the chapter on "The Masks of Ezra Pound," where Blackmur explains, for readers to whom it is evidently unfamiliar, a term that neither Richards nor Empson had used:

> *Persona*, etymologically, was something through which sounds were heard, and thus a mask. . . . Mr. Pound's work has been to make *personae*, to become . . . in this special sense . . . a person through which what has most interested him . . . might be given voice.

Yet Blackmur talking about poets was no more sophisticated than Empson. For him too, poets spoke to say something, and in general the poem was what they said: "An apple, Mr. Stevens says [in 'Le Monocle de Mon Oncle'], is as good as any skull to read." It might be "says" or something stronger: "For Keats, the Nightingale . . . let him pour himself forth." In any case, Keats uttered the ode, not a speaker.

By 1935, then, speaker and persona had made their appearance, but separately and very inconspicuously. Clearly, they had not yet made their way into critical practice, let alone theory.

It wasn't until I rounded up an old copy of Brooks and Warren that I found what I was looking for. I should have looked there first. Here were the terms I had found in place in the mid-sixties: Richards' *tone*, and with it, the speaker as we have come to know him. For the first time? Who can say? Literary critics have not as yet earned a concordance, and the teacher, as someone once remarked, sculpts in snow.

Cleanth Brooks and Robert Penn Warren's *Understanding Poetry* was first published in 1938, and its fourth edition is in print today—an astonishing record of pedagogical influence. Brooks and Warren brought the principles of neo-critical reading within the compass of teachers in every college, then in every high school. Revisiting it today, it's hard to appreciate the originality of their modestly titled "Anthology for College Students." The poems were accompanied by the explanations, questions, and exercises of a conventional textbook. Certainly the selection was new; metaphysical and modern poems were generously interspersed among the nineteenth-century favorites. But it was their arrangement that most plainly proclaimed a new agenda. They were not in chronological order, nor were they grouped by author nor by theme. A long "Letter to the Teacher" made the priorities clear: "Study of biographical and historical materials," served by chronological and authorial ordering, and "inspirational and didactic interpretation," invited by thematic grouping, were mere substitutes for the proper "object for study," "the poem in itself."

The poem in itself was now inherently dramatic (as Blackmur had said it sometimes but not always was). As a little drama, it had acquired a speaker. "What does section four [of 'Ode to the West Wind'] tell us about the speaker? Does the poem sufficiently present his situation? Or do you need to consult a life of Shelley in order for the passage to gain full significance?" The answer was not far to seek.

Though Richards had not doubted that a poet, like other human utterers, had aims and intentions, he had denied him the truth-value of what he said. Poetry was different from philosophy, from all expository prose; it made pseudostatements. (Eliot concurred, then demurred when he became a Christian.) Brooks and Warren made the application clear: there should be no "confusion between scientific and poetic communication." Poetry's pleasure and profit should be sought, not as of old in particular beauties or isolable *sententiae*, but in the poem as "an organic system of relationships," "object for study," objet d'art. In his *Principles*, Richards had named "message hunting." Brooks and Warren introduced the phrase to a generation of teachers and students—and poets—who learned from it not only how poetry should not be read but what it should not be.

And how does "the speaker" function to deter message hunting? *Mrs. Park, which of them is true?* Why should the speaker speak truly? The Duke of Ferrara did not. Once the poet was dissolved in the persona, his poems scattered under new rubrics like "tone" and "imagery," a student was no longer in a position to ask questions about the attitudes and convictions of a single human being. *We* speak to say something; "the speaker" might say something different in every poem. And though the poet-as-speaker might retain his aims and intentions, the student must experience them with some loss of urgency. The danger of "inspirational or didactic interpretation" is markedly reduced when the unacknowledged legislators of mankind speak at one remove. Only a fool trusts a man in a mask.

Yet again, not so fast. If any such implications existed, they were still in embryo. Brooks and Warren might say "the speaker," but they were far from saying it consistently. And they certainly did not think of their new phrase as a possible focus of critical or pedagogic attention. Their glossary contained no entry for "speaker" or "persona," and in their single explanatory sentence the poet came first. "Every poem implies a speaker of the poem, either the poet writing in his own person or someone into whose mouth the poem is put." The authors themselves shifted between speaker and poet almost at random.

> [Of "A Slumber Did My Spirit Seal"] Is the speaker saying that his loved one seemed so thoroughly immortal that he simply was asleep to the possibility that she could ever die?
>
> [Of "The Scholar Gypsy"] The poet says that his own age is confused by doubts.

There is, of course, a distinction to be made between the poet insofar as he speaks to say something, and the poet qua poet, shaping, ordering, choosing, and now and then the authors seemed to have it in mind: "Does the poet succeed in dramatizing the suggestion that the daffodils accept the speaker as a companion?" But the distinction collapses in practice. Back to the "Nightingale": "This poem is obviously a reverie induced by the poet's listening to the song of the nightingale," not the poet as craftman, but "the poet . . . just sinking into the reverie," the poet who "wishes for a dissolution of himself," and "breaks out of his reverie" in the last stanza. "Poet" melts imperceptibly into "speaker" as the discussion progresses, the total number of occurrences of each holding equal at eleven. In the book as a whole the usage is almost entirely fluid: if "the speaker" of the "Nightingale" has an "attitude toward death," it's "the poet" who has an "attitude toward fate" in Marvell's "The Definition of Love." Sometimes the likely distinction is actually reversed: for "Among School Children" it's "the speaker himself and . . . the woman he loves," yet for "Two Songs from a Play," so much less personal and circumstantial, it's "Yeats believes." Brooks and Warren are not yet committed to the speaker. "Is Johnson actually pointing a moral?" they ask of "The Vanity of Human Wishes"; when push comes to shove, as it generally does with the Doctor, it's back to the poet. Even an inspirational or didactic interpretation may get by if you agree with it: for "Shine, Perishing Republic," the questions are "Does this poet hate America? Is he trying to admonish his country?"

Brooks was no more consistent when writing alone and for grown-ups, and only slightly more conscious. In *Modern Poetry and the Tradition* (1939), written, presumably, while he was working on *Understanding Poetry*, we hear much more from poets than from speakers: "Marvell . . . compares himself and his mistress to parallel lines"; "Donne may argue as in 'The Nocturnal on St. Lucy's Day' that he is nothing." Speaker and poet comfortably coexist: of "Ode to the Confederate Dead," "The world which the dead soldiers possessed is not available to the speaker of the poem. . . . Moreover, the poet is honest: the leaves, for him, are merely leaves." Eight years later, in *The Well Wrought Urn*, the smokeless air over Westminster Bridge still "reveals a city the poet did not know existed," and it is "the poet" who begins the Immortality Ode "by saying he has lost something." By the next page, however, there has been a silent metamorphosis into "what the speaker has lost," and soon the usage is hopelessly confused: "Wordsworth says that the rainbow and the rose are beautiful"; "the moon is treated as if she were the speaker himself"; "the poet cannot see the gleam." Practice has not yet hardened into consistency, still less into precept. Elton's *Glossary of the New Criticism*, published the next year, glossed "tone" and "irony," but not "persona."

Brooks came closest to making the distinction explicit in the chapter on Gray's Elegy, where he reproved Empson for failing to realize that "we are not dealing with Gray's political ideas" but with "what the Elegy says," with "the *speaker's* choice." The emphasis is Brooks's own; we can imagine him underlining the word. The issue resurfaced only in an appendix, where Donald Stauffer was criticized for confounding "the protagonist of the poem with the poet, and the experience of the poem as an aesthetic situation with the author's personal opinion." But Brooks was only working toward such aesthetic purity; in the body of the book he had not yet attained it. Old simplicities die hard.

It was not until 1951, in Reuben Brower's *The Fields of Light*, that we were told straight out that a poem is not merely a drama but "a dramatic fiction," and that "its speaker, like a character in a play, is no less a creation of the words on the printed page." Brower's first chapter is titled "The Speaking Voice"; its first heading is "The Speaker." It is indeed an ur-text for persona, cited as such in Abrams' bibliography. Here the space allotted to "the poet writing in his own person" has visibly contracted; Brower is considerably farther along the road to the Universal Speaker.

> The voice we hear in a lyric, however piercingly real, is not Keats's or Shakespeare's; or if it seems to be . . . we are embarrassed and thrown off as if an actor had stopped and spoken to the audience in his own person.

Description hardens into prescription. Poets may seem to speak in their own voices, perhaps they even do so in fact, but they shouldn't. Brower can accept it when Shelley in "Ode to the West Wind" comes on in "his familiar character of priest-prophet," but with "I fall upon the thorns of life! I bleed!," "the dramatic fiction slips disturbingly: the allegory refers us too directly to Shelley's biography," though Brower concedes it is "only after the poem's high commotion is past that we feel the lapse." But however compelling the theatrical metaphor, those of us who remember how entirely, in the forties, we had learned to condescend to Shelley may suspect that it was less the slippage of the mask that embarrassed than the sentiment. There seems no reason, after all, why a priest-prophet in his familiar character can't feel sorry for himself. The unobtrusiveness of the human author has become a criterion, in poetry and in the novel as well; Brower reproves E. M. Forster for "somewhat portentous observations" which "in their unironic solemnity . . . are not altogether in character for the narrator of *A Passage to India*."

James would have committed no such gaffe. Four years later, Brooks and Wimsatt would identify the novelist's "problem of securing impersonality for his art," and ask, "How does the narrator avoid introducing himself into the work?" How? He does so by joining the speaker on stage. There sock and buskin conveniently separate him from authorial temptations to say what he thinks or feels and readerly temptations to experience his statements unprotected by irony. Mechanisms of detachment tend to cluster.

Yet actual critical practice continues to resist such aesthetic austerity. In Brower's verbs, poets still speak for themselves. As he compares sonnets by Donne and Hopkins, "Hopkins calls directly on God for help"; "Donne . . . for all his queries, [is] certain of his close and passionate relation to Christ," while "Hopkins [is] tortured at the very center of his faith." There are no apologies for his near lapse into biography. Though Brower asserts a distinction between speaker and poet, he makes it only when need compels, as it does in his discussion of "Love III," where his use of "story-teller," "narrator," "sinner," and "guest" (not, however, "speaker") only underlines the difference between Herbert's dramatized and universalized encounter with divinity and Donne's and Hopkins' direct and personal address.

Brower was far too good a reader to sacrifice that difference to a theory; writing naturally of "the intimacy of Donne's prayer" in Holy Sonnet X, he reserved "the speaker" for the overtly dramatized situation of "The Extasie." In fact, Brower seldom used the term. It appears in a discussion of the "Essay on Riches," to be immediately cancelled by a reference to "Pope's ridicule." It is notably missing in the extended treatments of *Absalom and Achitophel*, of Yeats's "Two Songs," even of "Surprised by Joy," though a footnote is there to admonish us that "a biographical reading, which the usual footnote to the poem invites, is altogether misleading and singularly unprofitable." Brower's transitional location between past naiveté and future rigor is marked by the doubled noun with which he concludes his discussion of the speaking voice: "the poet-speaker."

T. S. Eliot's "The Three Voices of Poetry," first published in 1953, is also cited as an ur-text for Persona. Actually to consult it, however, is to experience the retroactive power of an idea to compel us to misunderstand a text, indeed to reverse its meaning. Eliot in 1953 was writing plays, and far from making the dramatic voice the type of all poetic speaking, he was particularly concerned to distinguish it. He explicitly restricts the poet as persona to the third of his three voices, that actually to be heard on a stage. In the first voice, "the voice of private meditation," the poet is "talking to himself—or to nobody"; in the second, he is "talking to other people." Only in the third does the poet create "a dramatic character speaking in verse." Devotees of the universal persona may be startled to realize that by this Eliot does not mean dramatic monologue but actual drama, in which the poet is "saying . . . only what he can say within the limits of one imaginary character addressing another imaginary character," characters who have "equal claims" upon him, and whom, therefore, "he cannot wholly identify . . . with himself." In dramatic monologue, however, "it is surely the second voice, the voice of the poet talking to other people, that is dominant." Though metaphorically "he has put on costume and makeup," he hasn't really.

> Dramatic monologue cannot create a character. When we listen to a play by Shakespeare, we listen not to Shakespeare but to his characters; when we read a dramatic monologue by Browning, we cannot suppose we are listening to any other voice than that of Browning himself.

To the author of *Prufrock* it couldn't be clearer: "What we normally hear . . . in the dramatic monologue is the voice of the poet." Even in the play *The Rock*, the chorus was "speaking directly for me," speaking, moreover, in the second voice, the voice that Brooks and Brower found so off-putting but which Eliot here claimed as his own: "The voice heard in all poetry that has a conscious social purpose—poetry intended to amuse or instruct, poetry that preaches or points a moral"—that invites a reader, among other things, to consider whether what it says might be true. No wonder Eliot didn't say "the speaker."

But for all his influence, Eliot was not teaching English in American colleges. Brooks and Warren were; it is from their second edition, published in 1950, that I have quoted, and the memories of fifties graduates confirm that it was in that decade that the speaker permeated the diction of the English class. And as the decade progressed, critics became more aware of what they were doing; for their 1960 edition, Brooks and Warren revised their Nightingale section to eliminate those eleven occurrences of "the poet." They were less aware of why they were doing it. Though the invocation of "the speaker" harmonized with New Critical de-emphasis of biography and "conscious social purpose," the association was never explicit. Even in 1960 Brooks and Warren did not completely banish the poet; though Keats was speakerized, Marvell and Yeats were left alone.

Poems vary, however, in the insistence with which they solicit interest in their poet. Shakespeare's sonnets are notorious for inveigling critics into biographical lapses, and their treatment in what for convenience I will call the Brooks and Warren years demonstrates how consistently the use of "the speaker" correlates with the critic's biographical stance.

When Empson wrote in *Seven Types* that "Shakespeare is being abandoned by Mr. W.H. and stiffly apologizing for not having been servile to him," he was only continuing a tradition already well established when Wordsworth, or someone very like him, said that "with this key / Shakespeare unlocked his heart." (Naturally it was Browning who replied, "If so, the less Shakespeare he.") Even in 1941, in *The New Criticism* itself, John Crowe Ransom, trying to cool down Empson's "overreading" of Sonnet 73, was quite comfortable writing things like

> At this stage in the sequence, Shakespeare is melancholy. He finds the world evil and would like to die. His health is probably bad, for he refers to the likelihood of death.

Ten years later, Edward Hubler and Wilson Knight were still reading the sonnets as the expression of Shakespeare's personal concerns; neither used "the speaker." But by 1963 the speaker is claiming an authority critics cannot ignore, though they vary in how consciously they recognize it. In Hilton Landry's *Interpretations in Shakespeare's Sonnets*, the speaker takes over, imperceptibly to the author, but before the reader's eyes.

As to biography, Landry is a fence-sitter. Though he applauds critical "efforts to dispose of the biographical school of sonnet criticism," he "cannot agree . . . that the poet's interests are not deeply involved," especially in view of Sonnets 40 and 41. And for the first half of his book the ancient locution comes naturally, as he writes of "Shakespeare's reluctance to blame a friend directly," of "Shakespeare asking the handsome youth, 'What is your substance, whereof are you made?'" "The sonnets which open the sequence urge the patron repeatedly to marry . . . but that was before Shakespeare's own dark lady seduced the patron." On page 63, however, the speaker makes a silent entrance; Sonnets 40, 41, and 42 now become "a trio of poems in which the speaker comments on aspects of a sexual triangle." For some ten pages thereafter poet and speaker coexist freely, in relation to the same poems and sometimes in the same paragraph. Then the balance tips. References to "the poet" and "Shakespeare" diminish, then disappear. By the end of Landry's book, the speaker commands the field, with twenty-seven instances in twenty-four pages. There has been no discussion of voice or persona, but the poet has slipped away.

The next year, when Murray Krieger came to the Sonnets, he not only said "speaker" but could be explicit about it: "Shakespeare presents us with a true lover . . . as his poet-persona." Poet-persona, lover, and Shakespeare are distinguishable, though still close; both Shakespeare and the speaker are poets, after all, so "the poet" can be written with something of the old ease. They may even both be lovers; once Krieger even slips into writing not that the speaker but "Shakespeare calls upon his friend" to accept "the blessing of parenthood." But for the rest, his usage is both consistent and aware. How satisfyingly—and unexpectedly—the textual chase confirms personal history! It must have been just about 1964 that I got the news that poems were now to be talked about in a new way.

By 1968, the avowal of biographical interest has taken on a distinctly defensive coloration. Brent Stirling must confess on the first page of *The Shakespeare Sonnet Order* that "unlike some readers," he "would like to have some of the answers to the biographical mysteries." Stirling still feels easy saying "Shakespeare." So does Barbara Hernnstein Smith in her 1969 teaching edition: "The nature of Shakespeare's relation to the young man is addressed in many of the sonnets." James Winny, however, whose *The Master-Mistress* was published the same year, uses every argument he can think of to exclude a biographical reading, including the moral one (Shakespeare wouldn't have confessed anything so discreditable), and except when such references as "eternal lines" and "black ink" validate "the poet," he is careful to say "speaker."

In his 1969 *Essay on Shakespeare's Sonnets* and his 1977 edition of the poems, Stephen Booth has achieved full theoretical and practical consistency. Cooler than Winny, he jokes away any lingering biographical impurities. "Shakespeare was almost certainly homosexual, bisexual, or heterosexual. The sonnets provide no evidence on the matter." Since Booth's interest is in linguistic rather than human events, he does not often refer to whoever it is that utters the poems, but when he does, as in the discussion of Sonnet 35, the entity who "blames himself" is "the speaker."

Hallett Smith's 1981 book on the sonnets is perhaps the best illustration of the newly traditional diction of detachment. He too thinks he hears Eliot's Voices; he begins *The Tension of the Lyre* by quoting the first one, "the poet talking to himself." Invisibly and immediately, however, it is transmogrified, paraphrased into "poems in which the poet seems to be talking to himself." That "seems" sums up the speaker's forty-year progress toward universal imperium. For Smith, "the focus is on the feeling of the speaker," "the speaker's love is like a fever"; "there is little evidence in the first seventeen sonnets that the speaker feels love for the person addressed." And it's not only the speaker who's grown dim in the aesthetic distance, he's taken his friend with him, "the audience of the poem, fictional though it probably is." Pluralized, fictionalized, reduced to an It—what a fate for "the person addressed"! When at length Smith "must now consider the character of the poet (or speaker)," the parenthetical addition must disinfect so intimate a contact, and we are at once admonished to restrict our interest. "The 'I' of the sonnets . . . may or may not bear a close resemblance to William Shakespeare, but he is a *persona* with identifiable traits." We can guess which we are to prefer. Art's impersonality is more manageable than the untidy spectacle of poets who claim to look into their hearts and write. When Smith is momentarily brought "very close to the conclusion that the speaker in the Dark Lady sonnets is a man named Will, and that we are to take that person as William Shakespeare," his only recourse is to change the subject.

Poets tend to view things differently. Eliot had insisted his verse spoke for him. John Berryman added his own emphasis: "One thing that critics not themselves writers of poetry occasionally forget is that poetry is composed by actual human beings. . . . When Shakespeare wrote, 'Two loves I have,' reader, he was *not kidding*." A qualification followed—it was 1962, and the tradition was hardening: "Of course the speaker can never be the actual writer, who is a person with an address" and other impedimenta he can't carry into the poem. Distinguishing person and persona, Berryman quoted Ransom's phrase, "the highly compounded authorial 'I.'" But all he seemed to mean was that a poet (he was talking about Lowell's highly personal "Skunk Hour") may speak for others besides himself. It may even be the persona that makes the speaking possible: in a few years, Berryman would be writing the *Dream Songs*. When Robert Pinsky, poet as well as critic, identified the distancing persona as one of modern poetry's "strategies for retaining or recovering . . . the tones of the forbidden language of Arnold or Tennyson," Berryman was his premier example of how a poet through a persona "can use the style which annoys or embarrasses him, but which for some purposes he needs—needs more or less for its original, affirmative purposes." Needs as we all do; driven, we use irony to bypass irony. Reader, Henry was *not kidding*.

Only occasionally did critics join poets to retard the speaker's progress. Irvin Ehrenpreis resisted his invasion of eighteenth-century studies; in 1963 (the year of Landry's silent shift), his brief essay "Personae" insisted on what had never before required insistence, that the fictive work is written by "the real person," and "if he tells a story, we must ask what he (not his emanation) means by the story." But common sense appearing in an obscure festschrift and limiting its examples to Swift and Pope was not about to stop the tradition. Pinsky noted (in the mid-seventies) that speaking through a persona might "to a seventeenth-century reader . . . seem a bizarre way of writing poems of personal feeling"; he might have added that it might seem a bizarre way of talking about them. Indeed C. L. Barber, reviewing in 1978 Booth's books on the Sonnets, demurred briefly but explicitly from "those manuals of New Criticism" that "neatly separat[e] a 'speaker,' a dramatized presence, from the poet who mimes him," and argued gently that the "formalism" of Booth's interpretation ignored "human motives," "human gestures in the poems . . . that must reflect actual, . . . if somewhat obscure, personal relationships." Barber offered alternative interpretations which not only used the old locutions—as in "the poet's relation to the young man"—but depended on them. But these critical voices, eminent as they were, did not carry far. By 1981, the speaker's hegemony was so complete that John Reichert was impelled to ask, in a little-read but trenchant essay, "Do Poets Ever Mean What They Say?"

And it was in 1981 that my chase started, with the unyielding explanation of "Persona" I have quoted from the fourth edition of Abrams' *Glossary*—carried over unchanged, I was to find, from the third edition of ten years before. I had to take it as Abrams' own view; other entries made it clear enough when he disagreed with the ideas he summarized. Yet doubt nagged; could the critic I remembered really practice the antiseptic sophistication he seemed to mandate? I must find out how Abrams himself had been talking in the years when critics were learning to say "the speaker." Textual chases never end, but every chase at last must have a stop. Mine would stop here.

By now dates had become evidence; I did not expect to find a speaker in *The Mirror and the Lamp*. That marvelous book was published in 1953 and begun much earlier; I had read it as an unpublished doctoral dissertation in 1944. I checked; in it, Young, Boileau, and Pope (for a sample) came right out and "said" what they said in their poems; MacLeish made "a poetic statement"; Cowley even "sang," as poets were erstwhile wont to do. And so it was even in 1963; in the essay "Romanticism and the Spirit of the Age," Abrams regularly introduced poetic quotations by the simple "says" (Collins, Coleridge); Blake "complained to the Muses," and Wordsworth not only said and described, but insisted, dismissed, claimed and proclaimed, plainly pointed out, and bade farewell. Not for long, however.

I could almost have predicted the date; if 1963 was for Landry the year of the speaker, for Abrams it was 1965. In "Structure and Style in the Greater Romantic Lyric," we hear for the first time of "a determinate speaker . . . whom we overhear as he carries on . . . a sustained colloquy, sometimes with himself or with the outer scene, but more frequently with a silent human auditor, present or absent."

The verbs are now all the speaker's—it is he who "achieves an insight, faces up to a tragic loss, comes to a moral decision, or resolves an emotional problem." In *Frost at Midnight*, the Coleridge who said things so readily only two years before has become "the meditative mind," "the solitary and wakeful speaker"; to the speaker, too, is attributed the childhood under review. Abrams' account of the "Ode on a Distant Prospect of Eton College" is equally fastidious: the poem "evokes in memory the lost self of the speaker's youth," and not Gray but the speaker "watches the heedless schoolboys at their games." When it's not the speaker who gets the verb, it's by a common alternate strategy, the poem itself, as "Keats's first long poem of consequence . . . represents what he saw, then thought, while he 'stood tiptoe upon a little hill.'" And no sooner has Abrams quoted William Lisle Bowles's clear statement that his sonnets "describe his personal feelings" than he rephrases it with the familiar dubiety; the sonnets "present a determinate speaker, whom we are invited to identify with the author himself." The word "persona" makes its expected appearance two pages later. The tradition is, it would seem, firmly in place.

And yet within the year Abrams' own speaker had returned to the limbo whence he came. In the 1966 essay "Coleridge, Baudelaire, and Modernist Poetics," Wordsworth (in *The Prelude*) is describing, and without intermediary, "how, 'inspired by the sweet breath of heaven,' he assumed the prophet's sacred mission," and "calling on his fellow poet, Coleridge . . . to carry on with him 'as joint labourers in the work.'" Coleridge himself has reclaimed the right to say; the essay closes with him talking. "'Joy,' he says . . . 'is the spirit and the power, / Which, wedding Nature to us, gives in dower, / A new Earth and new Heaven.'"

Though his *Glossary* explanation appeared for the first time in 1971, by 1972 Abrams' own poets had got back all their verbs. In *Natural Supernaturalism: Tradition and Revolution in Romantic Literature*, Shelley remarks and diagnoses; Coleridge dismisses, reveals, and reviews his life; Arnold asks; Eliot remarks, Auden makes a wry comment, Plath testifies, and Stevens enquires, rejects, and says, all in verse, and all *in propria*, as we used to say, *persona*. Wordsworth himself explains, announces (repeatedly), says, goes on to say, goes on to *pray*, puts it, feels, proclaims, and cries. Though Abrams of course recognizes when his poet speaks "through the medium of an invented character," and though he more than once discusses "Tintern Abbey," there is no word of "the speaker who talks first to himself, then to his sister." When his sister is mentioned, in fact, the "his" refers directly to an antecedent "Wordsworth." Nor should we be surprised that Abrams couldn't keep his distance; that speaker is hardly consonant with the rich and humane contextuality of a critic the entire tenor of whose work opposes what he identified (in 1966, in "Coleridge, Baudelaire, and Modern Poetics") as "an aesthetic of an otherworldly, self-sufficient poem." It is characteristic, though odd, that when Abrams returned briefly to the idea of persona (in "Two Roads to Wordsworth," published like *Natural Supernaturalism* in 1972), it was to praise it as an antidote to too much New Criticism, a concept which can "rehumanize poetry by viewing the poet, in Wordsworth's phrase, 'as a man speaking to men.'" But the reference to persona, though appreciative, is momentary. As with Brower, subject and verb tell the story, and through the seventies Abrams' speaker does not revive. Abrams' own *Norton Anthology* briskly returns to Coleridge the childhood he lost in 1965 as businesslike notes to "Frost at Midnight" inform the student that "The scene is Coleridge's cottage at Nether Stowey," "The infant in line 7 is his son Hartley," "The 'stern preceptor' . . . the Reverend James Boyer," and the "sister beloved" his sister Ann. And in an essay written as recently as 1983, Coleridge says, Wordsworth proclaims, and to provide the grand coda: "Shelley announced that

The world's great age begins anew,
The golden years return."

And they yet may, if common sense keeps breaking in. But it's a long road back to innocence. I don't teach Great Books anymore, worse luck, but sometimes I teach Dante. This year, in a paper entitled "Textual Cocktails," I read that "the interplay of Dante-as-poet (as opposed to Dante-as-pilgrim, both poetic constructs of Dante-as-author), textualizes the *Inferno*." The young man who wrote that is a marvelous student and a marvelous person, brilliant, excitable, and excited about ideas. But I fear he has almost lost the capacity to ask naïve questions. I miss my community college students. Though they weren't used to literature, they were, some of them, perhaps for that very reason, ready to take it into their lives with an astonishing, hungry directness. I learned from them what I won't forget. Newly born Renaissance readers, they were coming into their heritage, reading for the reasons Horace and Sidney knew, for profit and delight. For them art could still hold the mirror up to nature. I learned to value that prelapsarian trust, to doubt that any paradise I could promise within the Poem Itself would be happier far. Could I sniff, farther down the road, an even newer criticism, one in which author, history, truth, meaning itself would dissolve, an insubstantial pageant faded? Subversion, as an activity, is overrated; the community college showed me that I did not want, and do not want, to undermine the assumption of very young people that great authors speak great words, and that great words proffer wisdom. Abrams would be the last to disagree that although we should not hunt messages, we should be willing to recognize and honor them when they are found.

Of course the speaker is often a useful concept, sometimes a necessary one. The pervasive attention to voice has increased the subtlety with which we are able to read literary texts as well as the length at which we can write about them, articulating nuances before undiscussed, if not therefore unapprehended or unfelt. But let's be sensible. Here, for example, is a new book attributing to Emily Dickinson "a voice, which though it is surely not hers, is so intimately defined by her habits of mind that it encourages friendship, familiarity, even affection." I'm told it's not hers, but I'm never told why. I'm supposed to know. Well, I don't know. Of course, as Abrams explained in the *Glossary*, "the I . . . is not the author as he exists in his everyday life," and "in each of the major lyricists the nature of the persona alters, sometimes subtly and sometimes radically, from one of his lyrics to the next." But do we really need to be told that the poet in everyday life never tasted a liquor never brewed, or wandered where the Muses haunt, especially since in the latter case the poet actually *was* with darkness and with dangers compast round? Our gain in subtlety is a loss in human community if we succeed in detaching the utterance from the uttering tongue and mind and heart, not occasionally and provisionally but as a matter of course. For we are all utterers—teachers, critics, poets, people—and at issue is the fullness of human commitment not merely to literature but to language, and language's commitment to what as human beings we think and believe and want and need to say. As to altering from one utterance to the next, everybody does that all the time, as any collection of letters—Flannery O'Connor's, say—will confirm. You'd have to be pretty unsophisticated to believe that "the speaker who utters Keats's 'Ode to a Nightingale'" is the author as he exists in his everyday life, but you'd have to be more sophisticated than I care to be to believe he's not Keats at all. I would prefer my students to recognize that poets are just like folks, arted up a bit, perhaps, but still doing for the most part the same sort of thing their teachers do when they write an article, that they themselves do when without thinking they alter their tone for a parent or an employer or a friend. And although it is certainly possible to draw therefrom the conclusion that every voice is fictional, I do not care to press the point. It seems unnecessary for students to question the coherence of their own personalities because they write differently for the college newspaper and for me. Unleashed, the idea of the speaker takes on a terrifying applicability.

From that speaker it is only a step to the "novelistic, irretrievable, irresponsible figure" conjured up by Roland Barthes, "the Author himself—that somewhat decrepit deity of the old criticism," who plays at seeing himself as "a being on paper and his life as a *bio-graphy* . . . a writing without referent," "a text like any other." Or Foucault: "It would be as false to seek the author in relation to the actual writer as to the fictional narrator; the 'author function' arises out of their scission—in the division and distance of the two." So quotation marks break out all over, as Derrida tells us that "it would be frivolous to think that 'Descartes,' 'Leibniz,' 'Rousseau,' 'Hegel,' etc. are the names of authors," and adds that the "indicative value" he attributes to them is only "the name of a problem." A problem indeed; a problem at once frivolous and dire, an intellectual heresy, a *trahison des clercs.* A concept that can assimilate the Milton who in darkness implored celestial light to shine inward to Lemuel Gulliver is a concept that devalues human personhood and human pain.

My voice has slipped; these notes have changed too much to tragic. Critics still use the names of poets naturally. Heartening inconsistencies still challenge critical rigor. Biography is back, albeit too often tricked out in such psychometaphysical garments as to obscure the human form divine rather than reveal it. If poets should reclaim the right (I quote Pinsky) "to make an interesting remark or speak of profundities, with all the liberty given to the newspaper editorial, a conversation, a philosopher, or any speaker whatever," even the inspirational and didactic may return: a recent issue of the *Hudson Review* contains an article on "the moral authority of poetry." And students, thank God, are ever virgin; each generation must be taught anew the mechanisms of detachment, or, as I'm told it's now called, distantiation. Left alone, it is no more possible to distance them from the human statement, from what Archibald MacLeish called "the human voice humanly speaking," than Brecht's epic gimmicks could insulate his audiences from Mother Courage.

Reading, rightly understood, is a relationship; we read, Auden said, "to break bread with the dead." "All methods of criticism and teaching are bad," wrote Northrop Frye, "if they encourage the persistent separation of student and literary work"; our job as teachers is to try our best to "weaken those tendencies within criticism which keep the literary work objective and separated from the reader." I would rather have students too naïve than not naïve enough. Distrust exacts a price, as when children are taught to refuse rides from strangers. We pay it as criticism metastasizes, as we read more and more cleverly, first looking behind masks, then discerning masks where no masks are, then persuading ourselves that the eyeholes are empty. Cleverness excludes, and distrust privatizes. Distrust of the text opens the way to elaborated and idiosyncratic readings and to a criticism that legitimizes them, even as it delegitimizes the common and accessible experience it stigmatizes as naïve. I want my students to hear voices, to recognize ambiguities—even, in moderation, ironies. I want them to experience the literary work as a thing well wrought. Yet I am conscious of the price. The "object for study" all too easily becomes "objective" in Frye's sense, a problem to be solved, not an utterance like our own.

In this process, I believe the speaker has played an unobtrusive but influential part. I have for my last years as a teacher my own project of subversion, my target the sophistication that compasses me round. Fortunately it's not impossible, if you're confidently old-fashioned enough, to reactivate a nineteen-year-old's naïveté. Dante, as ever, is a great help, Dante all tangled in biography and history, Dante the author, Dante the pilgrim, Dante the poet of many voices, who in Canto XX of the *Inferno* uses his own to tell us how to read a poem:

> *Se Dio ti lasci, lettor, prender frutto*
>   *di tua lezione, or pensa per te stesso*
>   *com' io potea tener lo visa asciutto. . . .*

"Reader, so may God grant you to gather fruit of your reading, think now for yourself how I could keep my cheeks dry. . . ." Do we think it was only the poet's emanation that wept? Think of the poet's emotion, reader, so you can share it. If you want to gather the fruit of your reading, take care how you interpose with poetic constructs, especially those you yourself have constructed. Listen very carefully to what Dante is saying. Consider, even, that it might be in some sense true.

Before I Read *Clarissa* I Was Nobody

Aspirational Reading and Samuel Richardson's Great Novel

JUDITH PASCOE

When I first came across Richardson's eighteenth-century blockbuster, I was standing in a campus bookstore in Philadelphia in the late 1980s. I had just enrolled in graduate school, chiefly as a dodge. My escape was from a high school classroom in Chesapeake, Virginia, or, to be more accurate, from a hallway lined with classrooms through which I pushed a cart loaded with Bunsen burners and test-tube holders. As an itinerant science teacher, I rattled my tinker's cart of lab supplies into the classrooms of teachers who were standing duty in the lunchroom or dropping cigarette ash on vocabulary quizzes in the faculty lounge. The me that stood in the bookstore in Philadelphia was ecstatic at having managed to swap my lab cart for a book satchel. Farewell to the boy who called me "Miss Tabasco"; adieu to the girl who carved initials into her forearm; good riddance to adolescent *Sturm und Drang*—I had achieved the cool remove of higher learning.

The bookstore was crowded, and I snatched paperbacks with abandon, working my way down the shelf of books earmarked for the seminar in which I had enrolled. *Robinson Crusoe, Moll Flanders, The Man of Feeling*—I was grabbing without paying much attention. A month before, I had received a notice from the course instructor who advised students to begin reading in advance, an admonition I took as seriously as a professional weight lifter would heed a warning about the strenuousness of beach ball aerobics. Reading was my leisure activity; I had no fear of being left behind.

The last item on the shelf was a book with the size and heft of a two-pound sack of flour, a Penguin Classics edition suffering from elephantiasis. I dropped my other books and started pawing through the one thousand five hundred thirty-four pages of Angus Ross's magisterial but reasonably priced edition of *Clarissa*. I knelt in the aisle and marveled at the weight of this book. The back cover boiled Richardson's novel down to a one-sentence plot summary, as if to rebuff the casual reader by denying the pleasure of surprise. Gazing into Richardson's novel, I saw myself as a creature deluded by false confidence, and my eyes had trouble focusing on the 10-point print. I reassembled my gathered pyramid of books and proceeded to the checkout line with *Clarissa* serving as the monumental foundation stone. Then, a chastened being, I began my new intellectual career.

The Penguin paperback edition of *Clarissa* represents a grand experiment in book production, a test to see how many pages can be glued to a thin cardboard spine. There are bigger paperback books—the greater Orlando phone book springs to mind—but no other paperback novel has such a commanding shelf presence. On its spine, the Penguin *Clarissa* showcases a smaller version of the front cover art—a miniature version of Joseph Highmore's portrait of Clarissa's family. Unlike most book spine art, which tends to zoom in on the most alluring detail of the full frontal artwork in a thumbnail square, the spinal Highmore provides a wider-angle view than the portrait's book front rendition. The Harlowe family cowers before the villainous Lovelace on both front and spine, but in the smaller version Clarissa's dress—which is of the voluminous hip-extending style that makes a woman look like she is transporting a sofa—billows out to its full extent.

But even the estimable Penguin edition does not encompass all of *Clarissa*, just all of the first edition. When I first read *Clarissa* as a graduate student, I went rummaging around in the dustier shelving reaches of a university library in order to find the section of *Clarissa* to which Angus Ross tantalizingly alludes while explaining why he chose to republish the first edition of *Clarissa* instead of the third edition in which Richardson strove to temper the appeal of his villain Lovelace and to enhance the sanctity of Clarissa so that readers would stop moaning about the two not winding up married. If I am to find fault with Angus Ross—and I do this hesitantly and deferentially—it is not because he crammed seven or eight svelte volumes into one corpulent book, since in so doing he made *Clarissa* available to the masses. No, the only reason I find fault with the Penguin edition is because Ross was too much of a purist: he reproduced the first edition, he said, because it is "appreciably shorter, often livelier" and because "to a large extent the added material seems relatively inert."

Inert? When I first read *Clarissa* as a graduate student, nothing could have seemed less inert than Letter 208. Letter 208, my first favorite letter, is arguably the most lurid letter in the novel since it contains Lovelace's outrageous flight of malevolent fancy against Clarissa's best friend Anna Howe. Lovelace plans for his coterie of rakes to carry out a triple rape of Anna Howe, her mother, and their maid-servant during a voyage to the Isle of Wight. To his friend Belford, Lovelace writes:

> I know it will be hard weather: I *know* it will: And before there can be the least suspicion of the matter, we shall be in sight of Guernsey, Jersey, Dieppe, Cherbourg, or any-whither on the French coast that it shall please us to agree with the winds to blow us: And then, securing the footman, and the women being separated, one of us, according to lots that may be cast, shall overcome, either by persuasion or force, the maid-servant: That will be no hard task; and she is a likely wench [I have seen her often]: One, Mrs. Howe; nor can there be much difficulty there; for she is full of health and life, and has been long a Widow: Another [*That*, says the princely Lion, must be *I!*] the saucy Daughter; who will be too much frighted to make great resistance [*Violent* spirits, in that Sex, are seldom *true*

spirits—'Tis but where they *can*—]: And after beating about the coast for three or four days for recreation's sake, and to make sure work, and till we see our sullen birds begin to eat and sip, we will set them all ashore where it will be most convenient; sell the vessel . . . and pursue our travels, and tarry abroad till all is hushed up.

When I first read this letter, which Richardson wrote for the first edition but then omitted in a half-hearted gesture toward brevity, I was sitting cross-legged on the floor in the library stacks. Someone lurking in the next aisle might have heard a sharp intake of breath quickly followed by a disdainful snorting noise as I got to the part where Lovelace imagines himself going on trial for the crime:

[B]eing a handsome fellow, I shall have a dozen or two of young maidens, all dressed in white, go to Court to beg my life—And what a pretty shew they will make, with their white hoods, white gowns, white petticoats, white scarves, white gloves, kneeling for me, with their white handkerchiefs at their eyes, in two pretty rows, as Majesty walks thro' them, and nods my pardon for their sakes!

The breeziness of Lovelace's sexual violence and the creepiness of his self-regard were probably enhanced by the experience of reading in a library where the custodial staff announced the approach of closing time by dousing the lights in the stacks. This sudden descent into darkness would be followed by cursing from the vicinity of the open carrels where readers had lost track of time.

Even though I was in danger of stumbling into a book trolley in the pitch blackness, I had not come looking for this missing excerpt out of solidarity with Clarissa, selecting this passage from all the others due to a shared sense of vulnerability. I singled out this most shocking letter because I liked shocking books, and so had perversely homed in on the scene that is most out of keeping with Richardson's oft-stated moral objective. According to Richardson, "[A]*musement* should be considered as little more than the vehicle to the more necessary *instruction*." When Richardson titled his novel *Clarissa, or, The History of a Young Lady: Comprehending the Most Important Concerns of*

Private Life, And Particularly Showing the Distresses That May Attend the Misconduct Both of Parents and Children in Relation to Marriage, he wasn't anticipating that some misguided graduate student would skim through the moral admonishments and head straight to the triple rape. "[I]f you were to read Richardson for the story," Samuel Johnson famously declared, "your impatience would be so much fretted that you would hang yourself." Johnson went on to insist, "[Y]ou must read him for the sentiment, and consider the story as only giving occasion to the sentiment." Balderdash, I might have said, if I'd been a bold graduate student, unafraid to disagree with the man who defined "balderdash" for eighteenth-century readers. The first time I read *Clarissa*, I read it like I was reading a Stephen King novel, and was only fretted for so long as it took me to come up with a seminar paper topic.

As a vulgar reader of *Clarissa*, a reader who sought out the most salacious missing letter, I was inadvertently participating in a debate among more astute readers of *Clarissa* which had grown heated in the years just before I entered graduate school. Richardson's novel enjoyed something of a critical moment in the early 1980s, with several of the brightest minds in eighteenth-century studies fixing their high beams on *Clarissa*. The dust jacket of Terry Eagleton's 1982 *The Rape of Clarissa* announced Eagleton's ambition to "reclaim Richardson for our time"; in Eagleton's analysis, Richardson's novel presented the story of the downtrodden oppressed (Clarissa) rising up against the aristocratic oppressor (Lovelace). *Clarissa*, for Eagleton, was a shot fired by the restive middle class against the corrupt and depleted nobility. In Terry Castle's *Clarissa's Ciphers*, also published in 1982, the focus was on Clarissa's suffering at the hands of Lovelace, and on her ingenious efforts to thwart his vile machinations. Both critics positioned themselves on the side of the angels, seeing it as their duty to counter a whole raft of past critics who, when they were not blaming the victim (Richard Cohen: "[A]t a deep and primitive level there is a sense in which Clarissa both asks and deserves to be raped"), were describing the rape of Clarissa with a clinical hauteur. Although I counted Dorothy Van Ghent's "On Clarissa" among the best essays written on the novel, I did not want to pitch my critical tent in the camp of someone who had written

> The central event of the novel, over which the interminable series of letters hovers so cherishingly, is, considered in the abstract, a singularly thin and unrewarding piece of action—the deflowering of a young lady—and one which scarcely seems to deserve the universal uproar it provokes in the book.

There was a take-back-the-night fervor to Eagleton's and Castle's discussions of Clarissa's rape; they were particularly incensed by William Warner's celebration of Lovelace as "the heroic practitioner of a Nietzchean style of subversive interpretation" and by his insistence that the rape of Clarissa had become "something extravagant, overdetermined, pleasurable." My interest in a letter that revolved around an imagined triple rape might seem to bear out Warner's point, but I avoided giving the appearance of fraternizing with the devil by focusing on Anna Howe, who, I argued, had been inexplicably and unjustifiably neglected by critics busy writing about Clarissa's suffering or Lovelace's subversion of language. What's all this about Clarissa and Lovelace, I demanded in my seminar paper. Why isn't anyone paying any attention to Clarissa's best friend, the character who gets the whole novel going by suggesting that Clarissa "write in so full a manner as may gratify those who know not so much of [her] affairs," who even requests a copy of the preamble to the Harlowe grandfather's will so that she can send it to her nosy Aunt Harman who is very desirous to see it? Inspired by the critic Judith Wilt, who had set bow ties spinning by daring to suggest that Lovelace hadn't been up to the job, that the rape had been carried out by his female accomplices, I used the triple rape scene to accuse Richardson of constructing an insidiously recurring leitmotif of incestuously tinged female relationships. Or at least I think I did. I preserved whatever I had to say about *Clarissa* on a 5-inch floppy disk, now an indecipherable hieroglyph. Everything I really need to know I learned in graduate school—but unfortunately I can no longer open the file.

I tend to romanticize the community of fellow readers I joined in graduate school, but it is fair to say that not all of them shared my commitment to Richardson. Less dedicated members of my eighteenth-century seminar might have been aided and abetted by George Sherburn, a Harvard professor who pared *Clarissa* down to the size of a book one could assign to undergraduates: 517 pages. Sherburn apparently decided his students needed a version of Richardson's novel that would not cause them to lose heart at first glimpse. This is speculation on my part, and I am attributing to Sherburn's students a shirking behavior of which I have been guilty myself in past confrontations with supersized novels. In turning Samuel Richardson's magnum opus into a biggish book, Sherburn was looking out for the interests of indolent readers like myself, but he was also following the lead of an earlier abridger, the editor of the 1756 *Paths of Virtue Delineated*, known, by subtitle, as *The History in Miniature of the Celebrated Pamela, Clarissa Harlowe and Sir Charles Grandison, Familiarised and Adapted to the Capacities of Youth*. Sherburn's estimation of the capacities of youth was generous in comparison; this more aggressive abridger turned the nineteen volumes of Richardson's three novels into a 232-page duodecimo. A writer for the *Critical Review* was glad to find Richardson's books "now reduced to such a size as may fit them for every hand."

Whatever approval Sherburn's edition initially met with, it was ultimately drowned out by the hissing and booing of Margaret Anne Doody and Florian Stuber in the normally tranquil pages of *Modern Language Studies*. "Sherburn's abridgment should no longer continue to masquerade as *Clarissa* in the canon of English literature," railed these critics in 1988, bolstered by the recent publication of the Penguin paperback. They went on to accuse the by-then dead Sherburn of sloppy scholarship, slovenliness in proofreading, deception, ruthless and clumsy editing, prudery, censorship, and the hostile trivialization of a great work of Western literature. They said that the flaws they found in Sherburn's edition were "symptomatic of a deep disease not subject to remedy" and that his version of *Clarissa* "should never be taught in any reputable college or university."

My secondhand copy of Sherburn's edition bears out their judgment. Unread by me, but purchased from a used book bin for $2.45 at some indeterminate moment in my distant reader's past, it was first the property of one Fred Warren who engraved his name on the cover in blue ballpoint pen, and what kind of a person, past the age of seven and a half, writes his name on a paperback's front cover instead of inside the front cover or on the half-title page or even on the title page? Despite evidence of this book's seedy provenance, and despite a constitutional aversion to abridgments in general, I do not, however, get exercised by Sherburn's edition. Could the same scholar who wrote *The Early Popularity of Milton's Minor Poems* have become fired with a Machiavellian zeal when, late in his career, he got around to abridging *Clarissa*? If he "slashed out paragraphs without giving any attention to the fabric of meaning," maybe this was because he couldn't make it to the novel's bolt end without losing track of some yardage. Clearly his heart wasn't in it. "*Clarissa* is one of the very greatest novels ever written," he wrote, according to two of Richardson's biographers. He went on to lament, "It cannot be improved by any sort of *abridgment*. I don't believe you can like what I have done. I don't myself."

No one who reads all of *Clarissa* can like what Sherburn did because reading all of *Clarissa*, as opposed to skimming quickly through the first several volumes in which everything that happens could (according to one of Richardson's contemporaries) be condensed into a single page, is a test of intellectual fortitude, a way of separating the chosen people from the churls who go about incising their names into paperback book covers, of distinguishing mature readers from youth with their limited capacities. As a person who finds few opportunities to feel smugly superior as I wander the halls of academe, or as I scarf goldfish crackers at department parties, I can count on my having read *Clarissa* (five times!) partly to compensate for my not having read *Ulysses* (which I carried across Europe on my honeymoon, and in which an obsolete franc note marks my failure to read past page twenty). When a visiting scholar who claims to be a specialist in the eighteenth century confides that he has never actually read *Clarissa*, I feel like lurching backward into the nonalcoholic punch bowl and shouting, "WHAT!! Never read *Clarissa*?" But instead I smile understandingly and turn my attention to the spinach dip. Whenever I read the latest academic effort to explain the rise of the novel in new terms, that is, to unseat Ian Watt, who wrote *The Rise of the Novel* in 1957, I notice that Richardson's *Pamela* gets thirty-five pages while *Clarissa* gets only the occasional passing reference, and I think, "Here is another person who hasn't read *Clarissa*." Leslie Fiedler wrote about *Clarissa* at length; in fact, *Clarissa* was the most important precursor text for his study *Love and Death in the American Novel*. Fiedler regretted that of Richardson's three novels, only *Pamela* is still read, "the other two now left to gather dust in libraries, though all Europe once wept over *Clarissa*." He went on to castigate "a living authority on the American novel" for wrongly characterizing *Clarissa* as wicked, calling the critic's ignorance of the novel unpardonable. But Leslie Fiedler, just before wagging his finger at his fellow critic's error, ended a summary of the novel's plot by wrongly claiming that Lovelace is killed in a duel by his closest friend. Fiedler let the mistake stand in his book's second edition, either because he had been humbled by his own scholarly error and was determined to let future generations know how the mighty had fallen, or because he was uncowed by the tiny number of people who had read to the end of *Clarissa* and so were likely to notice his mistake.

These days, I read *Clarissa* so that I can teach the novel to undergraduates. I justify teaching a whole class on *Clarissa*, urging students through the novel at the rate of one hundred pages per week, by making grandiose pedagogical claims in my course description. I say I will use the novel as a window onto eighteenth-century culture; I suggest its critical reception will allow me to delineate the major schools of twentieth-century literary theory. But that's just to impress the curriculum committee. The way I draw undergraduates in is by suggesting they will be initiated into the exclusive coterie of people who have read *Clarissa* in its entirety. You wouldn't think that this kind of bald elitist appeal would play very well at a state university in Iowa. My students are geographically unassuming. When asked to say where they hail from on the first day of classes, they mumble the names of their hometowns, and even when I try to whip up some feeling of civic pride—"Washington? the town with the new outdoor pool? with the giant slide and the tilty buckets?"—they still defer to the kids from the suburbs of Chicago. It can be a humbling experience to be an English major at the University of Iowa, to arrive with your reputation as a high school poet or prize-winning editorialist behind you, lured by the distant twinkle of the Writers' Workshop, only to find yourself taking "Reading Short Stories" in a grim classroom with misspelled signage: "Please do not adjust thermostat. If to hot or cold call maintenance."

It is usually to cold when I start teaching *Clarissa*. It is January in the Middle West, and people are sliding across the iced campus walkways, their faces freezing into death grimaces whenever a stiff wind gusts off the river. Inside the classroom, it takes several weeks of cheerleading to convince students that Richardson is worth reading, and I am not above trying to impress them with his mechanical achievement, that he wrote a sixteen-hundred-page closely typed novel in the days before typewriter, fountain pen, or rollerball. I do not make them trim their own goose quills and dip them in ink, but I dwell on Richardson's manual fortitude whenever possible. "Our author had a most ready pen," wrote Anna Barbauld, who edited Richardson's letters. "Indeed, it was seldom out of his hand, and this readiness, with the early habit of writing letters, made him take pleasure in an extensive correspondence, with which he filled the interstices of a busy day." My students fill the interstices of a busy day by watching *The Simpsons*, donating plasma for cash, and drinking excessively at local bars. I ask them to write about the exact circumstances in which they read *Clarissa*, wanting to make a point about the difficulty of reading *Clarissa* at this particular moment in time, when one could, instead, be playing video games or shopping online. In this way I bear witness to the student who reads *Clarissa* at a truck stop diner with an attached Harley-Davidson dealership. This student works out the power hierarchy in the Harlowe family while eating gravy biscuits amidst long haulers, then tucks his copy of *Clarissa* under his arm so he can peruse the Harley belt buckles next door.

Another student writes of reading *Clarissa* in the Arby's at the Old Capitol Mall: "It's quiet but not too quiet. Plus they have really good milkshakes. Many times I've enjoyed *Clarissa* and a Jamocha shake." Still another student reads *Clarissa* in the commons area of the student union, with her "very distracting & talkative boyfriend & the music & TV blaring." Richardson's first novel, *Pamela*, inspired a cult of readers who used the book to signal each other at pleasure gardens, flashing its cover suggestively as they passed each other in the lamplit walkways. "All that read were his readers," wrote Anna Barbauld. "Even at Ranelagh . . . it was usual for ladies to hold up the volumes of *Pamela* to one another, to shew they had got the book that everyone was talking of." Although I ask students to write about where they read *Clarissa* in order to highlight the difficulties faced by the serious student of Richardson, their descriptions allow me to imagine them as a secret society bound together by the black and yellow cover of the Penguin *Clarissa*. At semester's end, one student writes, "I became so engrossed with this book that after reading what I had to for the week, I went out to the bars, but came back to read more before I went to bed." There is the occasional naysayer—"I loathe *Clarissa*. I never want to see it again"—but the secret society of *Clarissa* readers are not put off by even the most fervent expressions of disdain. Over the course of the semester, many of them can be found in the smoking section of the Country Kitchen because, by one account, that is where the most interesting people sit. "If I needed a break," wrote one Country Kitchen *Clarissa* reader, "I would eavesdrop on the conversations of people with piercings."

My students read for the plot not the sentiment, and when one of them, inevitably, bothers to read the back book cover and finds out that some book designer at Penguin has killed the surprise, he becomes seriously splenetic, sulking at the periphery of the classroom, next to the nonadjustable heater which is chugging along like Mike Mulligan's steam shovel even though crocuses are blooming outside (to hot! to hot!). There's always one student in the room who knows that Clarissa gets raped and who also knows what happens next (I won't ruin it for the non-*Clarissa* readers—if you buy the Penguin edition, be prepared to clap a book jacket on the cover). But this knowing student is kind enough not to spoil it for his classmates who, in any event, sail right past the rape without realizing it has happened. In the most famous letter in the novel, on the 883rd page of the Penguin edition, Richardson communicates the rape of Clarissa by having Lovelace write:

> And now, Belford, I can go no farther. The affair is over. Clarissa lives. And I am
>
> > Your humble servant,
> > R. Lovelace

My students generally come to class after reading this passage with no idea that something momentous has occurred. They are initially resentful that, after having dutifully read 883 pages, they have been given so slight an account of the novel's central event. It is almost as if Orson Welles, instead of lingering over the sled at the end of *Citizen Kane*, had opted instead to put an advertisement for Rosebud sleds on a distant billboard in the corner of the screen. We talk about the contrast between this elliptical little letter and all the wordy letters that precede it, about why an author whose characters write at so great a length—a stickler for verisimilitude once proved that these characters could not have written so much and still have had time to live the events they describe—would be so reticent. My students come around to the view that Richardson's refusal to describe the rape of Clarissa, or at least his refusal of detail directly after the event has transpired, is a stroke of brilliance, that the rape is all the more shocking for its not being immediately described. Sometimes someone brings up Hitchcock's method of increasing suspense by letting the viewer's imagination fill in what the director refrains from depicting in gory detail. Okay, sometimes I bring up Hitchcock since everyone has seen *Psycho*. No matter—we are suddenly a community of readers with strongly held opinions about the rape of Clarissa. Before the semester is over, a few of my students become evangelical in their enthusiasm for the novel and try to bring others into Richardson's fold. One of them hails me at the Handimart fuel pump in order to report that her sister has tried to read *Clarissa*. "How far did she get?" I ask, trying not to let gasoline drip on my shoes.

My students are part of the wired generation that is leaving librarians with no one to shush, and *Clarissa* might seem immune to the kind of digital innovations that are making it possible to get a college degree without checking out a book from the library. Yet Richardson's behemoth has been well served by the technological advance guard. The good people at Literature Online stand poised to transmit a machine-readable transcript of either the 1748 *Clarissa* (all 5,914 kilobytes of it) or the 1751 third edition (with its 935 extra kilobytes). You, with the laptop computer and the internet link—you could be downloading *Clarissa* at this very minute. You, there, checking out the Rookwood auction on eBay—why aren't you reading one of the greatest European literary works of all time, the high-water mark of the English novel? Inspired by the success of Oprah reading groups, several municipalities have called on their citizenry to join together in a communal reading effort. A year or two ago, Chicagoans were urged to read Harper Lee's *To Kill a Mockingbird*; Boiseans were coaxed to take up Marilynne Robinson's *Housekeeping*. In Chicago, lapel pins were issued so that *Mockingbird* readers could identify each other in supermarket lines or across crowded buses and feel licensed to express their views of Boo Radley to complete strangers. There is a general unassailable consensus that reading is a good thing, that people who read together will exhibit a heightened civility, an increased brotherly love, an enhanced vocabulary.

When I see city officials focus their reading initiatives on a book like Harper Lee's, a good book, but let's face it, not much of a challenge even for the junior high schoolers to whom it is regularly assigned, I see a missed opportunity for bold governmental action. If everyone agrees it is a good thing to read *To Kill a Mockingbird* en masse, how much greater a thing would it be to tackle the longest book in the English language on a citywide basis? Reading *Clarissa* requires stiffened resolve, increased fortitude, heightened stick-to-itiveness—all qualities that would strengthen and improve a city's populace. Commuting distances would seem to shrink if carpoolers were consulting Angus Ross's glossary for the meaning of "pad-nag" or "padusoy." Cocktail parties would sizzle if martini-drinkers ventured strong opinions about epistolarity. Mine is an immodest, but by no means facetious, proposal. If Oprah favors books that feature sympathetic heroines who learn one of Life's Important Lessons, why is Oprah not leading her viewers to the book recommended by the 1762 *Treatise on the Religious Education of Daughters*, whose author found *Clarissa* "admirably calculated to instruct and entertain"? Richardson, could he come back from the dead, would be a delightful talk show guest, eager to oblige Oprah with a walking tour of his writing grotto. Witness the testimony of a Mr. Reich of Leipsic who once set out for England "purely with a view of cultivating a personal acquaintance with so great a man as Mr. Samuel Richardson," and who was subsequently served chocolate and encouraged to partake of the fruits of Richardson's garden, and who, when he came to rest in Richardson's grotto, kissed the esteemed author's inkhorn. Richardson was not the most camera-ready author, being by his own description short and rather plump, with one hand generally in his bosom and the other holding a cane which he leaned upon under the skirts of his coat as a stay against frequent tremors. But Richardson more than compensated for any physical deficits by his willingness to court female readers and by his tirelessness in discussing his own work. As Barbauld tactfully reports, "In the circle of his admirers, his own works occupied, naturally, a large share of conversation; and he had not the will, nor perhaps the variety of knowledge necessary to turn it on other topics."

Richardson was an insecure author, in constant need of bolstering, and he tolerated his readers' editorializing in exchange for their abundant praise. He worried constantly over his novel's excessive length, writing to his friend Edward Young, "[I] am such a sorry pruner, tho' greatly luxuriant, that I am apt to add three pages for one I take away!" Sarah Fielding's 1749 *Remarks on Clarissa* provided a gratifying response to the author's concern. "As to the length of the story," Fielding wrote in the guise of a *Clarissa* reader named Bellario, "I fancy that Complaint arises from the great Earnestness the characters inspire the Reader with to know the Event; and on a second Reading may vanish."

To read *Clarissa* once may be considered a duty, but to read *Clarissa* twice might be considered, especially in our day, a solipsistic retreat from the actual world. Leigh Hunt, walled around with all the comfort and protection his library could provide, wrote, "I entrench myself in my books equally against sorrow and the weather." If one wants to build a fortress with books, the Penguin *Clarissa* makes a handy brick, but Richardson's previous readers saw the book as a buttress rather than a retreat. Mary Shelley read *Clarissa* in 1816, then read the Italian translation three years later. In between readings, she lived through the suicide of her half-sister Fanny, the birth and death of her daughter Clara, and the death of her three-year-old son. In the journal entry that directly precedes Shelley's mention of reading *Clarissa* in Italian, she notes her husband's birthday, going on to write, "We have now lived five years together and if all the events of the five years were blotted out I might be happy—but to have won & then cruelly have lost the associations of five years is not an accident to which the human mind can bend without much suffering." For Mary Shelley, Richardson's novel served as sustenance rather than diversion. No novel allowed her an escape from the loss of two children, but Clarissa's suffering may have helped Shelley endure her own enormous grief. Richardson's refusal to grant his readers a happy ending was, for Mary Shelley, a companionable acknowledgment of human anguish.

I do not turn to *Clarissa* in times of duress, but then I am an unregenerate reader, too enthralled by Lovelace's legerdemain to linger over Richardson's edifying sentiments. Richardson wrote of his attempt to reach readers like myself, of "pursuing to their *closets* those who fly from the *pulpit*, and there, under the gay air, and captivating semblance of a *Novel*, tempting them to the perusal of many a persuasive sermon." He gathered *A Collection of the Moral and Instructive Sentiments, Maxims, Cautions, and Reflexions, Contained in the Histories of Pamela, Clarissa, and Sir Charles Grandison*, cross-listing the sentiments with citations for volume and page "both in Octavo and Twelves" so that readers could go directly to the most edifying excerpts. The purpose of gathering sustaining quotes from the novel, according to the preface to this compilation, was to "animate man to act up to his genuine greatness," and I hope, when I next turn the pages of *Clarissa*, to be the kind of reader who does not pass lightly over this passage which Richardson culls from volume 2:

> To *know* we are happy, and not to leave it to after-reflection to look back upon that preferable Past with a heavy and self-accusing heart, is the highest of human felicities.

Volume 2 is arguably the most tedious volume in *Clarissa*; I am accustomed to reading through it at great speed.

I would like to be a better reader of *Clarissa*, but the day may never come when I will not anticipate with greatest pleasure those moments in the novel when Lovelace prances about in a diabolical passion like Cyril Richard playing Captain Hook. I may persist in loving Lovelace like Percy Shelley loved Satan in Milton's *Paradise Lost*, against the author's intentions and counter to the work's noble aims. I may continue to love *Clarissa* partly for the same petty reason that I like *The Princess Casamassima*—because I've read it and not everyone has. In moments of honest personal inventory, I realize that I may never distinguish myself among readers of *Clarissa*, but, still, here we all are: Samuel Johnson, William Hazlitt, Mary Shelley, Samuel Taylor Coleridge, Thomas Babington Macaulay, Henry James, Virginia Woolf—along with Dan from Council Bluffs, Jessica from Cedar Rapids, and me.

Learning from Robert Fitzgerald

DANA GIOIA

I

Early one afternoon in September 1976, I was walking through the New Haven train station, trying to catch the Amtrak express to Boston. The weather was suffocatingly muggy, a gray Northeastern day when the sun is invisible but oppressive and the morning drizzle steams from the tarmac. For two hours the public address system had slurred assurances to the platform that the train would arrive in fifteen minutes. Finally I had wandered back to the terminal to fetch a cup of what I had seen advertised as "the world's finest coffee." Now with my lukewarm, watery purchase in hand, I returned through a sooty tunnel to my gate. The walls of this underworld were festive with defaced soft drink posters and lyric graffiti hastily spray-painted in what looked like Arabic. Although I walked alone through the subterranean gallery, the memory of other travelers greeted me in the delicate blend of urines that filled the damp air.

Climbing the concrete stairs to the gate, I tried to cheer myself by thinking of the friends I would visit on this last-minute trip to Boston. I had reached everyone except the person I wanted most to see, Robert Fitzgerald, who had two years earlier been my favorite teacher at Harvard. I had not seen him since leaving graduate school to pursue a career in business. I wanted very much to talk to him about the difficulties I was facing trying to write poetry while working in a large corporation. He would have practical advice, I knew, since as a young man, he too had pursued his literary interests outside the academy. Knowing I would miss him now in Boston, I wondered when, if ever, I would see him again.

Immersed in glum thoughts, moist with perspiration and self-pity, I rose from the redolent stairwell into the bright haze of the platform. Just as I turned to rejoin the refugees who stood dour and defeated at the far end, I heard footsteps echoing behind me from the underpass. Glancing down, I saw an older man climbing toward me from the shadows. Dressed despite the heat in a tweed jacket and navy blue beret, he seemed familiar, but I knew from experience how easy it was, alone in a new city, to mistake a stranger for some old friend. Then I noticed the dark-green Harvard book bag slung over his shoulder. As I stood staring, the apparition stopped to address me.

"Mr. Gioia," it said in the conspiratorial whisper I knew so well. "Who would have expected you?"

"Or you? Mr. Fitzgerald," I replied with the mock formality we always assumed on greeting one another.

We shook hands and walked down the platform together. A few minutes later, without announcement, the train arrived.

"Right on time," Robert said.

I realized he thought this was the 3 o'clock train whereas I knew it was the 1 o'clock express, two hours late. We had been trying to catch different trains. Now boarding the same one together, we spent the next two hours having the conversation I had hoped for.

Meetings with Robert were like that. They didn't just happen. They unfolded unexpectedly like sheer good luck. Sometimes the pure coincidence of the encounter was the amazing thing—like that tropic afternoon in New Haven. In the years that followed, I bumped into Robert by accident in enough unlikely places—from a windswept Avenue of the Americas to a sunny Vassar quad—to make me believe in a Homeric notion of fate. But usually the good fortune was simply the irresistible warmth of his company. I never met anyone who knew him—colleague, student, or competitor—who did not like him. Affection, however, was only part of it. Everyone who knew Robert well felt he was special, not only in himself but in the qualities he brought out in those around him. Such generous unanimity is rare enough this side of paradise, especially in literary circles where personalities so often clash and one finds no shortage of jealousy. What made this consensus truly unusual was that none of his otherwise articulate admirers, most of them writers, could explain exactly what made Robert so uniquely appealing.

Conversations about Robert with his friends often came around to that same question, and even intimates like William Maxwell, who knew him for half a century, ultimately declared the answer ineffable. There was his sprightly intelligence, but it wasn't just that. Neither was it his swift, understated humor nor his native gentleness and humility. There was something else—impossible to describe—hidden at the core of his personality that kept the visible gifts in perfect accord, for it was that harmony that made Robert so special. I have seen many conspicuously gifted people in literary and business life—individuals of awesome intellect, boundless energy, enviable intuition—but usually the stronger the faculty, the more it overpowers the rest of the personality. One hears in their presence a sort of psychic dissonance. Somehow Robert's many strengths harmonized so naturally that one simply wanted to sit back and enjoy the music of his company. Being with him, I understood for the first time how spiritual pilgrims recognized their next master. A few people truly do possess an aura, a tangible sense of their integrity which draws one in.

II

Good fortune also played a role in how I came to know Robert, because luck, more than careful planning, led me to take two courses with him in the same fall term of 1974. An unfashionable interest in prosody prompted me to enroll in "English 283: The History of English Versification," taught by a Mr. Robert Fitzgerald, a name I recognized then only as the author of a Homeric translation I had not read. Meanwhile the need to work up my Latin for the spring language exams pushed me into an advanced course on Roman poetry whose first session proved so intimidating that I fell by default (*o felix culpa*) into the less demanding "Comparative Literature 201: Studies in Narrative Poetry," taught by the same Mr. Fitzgerald. The seminar examined the *Odyssey*, the *Aeneid*, and the *Inferno* with the requirement that students be able to read at least two of the poems in the original. Utterly Greekless, I had just enough Latin and Italian to qualify and had already plowed dutifully through the first six books of the *Aeneid* twice in my old-fashioned Catholic high school. Comp. Lit. 201, I hoped, would be a good refresher course. It was, in retrospect, the course at Harvard that best fulfilled my grandiose fantasies of what an Ivy League seminar should be.

So daunting had the language requirement proven that only four students presented themselves on the first day in the spacious seminar room in Boylston Hall—three brilliant linguists and me. Mr. Fitzgerald, as we called him according to Harvard protocol (he did not become Robert until two years later), sat waiting for us at the head of the table. Dressed in a pinstriped suit, monogrammed shirt, and dark tie, incongruously he carried a Harvard Co-op book bag, which made him look rather like a banker who had grabbed his son's school satchel by mistake. Smoking a cigarette as he watched us settle in, he seemed elegant but unaffected. He then began quizzing us on our command of Greek, Latin, and Italian. Which did we know? How long had we studied each one? What authors had we read in the original? Which translations had we used? He listened carefully to our nervous, inadequate replies.

"Ah," he said at length, "then the ancient languages are not yet entirely forgotten." Turning to the blackboard, he wrote two Latin lines from Horace and asked, "Shall we begin?"

We met twice a week each time for two hours of relaxed but learned conversation. Halfway through each session the door would open quietly, and the capable Bette Anne Farmer, the Comp. Lit. secretary, would enter carrying a china tea service on a silver tray (which seemed an exotically luxurious touch of civility to a working-class Californian like me). Sipping our tea and listening to Fitzgerald discuss the special quality found in a particular line of hexameter, we experienced a combination of intelligence and humanity, scholarship and creativity for which our previous graduate work had left us unprepared.

No Greek mariners ever succumbed more quickly to a Siren's song than we to Fitzgerald's tutelage. To our public unease but private delight, he treated us as equals. (When asked to sign a student's copy of the *Odyssey*, he inscribed, "For ———, fellow student of Homer.") He was not voluble. He rarely dominated the discussions he encouraged. But when he talked, we listened intently. Fitzgerald spoke slowly in a voice so intimate it seemed almost a whisper. Instinctively, we leaned forward to catch each word, our anticipation being heightened by his habit of pausing slightly between phrases, sometimes even taking a small pull of his cigarette as he formulated his exact words. In another teacher this mannerism might have become bothersome, but with Fitzgerald these momentary punctuations underscored his perfect timing and hooked the listener onto the line of his thought. Even his dismissals were exact and decorous. Disagreeing with Denys Page's assertion that the *Iliad* and the *Odyssey* were written by different poets, Fitzgerald prefaced his detailed classroom rebuttal by saying gently, "Professor Page knew more Greek at eleven than I shall *ever* learn, but here his hubris has undone him." Listening to each beautifully shaped and skillfully paced sentence, we recognized a man who esteemed words. He exercised the same attention to his seminar conversation that he lavished on each line of poetry we studied.

Saying that Fitzgerald would linger over a particular line does not misrepresent his fastidious teaching style, which always focused on specifics. He combined the classicist's devotion to unraveling, word by word, the meaning of a passage with a poet's delight in how those words work together to create a memorable effect. He began almost every class with a line or two, some moment from the poem under discussion. It was almost inevitably some narrative detail or simile we might have overlooked. By working through the passage carefully in the original, he showed us how it mirrored some important aspect of the whole. Once, for example, he singled out the line in which Virgil described the serpents who rise from the sea to kill Laocoön and his sons:

Sibila lambebant linguis vibrantibus ora.

(They licked with quivering tongues their hissing mouths.)

After discussing the line as an example of Virgil's suggestive onomatopoeia, he also showed how it illustrated the secret of the Latin poet's characteristic music, which came from dramatic twists of word order. Here the first word of the line, the adjective "*sibila*" ("hissing") modified the final word, the noun "*ora*" ("mouths"). By bracketing the line with these syntactic partners, Virgil adds a subtle grammatical suspense to the more obvious narrative excitement of the description.

The risk in concentrating so much on textual detail is that the discrete observations never coalesce into a larger view. Fitzgerald quietly circumvented this danger with a skill that seemed effortless at the time. In retrospect, however, his apparently casual approach certainly involved both careful planning and a clear vision of how he wanted us to experience the interdependency of the three poems. What seemed like an offhand comment made one day would be picked up a few classes later with a surprising twist. A line from Homer he had asked us to pause over for its music would suddenly appear weeks later in a speech by Aeneas. A Virgilian simile he used to illustrate a strategy of Roman rhetoric would emerge almost word for word in Dante. Once, for example, he discussed an uncharacteristically epigrammatic sentence from Aeneas' speech at the fall of Troy praising its masterfully ironic use of repetition. This way of balancing a line, Fitzgerald suggested, had influenced Ovid and other poets:

Una salus victis nullam sperare salutem.

(The one safety for the vanquished is to expect no safety.)

Such pithy, end-stopped lines are rare in Virgil, and at the time this observation seemed only an interesting footnote. But when we began studying Dante, Fitzgerald started pointing out line after line that operated with similar turns. Here, for example, is the description of the Harpies attacking the souls of Suicides in Canto XIII of the *Inferno*:

Fanno dolore, ed al dolor finestra.

(They give pain and give to pain an outlet.)

These connections are the commonplaces of philology. Usually one registers them intellectually without letting them change one's sense of the poem. By allowing us to share in the discovery, however, Fitzgerald helped us understand how poets learn even the most specific tricks of language from their predecessors.

There was no battle between the ancients and the moderns in our class. If Fitzgerald traced the historical sources of these classic texts, he never let us forget their subsequent influence. They remained living poems, and he demonstrated their vitality by considering them from unusual perspectives. He analyzed the rhythm in Virgil's description of Neptune riding his chariot with reference to Gerard Manley Hopkins. Likewise he claimed Virgil's powerful representation of the Trojan ships under sail, "*spumas salis aere ruebant*" (which Fitzgerald later re-created as "they plowed the whitecapped seas / with stems of cutting bronze"), illustrated Robert Graves's theory that a poet's craft comes largely from knowing how to use the letter "s." One day he asked us to read Poe's "The Philosophy of Composition," a provocative assignment for a class in the epic since the essay maintains that a long poem is a contradiction in terms. Poe famously posits that no poem can be successfully sustained for more than about 120 lines. When asked in the next session what Poe's theory had to do with Dante, Fitzgerald replied with a question of his own. Had any of us ever counted the average number of lines in a canto of the *Commedia*? We quickly began counting and, of course, the average runs not much over 120 lines.

III

If Fitzgerald believed in teaching details, he also expected us to remember them. He required us, for example, to learn every character in each poem. This assignment did not include only the major figures but every soldier, shepherd, sailor, slave, or shade who appeared, even momentarily, from Aietes and Eurymedousa to Medon and Tehoklymenus—hundreds of characters in all. Though we complained at the time (as some of my classmates also did about the many passages he made us memorize), in retrospect, this demand was a clever tactic to teach epic poetry. There is a temptation to read verse narrative as quickly and carelessly as prose. But narrative poetry is more compressed than prose fiction, and details bear more weight. Fitzgerald slowed down our reading not only by compelling us to take careful notes but also by forcing us to differentiate characters like Ktesippos, Agelaos, Amphimedon, Antinoos, and Eurymakhos from one another—figures we would otherwise have lumped together indiscriminately as Penelope's suitors. Fitzgerald believed that a great poet never introduced a character without good reason. Our duty was to discover and remember how each figure fit into the whole. No literature teacher had ever asked us to do a task simultaneously so simple and so comprehensive.

But then none of us had ever had a teacher who placed such paramount importance on the narrative line. My literary education had trained me to consider plotting an obvious and superficial device unworthy of serious attention. Plots were what the unenlightened looked for in literary texts. One soon learned at college that showing too great an enthusiasm in the classroom for the story line of a novel or long poem bordered on bad taste. Structure, symbolism, stylistics, subtext—those were the proper subjects of criticism. Now I watched in bewilderment as our instructor, Harvard's Boylston Professor of Rhetoric, spent part of each session discussing nuances of plot with the same obvious care and delight with which he quoted the choicest lines of Greek and Latin verse.

The surface of the poem, Fitzgerald's method implied, *was* the poem. No epic survived the welter of history unless both its language and story were unforgettable. From a plot, posterity demands both immediate pleasure and enduring moral significance. An epic narrative must vividly and unforgettably embody the central values of a civilization—be they military valor or spiritual redemption. Only a few poets at a few fortunate points in history had met this challenge successfully. To understand these poems, Fitzgerald insisted, one not only needed to study the cultures and literary traditions which created them. One also needed to measure them against life. The ultimate measure of Homer, Virgil, and Dante's greatness was that their poems taught one a great deal about life, and that life, in turn, illuminated them.

It is embarrassing to admit now that Fitzgerald's position disturbed us. In Harvard seminars one took care to avoid that four-letter word, *life*. Our graduate program was training us to be professional critics, and the first lesson had been to keep literature separate from that sloppy, subjective category called personal experience. Sensing our skepticism, Fitzgerald borrowed a trick from Homer. He persuaded us through stories. He described how seeing Thiaki, Homer's Ithaka, had not only helped sharpen the language for his translation of the *Odyssey*, but had also clarified the meaning of certain moments in the poem. Likewise he confessed how little he had cared for the *Aeneid* until he read the poem by lamplight in a Quonset hut during the Pacific campaign. Stationed as a naval officer on the battle-torn island of Guam preparing for the invasion of Japan, he learned to appreciate the weight of Virgil's moral concerns.

My favorite anecdote came when Fitzgerald was explaining Odysseus' special relationship to his protectress, Athena. At key moments in the *Odyssey*, the goddess visits her hero in disguise. We had just come to the episode in Book VII in which Athena appears to Odysseus as a young girl in pigtails when Fitzgerald told us about his trip to Crete to see Arthur Evans' reconstruction of Knossos. Traveling alone and knowing no modern Greek, he had felt isolated and forlorn the first evening as he walked the streets of Heraklion. Pausing to look in a store window, he heard a voice say in English, "Good evening, sir." He looked up to see a twelve-year-old girl in pigtails standing in the doorway. She had learned English, she explained, while visiting relatives in America. Their conversation cheered him immensely. As they parted, he asked her name. She responded with a common Greek appellation, "I am Athena."

Years later I heard an astronomer explain that the "simplicity and elegance" of a scientific solution represented the best criteria for its adoption. Gradually the simplicity and elegance of Fitzgerald's approach to poetry led me to question my own needlessly complicated methods. I realized how much my critical education had alienated me from my own experience of literature. Fitzgerald's unorthodox and often subjective remarks on poems almost always focused on the features I found most moving and memorable. There had to be some way of reconciling one's intellectual, emotional, and moral responses to literature. "*Hoc opus, hic labor est*," as Virgil said—"This is the trouble, there is the toil." Achieving that reconciliation would become my challenge. In the meantime, it was difficult to despair about the state of literary education while studying the classics with Fitzgerald. "Fortunate he who's made the voyage of Odysseus," wrote George Seferis. What an island of good luck it was to have spent so many afternoons with that small band in Boylston Hall.

IV

But I exaggerate. Only Tuesday and Thursday afternoons were spent in philosophic equipoise. On Monday and Wednesday I left Harvard Yard, crossed traffic-choked Massachusetts Avenue, and rode the elevator to the top of Holyoke Center, a bristling modernist high-rise designed by crossing Mies van der Rohe with a porcupine. Here in Fitzgerald's "History of English Versification," I found a more familiar Harvard—crowded, boisterous, and competitive.

On the first day the small room was jammed with students. Like me, most of the men were dressed in that fall's unofficial Harvard uniform—blue jeans, button-down shirt, and corduroy jacket. More diverse, the women displayed two sartorial varieties—preppy and *artiste*. As we waited for Fitzgerald to arrive, no one spoke, but a few glanced systematically from face to face around the table making a dispassionate appraisal of their peers. The crowd grew. Soon students stood two deep along the back and side. I was confused. Why did so many people want to study prosody? And why did everyone look familiar—not so much as individuals but as a group? Finally, breaking the silence, I asked the fellow next to me why this specialized course was so popular.

"Don't know about them," he replied without looking at me, "but I couldn't get into English C. No connections."

"What's English C?" I asked.

"Creative writing," he replied, still looking straight ahead.

"Is that hard to get in?"

"Impossible," he explained, turning ever so slightly my way. "Unless you've got connections."

"But what does this class have to do with creative writing?"

"Don't you know?" he said—now looking straight at me with surprise, Harvard's rarest emotion.

"Know what?"

"Why everyone's here," he responded. "In this class you get to write poems."

Suddenly I realized why everyone looked so familiar—the Viking in the motorcycle jacket, the brunette with waist-length hair, the prematurely gray preppy. They made up the crowd at all the campus poetry readings. These were Harvard's aspiring *literati*.

When Fitzgerald arrived, he surveyed the mob with a veteran's weary resignation. Donning a pair of black-rimmed glasses, he took out a reading list and described each of the eight books on metrics we would be assigned. In addition, we needed to study the three volumes of Saintsbury's *History of English Prosody* on reserve at Widener Library. And, yes, we would also read chronologically through all five volumes of Auden and Pearson's *Poets of the English Language*. Already a few faces looked worried. The course sounded as technical as "Introduction to Particle Physics."

Turning to the blackboard, Fitzgerald then explained with many dusty chalkings and erasures his personal system for notating English scansion. Apologizing for its apparent complexity, he reassured us how quickly we would master it through the many written scansions he would assign for each class. There would also be a long term paper on the prosody of a classic poem. And, yes, some memorization. (A student standing near the back door quietly escaped.) Finally, he added that every week we would also be expected to write from fourteen to twenty lines of verse. Here faces brightened.

"I say 'verse,'" he explained, "because I expect nothing so exalted as poetry from these assignments. Each week I will ask you to craft a short passage according to the rules of a particular form. Do not worry about creating art. Worry only about making sense and displaying impeccable prosody." He then turned back to the blackboard and spent the next hour explaining the principles of Greek and Latin metrics. By the end of the period, the board was covered with prosodic graphs and long lists of terms like "hemistich" and "antepenult." There were also many lines written like PEISTEON KEI MEDEN HEDU PANTA GAR KAIRO KALA, which was helpfully labeled as "trochaic tetrameter catalectic."

By the time Fitzgerald dismissed us with several handouts to scan, a hundred pages of Saintsbury to read, and two verse exercises (three stanzas in strict Sapphics and fourteen lines of Catullan hendecasyllabics), the class had become considerably less crowded. On my way out someone nudged me from the side. I turned to see a small, wiry, dark-haired fellow who looked like a spider. Not like a tarantula or anything deadly. Just an ordinary spider. "Don't worry," he whispered. "He's just trying to scare us."

My interlocutor was correct. At the next session there were just enough students to fill the large seminar table. Fitzgerald's performance had successfully frightened off the unserious. (I was not surprised to learn years later that both parents had briefly been actors.) Our teacher now relaxed into a more wry and congenial presence. Although intellectually demanding, his manner was always gentle and never insistent. Even his rebukes were decorous. Returning an almost illegibly faint typescript to a student one day, Fitzgerald remarked, "A young writer may not be able to change the world, but he can change his typewriter ribbon."

V

Fitzgerald's "History of English Versification" has proved so influential on certain young writers—and through them on current poetry—that it merits some description. As the course title indicates, the structure was chronological. We systematically surveyed the major metrical systems and verse forms of English poetry from Anglo-Saxon alliterative stress meter to modern free verse. Fitzgerald's perspective, however, was inevitably comparative. He consistently examined

English prosody in a broader European context. After presenting a passage of English poetry, he would often add relevant lines of Greek, Latin, French, or Italian—quotations, that is, from the foreign literatures British and American poets were most likely to have known in the original.

I recently found a mimeographed handout in my old class notebook. Labeled "The English Heroic Line: A few models, analogues, examples," the sheet lists twenty-five individual lines of verse chronologically arranged from Dante (*"Mi ritrovai per una selva oscura"*) to fellow faculty member Robert Lowell ("The Lord survives the rainbow of His will"). The first eight examples come from Italian or French—roughly one-third of the total. That fraction accurately reflects the importance of foreign poetry in a class ostensibly on English versification. "You cannot learn to write by reading English," claimed Ezra Pound. Fitzgerald implicitly agreed. His polyglot approach demonstrated how often poetic innovation in English resulted from borrowing an established convention from Latin, French, or Italian. One language's old news becomes "news that stays news" in another.

Scratch a prosodist, and you will usually find a Platonist—except with Fitzgerald. His perspective was not merely Aristotelian but deeply Thomistic. He rarely presented abstract metrical patterns in class. He preferred to study individual lines of poetry. General rules were deduced from individual examples and patterns modified to fit specific poems. Scansion played a central part in his method, but he employed it as a way of apprehending the details of the poem—a sort of auditory close reading. His approach suggested that metrical form did not meaningfully exist outside specific texts. It needed to be embodied in an actual poem.

Free verse teetotalers innocently imagine that metrics is an abstract, intellectual enterprise. For most young poets, however, studying prosody proves an intoxicating experience, a debauchery of verbal dance and music. Fitzgerald understood his subject's drunken appeal. If he never preached temperance, he did emphasize responsible drinking from the Pierian Spring. He constantly reminded us that meter was only one of several features operating in a poem. "Verse is not just meter," he observed, "but also diction, rhetoric, and syntax." Separate the elements, even for pedagogic purposes, and one risked teaching abstract simplifications. The beauty of the poetry arose from the intricate dance of its parts. The study of versification was best understood as a privileged perspective from which to consider the larger question of poetic language.

Underlying the entire course was a profoundly Catholic sense of form as a sacramental instrument of perception. In class Fitzgerald never mentioned Jacques Maritain (though he often cited the French philosopher's two shaping influences, Aristotle and St. Thomas Aquinas). Maritain's neo-Thomistic ideas, however, were reflected in Fitzgerald's analytical procedures. Reviewing Maritain's *Creative Intuition in Art and Poetry* twenty years earlier in *The Hudson Review* (vol. 6, no. 2, Summer 1953), Fitzgerald had spent considerable space on Maritain's exegesis of Aquinas' three requirements for beauty—*integritas* (wholeness), *consonantia* (harmony), and *claritas* (radiance). Many readers unfamiliar with philosophy or theology will recognize Aquinas' famous formulation from James Joyce's *A Portrait of the Artist As a Young Man*. In his review Fitzgerald not only provided his own translation of Aquinas' original definition, but also quoted a lengthy passage from Maritain that suggests, in an essential way, his own deepest convictions:

> If we were able fully to realize the implications of the Aristotelian notion of *form*—which does not mean external form, but on the contrary, the inner ontological principle which determines things in their essences and qualities, and through which they are, and exist, and act—we would also understand the full meaning intended by the great Schoolmen when they described the radiance or clarity inherent in beauty as *splendor formae*, the splendor of the form, say *the splendor of the secrets of being radiating into intelligence.*

The italics in the final phrase are not found in Maritain's original; they were added by Fitzgerald. For him, poetic form was not an external element but an inner process coming perceptibly into being. One recognized a genuine work of art by its *radiance*, the splendid clarity communicating not only its identity but its mystery. What we apprehend in art, therefore, is always greater than what we understand. Even in poetry, an art drawn from speech, most of a poem's essence remains, to use Rilke's term, "unsayable." We approach art not only with our intellect, but also with imagination, intuition, and the instinctive knowledge of our physical senses.

There are currently thousands of poetry-writing courses in America, and virtually all of them employ a variation of the same format—the workshop. Developed at the turn of the century as a progressive teaching method, the workshop made group discussion of student work the focus of writing courses. Fitzgerald's teaching method bore virtually no relation to the workshop technique. Although we wrote one or more poems each week on assignment, we never discussed our work in class. At the beginning of each session, Fitzgerald would return our homework covered with markings penciled in his elegant, small hand. First, he would point out any metrical mistakes or, to use his term, "infelicities." His technical comments were always specific. He scanned every line and syllable one wrote. "This anapest is too clumpy and blocky," he noted on one of my assignments, then followed a few lines later with "This anapest the same." He would also mention anywhere the verses failed to make literal sense. His commentary usually stopped there. He maintained no pretense that we were writing deathless poetry—a liberating assumption for students writing on assignment. He insisted only that we seriously grapple with each form and handle our language responsibly.

Occasionally Fitzgerald began class by writing a student line or two on the blackboard for special praise or censure, but he never identified its author. The line was offered as an example either of a fault we needed to avoid or a virtue deserving common pursuit. By freeing students from public evaluation of their work, he eliminated the complex group dynamics and self-esteem issues that bedevil most workshops. His focus was always on the work not the workshoppers. He, moreover, focused on classic poetry not student poems-in-progress. Like a clockmaker taking apart an expensive timepiece, he meticulously unfolded each masterpiece so that we could see the complex but purposeful workings. He consistently set our standards at the highest levels. Young writers are instinctively competitive. Fitzgerald did not deny our competitive urges. We were encouraged, however, not to measure our poetic performance against one another, but against Shakespeare, Milton, Keats, and the other classic authors of our language.

Fitzgerald also developed the only sensible system I have ever seen for grading student poems. Part of its charm was that he never explained it. In addition to his comments, each poem he returned bore a series of capital letters in the top right-hand corner. We recognized these abbreviations as grades, but it took a few weeks to figure out his system. His grading scale—from best to worst—ran NAAB, NB, NTB, and PB. I'm happy to say I never got a PB, though I did once acquire an inglorious NTB. I only managed NAAB twice. With a candor characteristic of its creator, Fitzgerald's system concedes that the absence of badness is the proper aspiration for a student poem.

In my own case, the benefits of Fitzgerald's tutelage can hardly be overstated. By the time I arrived in English 283, I had been trying to write formal verse on my own for nearly six years. An autodidact may not always have a fool for a teacher, but he often has an incompetent. With the innocent arrogance of youth, I thought I knew a great deal about prosody. In retrospect, my comprehension was undisciplined, incomplete, and approximate. Fitzgerald's rigorous but congenial approach was exactly what I needed. He quietly insisted that our work be held to the only proper standard of poetry: every word, every phrase, every line must be right. Any less exacting standard was unworthy.

If Fitzgerald's standards were rigorous, his aesthetic principles remained liberal. While insisting we master the old measures with scrupulous exactitude, he never discouraged us from working in free verse—or any other technique. He declined to proselytize for a single style. He advocated only precision, compression, and elegance. At Stanford, where I had spent my undergraduate years, free verse and formal poets had occupied opposing camps. As a young writer who wished to work in both modes, I did not understand why one style should preclude the other. (Little did I guess then that the already incipient Poetry Wars would only grow more widespread and intense over the next two decades.) At Harvard, however, neither Fitzgerald nor his fellow instructor, Elizabeth Bishop, considered metrical poetry and free verse as mutually exclusive techniques. They were complementary ways of writing poetry. The important thing was to use each technique well.

Fitzgerald's taste was both broad and refreshingly unfussy. To give an idea of his range of response, let me offer a few examples from a single afternoon's session. The subject was the relation of free verse technique and prose style. Fitzgerald began by quoting from three letters Gustave Flaubert sent to Louise Colet. ("A good prose sentence should be like a good line of poetry—*unchangeable*, just as rhythmic, just as sonorous.") Then we moved to Hopkins' famous letter to Robert Bridges on sprung rhythm. ("It is nearest to the rhythm of prose, that is the native and natural rhythm of speech. . . .") Then he quoted a passage from Shakespeare's *Henry IV*, Part II in which verse and prose were intermingled. Fitzgerald now followed with a few sentences from Ford Madox Ford's *The Good Soldier* that could be satisfactorily rearranged into free verse. Finally, he arrived at Eliot's "Ash Wednesday" to discuss the rhythms of syntax. Having analyzed these passages, Fitzgerald then led us into a consideration of the differing free verse techniques of Wallace Stevens and William Carlos Williams. There was nothing narrow or doctrinaire about Fitzgerald's curriculum.

Tradition, wrote T. S. Eliot, "cannot be inherited, and if you want it you must obtain it by great labour." Fitzgerald's courses in versification and epic carefully outlined the nature of that labor. A less abundantly gifted teacher might have minimized the effort and endurance required to master the craft of poetry. Fitzgerald painstakingly noted the challenges that existed at every level of proficiency. Twice he quoted the maxim Seneca drew from Hippocrates, *Ars longa, vita brevis*. Neither Seneca nor Hippocrates, he reminded us, implied that art endures, as the phrase is so often misconstrued. Instead, the Latin meant, as Chaucer so aptly translated it, "The lyf so short, the craft so long to lerne." The humane arts are immensely difficult to master.

They require a life of constant application. If Fitzgerald warned us of the struggles ahead, he also showed us the multitudinous pleasures of the craft. We felt—perhaps for the first time—the kinship of artists dedicated to a common pursuit. "Sweet are the pleasures that to verse belong," wrote Keats, "And doubly sweet a brotherhood in song."

VI

Almost from the first I had recognized that Fitzgerald was powerfully refining my sense of poetic craft. What I did not know then, however, was the profound effect he exercised on a generation of Harvard poets. Culture depends on human energy, and there are particular moments and places where artists meet in ways that decisively shape their futures. In retrospect, Fitzgerald's classes in Cambridge, especially his "History of English Versification," provided one such influential nexus. (He succeeded Archibald MacLeish as the Boylston Professor in 1965 and served until his retirement in 1981.) He became a crucial mentor to a disproportionate number of the young poets who later emerged as the so-called New Formalists. No one imagined such a movement at the time, and it is unlikely that Fitzgerald intended to create a revival of formal and narrative verse. Confessionalism and Deep Image were then the reigning fashions, and free verse was the almost universal style among poets under fifty. Fitzgerald was modestly famous but almost entirely as a translator of the classics. Already in his sixties, he seemed an unlikely influence on the young. Moreover, Fitzgerald's presence at Harvard in the early seventies—like Elizabeth Bishop's—was overshadowed by Robert Lowell, who was then unquestionably America's most famous poet. A quarter century later, however, the extent of Fitzgerald's influence appears a verifiable fact of literary history.

A significant number of his students—most of whom did not yet know one another—became actively involved in reviving rhyme and meter during the 1980s. A short list of Fitzgerald students conspicuously interested in formal poetry would include Robert B. Shaw, Brad Leithauser, Mary Jo Salter, Rachel Hadas, Elise Paschen, David Rothman, and myself. Although these poets share a common fascination with form—traditional or experimental—anyone familiar with their work may be more deeply impressed by their diversity. Fitzgerald inspired his students to explore form without imposing his own sensibility on them. (By contrast, Stanford formalists of the same period, as Robert Shaw has noted, display considerably more stylistic uniformity.) If one adds to this core group his former students who do not customarily work in meter but nonetheless demonstrate formal proclivities—poets like Judith Baumel, April Bernard, Katha Pollitt, and Cynthia Zarin—then the diversity of his influence becomes extraordinary. These students also reflect Fitzgerald's influence in another way. Many of them have designed courses on poetic form consciously modeled after the "History of English Versification." Fitzgerald's ideas on prosody and poetic language, therefore, are now reaching a new generation of young writers across the country. "If he was our Odysseus," one former student told me, "he had more than one Telemachus."

There is so much else I could write about Robert. If I have said almost nothing about his personal life, it is because he deserves a full-length biography. His childhood was scarred by a series of family tragedies. When he was three, his mother died in childbirth. Five years later his only brother perished in the influenza epidemic. Meanwhile his father was invalided by osteomyelitis and eventually died when Robert was only seventeen. These losses might have crippled a less distinguished soul. One could also write a book about Robert's literary friendships. His intimates included Flannery O'Connor, James Agee, William Maxwell, Robert Lowell, John Berryman, Eileen Simpson, Dudley Fitts, Paula Deitz, Frederick Morgan, James Laughlin, Allen Tate, Caroline Gordon, and Vachel Lindsay—not to mention his close but difficult relations with Ezra Pound. Likewise, a proper appreciation of Robert's work in poetry and translation remains to be written. He stands as American literature's preeminent translator of classical poetry. His reputation rests not only on his celebrated versions of the *Odyssey* (1961), the *Iliad* (1974), and the *Aeneid* (1983), but equally on his powerful, stageworthy renditions of Sophocles and Euripides, which remain unsurpassed after half a century. From the first these translations won the praise of cognoscenti, but they have also earned huge popular followings. His *Odyssey*, for example, has sold nearly two million copies—making it one of the century's best-selling books of verse. Finally, there is Robert's Catholicism, which exerted a powerful effect on many students—myself included. He was the only professor I had in eight years of college and graduate school who was an openly practicing Catholic. Quietly devout, he was also deeply knowledgeable about Catholic intellectual tradition. His own verse occupies an important place in the history of American Catholic poetry. At Harvard he became a role model for many religious artists and intellectuals—including Jews and Protestants. I could have written on any of these important areas, but I felt it best to concentrate on the one aspect of his life I knew best—his teaching of poetry.

Teaching hovers between two realities. First, there is the material overtly being taught. Then there is what one really learns, which may have little to do with the announced curriculum. So much of what one absorbs comes neither from lesson nor lecture but from example. The way a person teaches inevitably becomes an essential part of what is taught. Robert Fitzgerald was a splendid teacher in both ways. His courses broadened our knowledge of poetry and deepened our pleasure in the art. Meanwhile his personal presence provided an unforgettable example of an artist intellectual who was both genuinely good and deeply learned. Whenever I read Maritain's phrase, "the secrets of being radiating into intelligence," I think at once of Robert and the aura of wisdom and grace he brought into class. It is a light I still learn by.

A Pilgrimage to Santayana

Irving Singer

When historians in the twenty-first century assess the nature of twentieth-century philosophy from their own perspective, they may have some difficulty in placing the mind and works of George Santayana. There are two ways in which we might appraise his contribution. We could take him as a writer about the human condition who also did philosophy, or else as a theorist in various branches of philosophy who wrote essays, literary criticism, history of ideas, social commentary, volumes of poetry, a best-selling novel, and so on. Both approaches to his talent must be employed, and interwoven, in order to attain a clear idea of what Santayana accomplished in his books.

More than any other great philosopher in the English language, Santayana not only harmonized the two types of writing—the literary and the philosophical—but also made harmonization of this sort a fundamental resource in his doctrinal outlook. In the preface to *Scepticism and Animal Faith*, he writes that if the reader is tempted to smile at the idea that he is offering "one more system of philosophy," he smiles as well.[1] Despite its systematic structure, Santayana's philosophy was intended to be an expression of the author's personal experience and imaginative interpretation of his life as he lived it. Neither

---

1. George Santayana, *Scepticism and Animal Faith: Introduction to a System of Philosophy* (New York: Charles Scribner's Sons, 1923), v.

in his works nor in anyone else's, he thought, could a reader find the certitude and objectivity that so many others promised.

In taking this attitude, Santayana believed that philosophical speculation was inherently a literary pursuit and therefore a branch of the humanities rather than of the sciences. Santayana sought to further humanistic acuities that would permeate philosophy as they also permeate the fine arts and the various forms of criticism that interpret and evaluate them. He denied that these different facets of human inspiration could be reduced or rendered subservient to technical procedures that science (correctly) employs for its own expertise. He recognized that the life of the mind, above all in the humanities, becomes stunted when artificial barriers are reared between philosophy and literature or philosophy and history or, in a different dimension, between creative and critical insights. Ideally these would not be separated from one another. To the extent that they establish a harmonious interpenetration, they enrich each other.

Above all in the United States, but now in most other countries, intellectual and academic fields have become increasingly splintered in the twentieth century, even split into hermetically distinct compartments. The long humanistic tradition that linked the early Renaissance to the art and history of the ancient world, and then continued to evolve for the next five hundred years, has suffered disabilities from which it may never recover. In the past few decades, the danger to the humanistic spirit has accelerated greatly. As a reminder of what we have had, and as a model for what we may yet regain as a supplement to the new achievements on which we can rightly pride ourselves, Santayana's books merit the renewed study that some scholars are now giving them. Though far from completed, the new critical edition of his works has already encouraged this return to Santayana and what he represents as a philosopher.

In a book published in 1949, Somerset Maugham laments that it was in the service of philosophy that Santayana used his "great gifts, gifts of imagery, of metaphor, of apt simile and of brilliant illustration." Maugham doubts that philosophy needs "the decoration of a luxuriance so lush." He regretfully concludes, "It was a loss to

American literature when Santayana decided to become a philosopher rather than a novelist."[2]

In saying this, Maugham fails to recognize that Santayana's literary gifts were not employed for mere decoration, even when his prose was lush and luxuriant, but rather as the means by which he could express his view of the world in a way that transcends any preconceptions about what either literature or philosophy "ought" to be. Santayana's fusion of the two disciplines was an enrichment, not a loss, to both American philosophy and American literature.

Writing in 1937, John Crowe Ransom said, "Among philosophical personalities probably the most urbane and humanistic since Socrates is Mr. Santayana."[3] In one of his letters, Santayana remarks, "In my old-fashioned terminology, a Humanist means a person saturated by the humanities: Humanism is something cultural: an accomplishment, not a doctrine."[4] In renouncing humanism as a doctrine, Santayana was asserting his usual belief that the imagination must never be constrained by any fixed or codified tenets. By serving as an accomplishment, humanism would illustrate the fact that virtually all areas of learning can find a home within the mentality of a person who is truly cultivated and radically enlightened. Santayana's writings themselves embody the highest aspirations of this humanistic faith, and throughout its subtle modulations his thought serves to buttress even the most diversified types of humanism.

Nevertheless, Santayana's philosophical novel *The Last Puritan* was generally neglected by professionals in literature as well as philosophy for almost sixty years after it was first published, and during

---

2. W. Somerset Maugham, *A Writer's Notebook* (Garden City: Doubleday & Company, 1949), 341.

3. John Crowe Ransom, "Art and Mr. Santayana," in *Animal Faith and Spiritual Life: Previously Unpublished and Uncollected Writings by George Santayana with Critical Essays on His Thought*, ed. by John Lachs (New York: Appleton-Century-Crofts, 1967), 403.

4. *The Letters of George Santayana*, ed. by Daniel Cory (New York: Charles Scribner's Sons, 1955), 40.

most of that time there existed no inexpensive edition that English-language readers could readily acquire. For the most part Santayana's other works were ignored not only by the prevailing tendencies in contemporary thought but also by the popular culture. His ideas survived mainly in a few well-turned epigrams, such as the famous line (often misquoted) from *Reason in Common Sense*: "Those who cannot remember the past are condemned to repeat it."[5] These words were traced in large letters on a placard just behind the altar in Jonestown, Guyana. After the massacre they were visible in photographs of the site that appeared in newspapers. They were, in fact, the only text to be seen—like holy script wrenched out of context.

This desecration of Santayana's perceptiveness, and the unfriendliness toward his philosophy in academic circles, may yet be rectified. My hope is partly based on healthy changes that are now occurring. More than at any time since Santayana's death in 1952, work is being done in the kind of humanistic approach that Santayana favored. In various ways, though not massively as yet, American philosophy is returning to questions about the nature and quality of human experience, of living the good life, of creating or discovering values and expressing them in action as well as works of art. In Santayana's day the subject matter would have been called morals. The French still use the word *moralité* in this fashion, though the practice itself seems to be almost as imperilled with them as it is in the United States. The study of morals includes what philosophers currently categorize as "normative ethics." It is best investigated by thinkers who are at home in all the areas of the humanities—in history, literature, and the other arts as well as in the broadest spectrum of philosophical speculation.

In this realm of the intellect Santayana's contribution is, I believe, superior to the efforts of any other American philosopher. I do not minimize the importance of his work in more technical branches of philosophy—in ontology, epistemology, aesthetics proper—but

---

5. George Santayana, *Reason in Common Sense* (New York: Charles Scribner's Sons, 1905), 218.

Santayana's achievement as a humanistic thinker is what I admire most of all.

In book after book, beginning with *The Sense of Beauty* in 1896 and continuing throughout his career as a philosopher, Santayana charted the ever-present functioning of what he called "the constructive imagination" in human existence.[6] "The systematic relations in time and space," he wrote, "and their dependence upon one another are the work of our imagination . . . unless human nature suffers an inconceivable change, the chief intellectual and aesthetic value of our ideas will always come from the creative action of the imagination."[7]

The work Santayana did in this area primarily interested two mentors of mine at Harvard, Walter Jackson Bate and Henry David Aiken. From them I first learned how to appreciate his thought. Their enthusiasm eventuated in my pilgrimage to the man himself, and that propelled me into further explorations in his writings. When I studied at Harvard shortly after the Second World War, Aiken was the most dynamic teacher in philosophy there at the time, and virtually the only one whose interests ranged through all the fields of the humanities. He was the resident aesthetician and a former student of David W. Prall and Ralph Barton Perry. Prall had taught courses similar to Santayana's, and Perry had been a disciple of William James. Through this derivation one could feel that Aiken, at his best, exemplified the spirit and many of the ideals of the Golden Age of Harvard philosophy to which Santayana belonged.

As an undergraduate I had the good fortune to meet Walter Jackson Bate and to become one of the students he befriended. His specialty was English literature of the late eighteenth and early nineteenth centuries, but he saw in Santayana's belletristic style a living proof that philosophy could still express itself in vibrant and graceful prose. For

---

6. George Santayana, *The Sense of Beauty: Being the Outlines of Aesthetic Theory*, ed. by William G. Holzberger and Herman J. Saatkamp, Jr. (Cambridge: MIT Press, 1988), 49.

7. Ibid., 88, 20.

Bate as for Aiken, philosophy remained a humanistic activity rather than a conglomeration of inquiries into logic, linguistics, or the foundations of science. They revered Santayana as one of the last humanists in this sense of the word. Aiken and Bate were both convinced that liberal education attains its greatest sustenance in writing such as his.

Neither Aiken nor Bate found Santayana's beliefs wholly tenable. At different times in his career, Aiken preferred the philosophy of Hume, the pragmatists, English and American logical analysis, and (for a while) Continental existentialism. At an early age, Bate had fallen under the influence of Alfred North Whitehead, whom he knew in the Society of Fellows at Harvard. Whitehead's idealistic organicism plays a substantive role in Bate's work, whereas Santayana's combination of Platonism and materialism does not.

For Bate as for Aiken, Santayana nevertheless served as a model of what could be attained by literary philosophy and philosophical literary criticism. Aiken detailed Santayana's comprehensive importance in an essay entitled "George Santayana: Natural Historian of Symbolic Forms," and Bate chose him as the only twentieth-century philosopher writing in English who was worth including in his anthology of the history of criticism.[8] Whitehead himself, when asked which living philosopher was "most likely to be read in the future," is reported to have answered: Santayana.[9]

When I began to read Santayana, in one of Aiken's courses, books like *Reason in Art*, *The Sense of Beauty*, and *Interpretations of Poetry and Religion* initially seemed to me somewhat archaic and very unequal in quality. Much of their contents I could not understand, and long stretches appeared precious and overblown. I could see the

---

8. Henry David Aiken, "George Santayana: Natural Historian of Symbolic Forms," in his *Reason and Conduct: New Bearings in Moral Philosophy* (New York: Alfred A. Knopf, 1962), 315–48; Walter Jackson Bate, *Criticism: The Major Texts* (New York: Harcourt Brace Jovanovich, 1970), 652–56.

9. Richard Colton Lyon, preface to *Santayana on America: Essays, Notes, and Letters on American Life, Literature, and Philosophy* (New York: Harcourt, Brace and World, 1968), vi.

many evidences of a brilliant mind, but I was not able to perceive the coherent structure that unifies Santayana's statements in even these early works. During a year that I spent at Oxford doing graduate study, I read *The Last Puritan* as an antidote to the philosophy of ordinary language that was practiced there in those days (1949–50). The novel left me unsatisfied, however, and it was almost out of determination to discover what I had been missing that I decided to look for Santayana himself when I would be in Italy the following summer.

I had no idea where he was living, but someone suggested that the authorities at San Giovanni in Laterano—the Mother Church of Rome—would surely know. I went there and talked to a priest who became very indignant when I referred to Santayana as an American philosopher. "He is *not* an American," he said. "He is a Spaniard." I muttered something about Santayana's having lived in America for forty years, but the priest continued to glower, and so I turned away. But then an inner voice must have moderated his anger at my obvious ignorance. He called me back and told me that Santayana was living in the sanatorium of the English Blue Nuns adjacent to the Church of Santo Stefano Rotondo.

I was surprised at how easy it was to meet Santayana. Having learned that I was a graduate student at Harvard, he sent word that he would welcome a visit the following afternoon. I hardly knew what to expect. The only great philosopher I had ever met was Alfred North Whitehead. In December 1947, when I was still an undergraduate, Bate had pushed me into a telephone booth and insisted that I call the Whitehead residence. Mrs. Whitehead answered the phone and arranged for me to see her husband immediately. I had an hour's conversation with him two weeks before he died. Dressed in a dark suit and wearing a bright blue cravat, the eighty-year-old Whitehead looked cherubic. Having tea with him was like chatting with a modest and extremely gentle parson who had somehow been transplanted from Cambridge, England, to Cambridge, Massachusetts. He was reluctant to talk about himself or his ideas. He remarked that he no longer read the books and articles on his philosophy that were sent to him—"I just turn the pages occasionally," he said—but he was eager to know what was going on in the world of philosophy in general. He kept asking what the young people at Harvard were interested in nowadays.

My visit with Santayana was totally different. Since it was a hot day in August and my wife and I were bicycling through the countryside, I arrived dressed in scanty Italian shorts. When Santayana opened the door to his room in the sanatorium, his first words were: "I am so glad that you are dressed informally. For I am always, as you see, in my pajamas." For about three hours Santayana regaled us with reflections about everything that came to mind. He seemed to want to talk only about the world as he experienced it, about himself and his ideas. He asked very few questions that might encourage a response to his monologue. I later learned that in this period of his life (he was then eighty-six) Santayana was having difficulties with his hearing. Like many people who are afraid that they will not be able to catch what is being said, he doubtless spoke more continuously than he would have in earlier days. When Gore Vidal paid a visit in 1948, Santayana told him, "I shall talk and you shall listen. . . . You can ask questions, of course. But remember I am *very* deaf."[10]

But possibly that was not the only explanation. Years later Isaiah Berlin told me something relevant that he had heard, in what I assume was the late 1930s, from Mary Berenson, the wife of Bernard Berenson. She mentioned that Santayana had been their houseguest for some time at the Villa I Tatti outside Florence. When Santayana returned to Rome, he wrote her a routine thank-you note. In it he said how much he enjoyed conversing with her husband, whom he knew as a fellow student at Harvard, and he added words to the effect that he had not realized that Bernard was such a good talker. According to Berlin, Mrs. Berenson then exclaimed, "Good talker! How would he know? He wouldn't let anyone else get a word in edgewise. He did all the talking himself and never stopped."

---

10. Gore Vidal, *Palimpsest: A Memoir* (New York: Random House, 1995), 159.

For our part, my wife and I were so thoroughly captivated by Santayana's discourse that we had no desire to interrupt. We felt honored that he was willing to lavish upon us this flow of animated language that issued so effortlessly from him. At his ease in an armchair close to his narrow bed in the small room that he inhabited, he treated us like friends or grandchildren to whom he could speak freely. He learned very little about us to justify his friendliness, but possibly the link to Harvard was sufficient. He showed hardly any curiosity about what was happening there, and the Wittgensteinian philosophy that I had been studying at Oxford intrigued him not at all. He seemed rather scornful of Sartre's kind of existentialism. He referred to Daniel Cory, who was his closest disciple and who later became his literary executor and biographer, as a "half-educated man."

Among the students Santayana had at Harvard, he named only two who were now famous: T. S. Eliot and Walter Lippmann. He was very much concerned about world affairs. The Korean War was at its height, and he was worried about the possibility of an American defeat. He continually used the first person plural in referring to things American—"our forces in Korea," "the war we are in"—and I wondered what the priest would think of his blatant Americanism.

The English that Santayana spoke seemed clearly American in its accent, but with a slight English articulation that sounded very beautiful to me. The Colombian philosopher Mario Laserna recently informed me that when he met Santayana in 1948 they talked in Spanish. I asked Laserna what kind of Spanish accent Santayana had. To which he replied, with some amusement, "An *American* accent!"

At one point I said something about *The Sense of Beauty*. Santayana answered that he wrote the book only because he was coming up for tenure at Harvard and his friends had warned him that in order to keep his job he would have to publish a scholarly work. "But what can I write about?" he had asked them. "There's that course of lectures you've been giving on aesthetics," someone suggested. "Why not that?" Santayana laughed as he added that he followed this advice just to stay on at Harvard. Then he remarked, "But I hadn't *seen* anything." Either at that point or later in the conversation, he leaped up and threw open his casement window in order to show us the view of Rome—although he himself was partly blind.

After a couple of hours had elapsed, a sister entered with Santayana's sparse dinner on a tray. My wife and I quickly rose to leave. Santayana got up too, but talked on for another forty-five minutes. Although his food was getting cold, as we pointed out, he refused to take any notice of it. Standing awkwardly, I allowed my eyes to wander through the room. They lighted on two travel-weary suitcases tucked under a table. Santayana followed my gaze. "I know they're old and battered," he said, "but they've been all over Europe with me." It was as if he felt a need to justify possessing such unsightly articles. His caring about this diminished slightly my admiration. It was fully restored, however, when I mentioned that we hoped to return to Rome in a year or so and would like to see him again. A meager smile appeared on his lips and a look of serene indifference shone in his eyes as he replied, "I may be here."

The following day our friends David Wheeler and his future wife Bronia also visited Santayana. They talked with him about Proust and Kafka, and reported that he listened attentively to their ideas. He said to them, half quizzically, something he had also said to us: "I don't suppose anyone still believes in immortality." When Bronia insisted that she did, Santayana brushed this aside and asserted that the only kind of immortality he could believe in was the eternal and immutable fact that he had lived in time exactly as he had. Nothing else made sense to him. This comports with what he wrote about life and death in *The Realm of Essence*: "Our distinction and glory, as well as our sorrow, will have lain in being something in particular, and in knowing what it is."[11]

I left Santayana with the feeling that he was a lonely man, an old philosopher who would soon be dying by himself in Rome. The brilliance of his conversation was largely lost on me. It was only afterward, when I had studied his major works, that I realized how profound a

---

11. George Santayana, *The Realm of Essence, in Realms of Being* (New York: Charles Scribner's Sons, 1942), xiv.

thinker he was. By then I had forgotten almost everything he had said during our visit. What remained, however, and has been strengthened throughout the passing decades, is my conviction that Santayana was—in Henry James's characterization of what every would-be writer should be—"one of the people on whom nothing is lost."[12]

12. Henry James, "The Art of Fiction," in his *Literary Criticism*, 2 vols. (New York: The Library of America, 1984), 1:53.

PART THREE

Tributes

Last Days of Henry Miller

BARBARA KRAFT

That last year he shuffled between his old-fashioned, high-set, walnut-dark bed, the desk at its foot, the Ping-Pong table in the lanai on which he now painted, a more sedentary kind of play for an octogenarian, and the dining table, in fact, a redwood picnic table covered with a cloth. This is where he held court every evening attired in his bathrobe, plaid or blue terry cloth, pajamas, fluffy white bedroom slippers and white socks. He was a tough old bird, rather like a turkey, with his croaky voice, heavily veined, creped hands, parchment-thin skin, wattled throat and indomitable, naked head.

As his body failed him, the eyes, the ears, the bowels, the bladder, the bones, he shrugged his shoulders and with head held high said, "We must accept what comes, don't you know." And then he would return to the arduous business of folding the napkin in front of him. The long-fingered, still-graceful hands, bruised and etched with coagulated arteries, slowly smoothing the cloth, folding it in half, in quarters. This accomplished he would labor to roll the napkin up, fitting it, at length and with considerable effort, into the monogrammed silver napkin holder that marked his place at table. One tiny island of control that could still be mastered with great concentration.

The word he used to describe his condition was *apocatastasis*, a Greek word meaning "restoration" and referring to the eternal round made by the planets which restores a state of being. The word also refers to the doctrine that Satan and all sinners will ultimately be restored to God. Though Henry accepted what was happening to him, there were moments when he flapped his wings in annoyance, an appropriate response for a man who had steadfastly refused to be overcome by anything. "You think for the man of great spirit it [death] should be a graceful thing. A just going to sleep and yet that isn't necessarily true. It could be awful, ignominious."

His humble efforts to carry on with his life were at times moving, at times exhausting, at times hysterically funny and at all times immensely and universally human. For Miller was not and never desired to be "somebody" in the sense that today everybody is somebody. Either through their own earned or unearned celebrity or through some vicarious attachment to celebrity. Miller was anybody and everybody, a meat-and-potatoes man, an ordinary bloke according to the literary critic Alfred Kazin, a man who would rather be at peace with himself than a writer according to his friend, the writer Wallace Fowlie. Although, with all due respect to Mr. Fowlie, Miller's rapprochement with peace was achieved by writing which ordered and transformed the Milleresque chaos into a turbulent and teeming celebration of life on its own terms.

Henry described himself as a plain, down-to-earth, simple man. He was also a genius who, if reincarnated, wanted to come back not a genius but an ordinary man, a horticulturist, as he told me one evening over dinner. No, I was not one of Henry's "ladies"; I was one of his "cooks," and Friday was my night chez Miller.

On this particular Friday evening, some six months before he died, I had to awaken him to come to the table. A punctilious man, he was orderly in all his habits. His pens, pencils, and paper in their proper place on his desk, his watercolors, his paintbrushes neatly arranged on the Ping-Pong table, his dinner served at 7:00 p.m. The dedication to list making over the years. The famous, framed lists of places he had been, of places he had not been, lists of favorite foods, lists of favorite piano music, lists of women he had never slept with. Behind that Buddha-like equanimity lurked a Germanic heritage.

Usually he was up waiting for me, but of late he had become so weak that he was no longer able to navigate alone the distance between bedroom and dining room. Debilitated by malnutrition, not an uncommon affliction of old age, and a kind of palsy, possibly caused by petit mal seizures, he was quite frail. His hands trembled, he was paralyzed on one side, deaf in one ear and blind in one eye, so he said, although he regularly commented on what I was wearing down to a pair of green suede cowboy boots I once showed up in. When sight failed him, his sense of smell came to the fore. "I can smell your perfume, Barbara. Hmmmmm. I can barely see anymore but I can still smell." The full lips gathered into a lopsided grin, exposing teeth that remained remarkably virile.

I roused the slight body that was all but invisible under the satin-covered, down comforter and eased him into the waiting walker. Earlier Charles, a tall black man whom Henry referred to as his "Negro," had been in to bathe and shave him. This was a daily routine.

At dinner that night he spoke about how he would come back "a man who tends flowers. Not a genius, or a writer, that's the worst." Pressed, he elaborated on what writing entailed, his eloquent, age-marked hands raised in decisive exclamation. "It's a curse. Yes, it's a flame. It owns you. It has possession over you. You are not master of yourself. You are consumed by this thing. And the books you write. They're not you. They're not me sitting here, this Henry Miller. They belong to someone else. It's terrible. You can never rest. People used to envy me my inspiration. I hate inspiration. It takes you over completely. I could never wait until it passed, and I got rid of it."

But he never did get rid of it. Of inspiration. Nor did he rid himself of his obsession with woman, with *eros*, with life itself. Woman, *eros*, and life were vital to Miller's sense of himself, imbued with a mystery and a magic which compelled and obsessed and bemused him without letup until June 7, 1980—the day his eternal round was completed.

"I keep my nose to the grindstone," he said. "Old age is terrible. It's a disease of the joints. It's awful when I get up in the morning. I can barely bend over to brush my teeth. It's only when I get to work solving problems that I forget about it."

Beset by a multitude of infirmities the last decade of his life, Miller worked as furiously as ever producing several books (among them the three-volume *Book of Friends*) and hundreds of watercolors. He continued to maintain his voluminous correspondence with the world and entertained a seemingly inexhaustible stream of visitors who ranged from Vietnamese immigrants to celebrities like Ava Gardner, Governor Jerry Brown, and Warren Beatty who was then filming *Reds* in which Miller appeared in a cameo role. In between were people who came to interview him, academics who came to write about him, and film crews eager to commit to videotape the passing of an era.

Some he performed for, some he insulted, others he beguiled. He had a striking photograph of the young Ava Gardner in his entrance hall which hung next to a framed list of his favorite cock and cunt words. When the lady came to visit in the flesh, Henry overheard her chauffeur asking, as they left, where she wanted to go. According to Miller, she responded, "Anywhere. Just anywhere." Henry found that a remarkable answer. In August of 1978, Jerry Brown, accompanied by his entire entourage, paid a call at Ocampo Drive. Miller was in one of his wicked moods, being wicked was a pure delight to him, but he was never malicious. He greeted Brown, saying, "You know I think politicians are the scum of the earth, next to evangelists. I can't stand Billy Graham." Henry had a way of benignly saying outrageous things. Having said them he would sit back, a cat pawing a mouse, a crooked smile playing expectantly around his lips, waiting for the response his words would elicit.

Old friends came to see him, and there were plenty of new ones as well. I belonged to this latter category as did Brenda Venus, who was the last love of Henry's life. A beautiful woman, with shining black hair that fell just above her waist and the soft speech of the South, Henry credited her with keeping him alive. "Without her I wouldn't be able to go on." Brenda, who admitted to thirty-one, had introduced herself to Henry by way of a manila envelope containing provocative photographs. He was enchanted, and a meeting quickly followed. Brenda was to become the recipient of hundreds of Miller letters (published in 1986 by William Morrow as *Dear, Dear Brenda*), as had been Anaïs Nin before her. A voluptuous woman, deceptively petite at the same time, Brenda had a sultry, smoky kind of beauty which coexisted with remarkably delicate features. It was as if aspects of both June Miller and Anaïs Nin had been reincarnated in her, and there is no doubt in my mind that God sent this particular Venus to ease Henry along the path to his final destiny.

He wrote Brenda four or five letters a day, and there were many evenings when he would press a batch of these feverish missives into my hand to mail on my way home. He reveled in the pain and pleasure of this, his last *affaire de coeur*, fretting when Brenda didn't call or couldn't come to see him, as miserable as a boy in the clutches of Cupid's first embrace. He prided himself that he treated her like a queen and often commented with wry bewilderment, "It is only now that I have finally learned how to love a woman. After five wives and when I'm beyond doing anything, now I've finally learned how to treat a woman." Seeing Brenda to the door was one of his gentlemanly, sunset gestures.

Brenda received a goodly number of Henry's watercolors and lithographs as did the rest of us who were a constant in his life. When he gave a painting, he would apologize at the same time. "In a way I hate to give you this," he would say. "You'll have to have it framed and it's expensive. Do you mind?" He was a generous man and a thoughtful one too. One evening as he was signing a lithograph to give to Charles, he stopped suddenly because he simply couldn't remember the man's last name. "You don't think that sounds condescending, do you? To write 'To Charles' without a last name?" Picking up his pen he added "with affection," and said, "Now, there won't be any doubt." He was very fond of Charles, whose last name I never did learn as he was one of the day people and I one of the evening ones. He liked Charles not only because Charles took care of him a few hours every day but, and perhaps more importantly, because Charles was not always smiling at him. Henry hated what he called idolaters, strongly suspected academics, and detested being fussed over in any way.

As a result, there was no permanent help in the household which bumbled along haphazardly day to day. Besides Charles there were a sporadic secretary, the "cooks," and various itinerant people who slept there for a night or more as they passed through on the way to somewhere else.

The cooks were chosen from a list of people Henry enjoyed conversing with and evolved into a staple of his routine once he became housebound. Always a pragmatic man in practical matters, this is one of the ways Henry stayed plugged into the world. The list was long and the cooks rotated, although a few of us had fixed nights every week, Friday being mine. I was introduced into this system via a telegram from Miller's son Tony shortly after my first meeting with Henry. Subsequent to a radio program that I wrote and broadcast which was something of an analysis of the work and the man, I received an invitation to dinner from Miller's secretary. He had listened to a tape of the program and wanted to meet me. I went but not without some trepidation as I had heard he could be very difficult and blunt if he didn't like someone. As it turned out we had an immediate rapport, and I left thoroughly enchanted but hardly expecting that I would be invited a second time. A week or two later, I received a telegram from the Miller household: "Henry would like to know if you're available to cook this Saturday evening. Please respond immediately." His lifelong aversion to the telephone as a means of communication resulted in the legacy of his voluminous and prolix correspondence.

As for the cooks, many of whom were women, but not all, he once had the notion of inviting them to come at the same time to meet one another but decided in the end that it wouldn't work. "Women get along with women when they're alone, but when a man is around they are jealous and vie for the attention, don't you think?"

A modest man, surely the most unaffected, unselfconsious human being I have ever met, Henry resided downstairs in the Pacific Palisades home he had bought in the sixties to house his former wife Lepska (they had divorced in the early fifties), their two children, Tony and Val, and himself. And in later days, although there was a buzzer next to his bed, he refused to use it. When he wanted to summon his secretary or someone else in the house, he would call on the telephone (there were two lines): "This is Henry, you know Henry who lives downstairs."

Those last few months when Henry began to fail badly, I finally prevailed upon him to let a young man who was a friend of his, Bill Pickerill, move in on a permanent basis. He stubbornly resisted until I finally came up with the idea of telling him Bill had no place to live. This of course wasn't the case. Only then did he acquiesce, saying, "Well, why didn't you say so. Bill always has a home with me."

While Bill brought a semblance of order and regularity to the household, chaos gradually took up residence in Henry's innermost being. Many of the watercolors he did at this time had the word chaos scribbled across them and were reflective of the inner disquiet that took him backwards and forwards in time. "It's terrible to lose one's sight. I'm deaf and now I can't see. For someone who lives in the intellect it's awful. I've been having hallucinations, apparitions. So real that I sit up in bed and hold out my hand only to realize that I imagined the person. It's the damnedest thing."

One morning he awoke hungry and penniless in the Paris streets of the thirties, asking everyone who came into his room if there was any money in his wallet, in theirs, for breakfast as he was famished. While he could no longer read the newspaper, he adamantly maintained the habit of it, holding it more often than not upside down at the breakfast table, refusing to relinquish it or to allow anyone to turn it right side up. Still the news of the day somehow managed to filter through where it metamorphosed into wild, chaotic tales in his dreams. He regaled us all one evening with a story of how he had been blindfolded and abducted from a movie theater by the Iranians earlier in the day. This adventure occurred at the height of the Iranian hostage crisis which ended the Carter presidency.

One of the last watercolors he produced showed the figure of a man looking off to the right, a female figure looking straight ahead and, between the two, a diminutive male figure sketched in blue mimicking the pose of the larger male. Scattered around the painting was the usual Miller iconography: a six-pointed star, squibbles locked into masses of red paint and blurbs of color suggestive of a dove, a fish. Underneath all of this was a four-legged, grimacing beast with the name Sarasota written inside its body. The beast's teeth were bared in a fierce expression, and I often thought that was how Henry himself actually felt at this time. A beast with bared teeth. Henry said he had no idea what Sarasota meant or referred to. Nor could he relate to the word "void" which also found its way into the late watercolors. When asked over dinner one evening what it meant, he squinted up his eyes, scratched his head in perplexity and said, "I can't get it. I don't know what it is."

One of the dubious benefits of having been a female friend of Henry Miller was and is the raised eyebrows, the insinuations, the questions: "Were you one of his women? Did he talk dirty to you?" As most people have never ventured beyond the *Tropic* books into the more epiphanic pages of works like *The Colossus of Maroussi* or *Stand Still like the Hummingbird*, it is perhaps understandable that these questions were and are preeminent.

We had our obligatory "dirty" talk once only, early on, over a dinner of steamed zucchini, noodles Romanoff, tomatoes Provençale, melon and ice cream. The conversation evolved out of a general one that touched on favorite Miller lovers like Abelard and Héloïse and Tristan and Isolde, on Anaïs Nin, on men and women and their differences. I myself prompted the conversation by reading him a short, erotic story I had recently written which led him into a discussion of how a man likes to take a woman. "Anyway," he said. "The more bestial, the more exciting. A man likes it standing up against a wall, bent over like an animal. There are times for a man when all he wants is a cunt. Any hole will do—dog, cow, goat. An opening in a fence even. Men want to fuck and get it off; women want to be made love to, to be held."

He then told a typical Miller story. He had been separated by circumstance from his wife for about ten days (a gentleman in his own way, he didn't say which one of the five he was referring to). "I was feeling horny," he said, "as we had a very satisfying sexual relationship." He claims he was at a county fair where he went into a barn that held all sorts of animals. Climbing up on a box he pulled a goat over so that they were on the same level. In the end he couldn't go through with it. "I was afraid someone might come in." Fact or fiction? Who knows. As he wrote in one of the essays in *The Wisdom of the Heart*,

"Fiction and invention are the very fabric of life. The truth is in no way disturbed by the violent perturbations of the spirit."

Women perplexed Henry, possessors of a mystery that fascinated and eluded him. While he believed in duality and spoke loftily about the difference between *eros* and *agape*, it was almost impossible for him to conceive of a woman being capable of pure love. He did not see women as spiritual beings. He remained intrigued to the end that a woman could be simultaneously lascivious and innocent and reminisced about the woman who had once come into his Paris flat, sat down on a chair, lifted her skirt, spread her legs wide and opened herself up for him. "She was so fragile. A jewel, a flower. Delicate. No matter what she did." He was as captivated by the memory of this experience as he had been nearly half a century earlier when it had occurred.

The traits he admired most in women were sincerity, beauty, and, like his friend Blaise Cendrars, innocence. "Women have to be beautiful. I don't just mean physically beautiful, but beautiful in their being. They have to have a soul also, you know. I don't care for beauty raw and nothing behind it. I never did. I was never attracted to that."

We discussed the notion of innocence more than once. I arguing that purity was a more desirable state than innocence as innocence was a condition devoid of experience, Edenic, whereas purity connoted both experience and wisdom; that no one, man or woman, could or should remain innocent; that ideally innocence evolves into a purity of spirit through the transformation of experience and age. He himself exemplified what I was trying to express. We never resolved this argument, although we returned to it on many occasions, as Henry was loath to part with his romance with innocence. He did agree, however, that to have experience and attempt to remain innocent was costly, saying, "To remain innocent one has to put on blinders and not look to the left or the right."

He numbered among his idols Nietzsche, Hamsun, Whitman, and Lawrence but was brought up short when asked about goddesses by a German television interviewer. After a long pause, he responded, "The only one would be Héloïse. Do you know what she said to Abelard? And this when she was a Mother Superior and not a young woman anymore. She wrote to him 'Would that I loved my God as I love thee.' Can you imagine that. Wonderful."

Henry's real passion was for his work. He was also a man who liked himself and venerated life. Why else marry five times and father three children? He believed that art was glorification and that paradise was a creation of the individual mind, available to anyone, anywhere, regardless of the circumstances in which they found themselves. "I guess I do love my work," he said in talking about *Insomnia*, one of his favorite books. "I don't often reread what I've done but sometimes when I do I think 'Did I really do that?' And then I can't believe that I did it. Yes, I do love my work. You know if you don't like yourself, how can you like anyone else? When I look into the mirror I like myself. I love what I see. Even if I look terrible, it doesn't matter. And it's not ego I'm speaking of, it's id. I think everything comes from the id."

Over years of Friday night dinners I enjoyed Henry's stories and adventures which he spun out with zest and enthusiasm, laughter, and often bafflement. And I would like to believe that a residue of his individualistic, and in that sense American, wisdom has remained in me, lingering like the aroma of the meals I prepared for him. While he was restricted to a bland diet, I tried to make his meals interesting, flavoring them with fresh herbs and garlic, which is good for high blood pressure among other ailments. Occasionally I would ignore the diet altogether and fix a treat. He loved filet mignon (tournedos), which I served along with mashed potatoes mixed with leek-soaked milk. He was very appreciative of good food and nearly always commented on what he was eating.

When I arrived in the evenings, he enjoyed coming out into the kitchen for a Dubonnet before dinner. While I chopped and stirred, he would sit in his walker and chat with me. "You don't mind do you? Some people mind, don't you know. They get all confused." The conversation was always alive and vibrant, in the kitchen, at the table, meandering over familiar Miller terrain: Lou Andreas Salome, Nietzsche, Madame Blavatsky, Emma Goldman, the absolute, astrology, freedom of the spirit, love, the inaccessibility of truth, fabulating (lying), Anaïs, compromise, unconditional surrender.

While he accepted that truth ultimately lay beyond our mortal grasp, it was still an important concept to him. "Truth is wonderful," he would say. "It embraces everything and it's worth it and that from a man who can tell some tall lies. I can't tell you what it means to me to get letters from all over the world about just that—that I told the truth."

He had little sympathy with the young who took drugs, became groupies, and generally dropped out; he viewed such behavior as pure escapism. The self-destructive behavior, in particular the use of drugs and alcohol, that is characteristic of so many of the young since the sixties—behavior also characteristic of so many of this century's best-known American male writers—was antipathetic to Miller. Free of the angst, guilt, and self-doubt that tortured the majority of his contemporaries, Miller's work was consistently a celebration of the human condition in all of its exigencies. As he said to me in an interview we did for National Public Radio (and subsequently published in the *Michigan Quarterly Review*, Spring 1981): "If you're going to be a whore, be a good whore, a great one. If you're going to be a saint, be a wonderful saint. Be it! Be it, whatever you are, to the hundredth degree. Whatever it is you are, accept yourself, first of all."

Another thing that he had no patience with was government support of the artist. He was convinced poverty brought forth great work. "When I wrote the *Tropic* books I was a desperate man . . . I owe everything to poverty. I wouldn't have become what I became without it." There was a time, before he left for Paris, when Miller begged in the streets and nearly became a professional as he put it. Then one night he quit. He was in the habit of walking uptown as the theaters emptied, panhandling the crowd on his way back to Brooklyn. This particular night had not been lucrative and he was on his way home with only a nickel in his pocket for the subway. It was late, and by the time he reached his stop it was pouring rain. He noticed a man in white tie and tails getting off whom he assumed had been to the opera.

When Miller approached him, the man pushed Henry aside rudely and walked on without a word. Then, with his back to Miller, he reached into his pockets and threw a handful of change into the mud-filled gutter. "I was really degraded, humiliated, you know. But there I was down on my hands and knees, picking up the change and wiping the mud off. Right then and there I swore I'd never beg again, and I didn't. I've known it all. Every humiliation, degradation, poverty, starvation." This perhaps accounts for his dignity. Such experiences, as Nietzsche pointed out, either kill a man or strengthen him.

Henry's dignity never deserted him. During the final months of his life, he sat at the table with head bowed forward, barely able to lift the fork from plate to mouth, drifting away and then pulling himself back, saying, "Were you talking about me?" He hated to have the conversation pass him by. He had difficulty sitting upright and listed like a ship straining against its moorings in a heavy wind. "Am I leaning to the left? I feel as if I'm going to fall."

On one occasion he tried to describe his state of mind over the preceding days. With a bewildered expression on his face, he shook his head sadly and said, "It's been like an adventure. I don't know where I am, where this place is, what this house is. It's the damnedest thing." I explained that it was his house and that I had been there all day, sitting by the pool. (For the past several weeks, since it was evident the end was near at hand, I had spent as much time as possible at the house.)

"The pool," he asked incredulously, "there's a swimming pool here?"

"Yes."

"Were there other people here?"

I named the three or four people who had dropped in during the day.

"That's all," he said. "What a shame. Weren't there others?"

I told him that the pool was his, not a public pool, which surprised him.

"Mine?" he asked.

"Yes, you own it."

"You don't say. I own it!"

"Yes and this house too."

He rubbed his eyes and ran his hands over his head, a familiar, caressing gesture by now, smoothing his nonexistent hair, and said, "Amazing!"

He fell frequently, often rolled out of bed at night, and was a mass of cuts, bruises, and sores. When he was lifted from his walker to his chair at the table he would cry out in pain, yet the ritual of the dinners continued. His words came out garbled, his thoughts fragmented and undecipherable and there were long, impenetrable silences. The "don't you knows" were few and far between. Often his head would hover motionless an inch or two above his plate. When this happened a collar would be put around his neck, the kind used for whiplash victims, to give him some support. He dropped his fork, and spittle dribbled from his mouth. Somehow he was aware of this and repeatedly tried to raise his napkin to wipe his face. Those hands, they were like nervous, independent beings, agitated creatures in continual, fluttering motion, flitting here and there, lighting on his head, adjusting his hearing aid, smoothing his napkin, rubbing his eyes. He feared he was losing his mind and dictated letters to this effect to Brenda and to his friends Lawrence Durrell and Alfred Perles. "I think I'm going mad. I'm afraid I'm losing my mind."

Nearing the end, a crazy strength coursed through his failing form, the terrible energy of the dying. One night, forgetting he could no longer walk, he managed to get into the bathroom where he closed the door before collapsing. The bathroom, as legendary as his lists and charts and part of the Miller lore, was covered floor to ceiling with photographs of friends, naked women, idols such as Nietzsche and Lawrence and gurus like Krishnamurti and Gurdjieff. When he was found by Bill Pickerill, he was gesticulating and talking to some image on the wall, calling, "Monsieur, Monsieur." According to Bill, Henry looked up calmly and said, "Oh, Bill, I'm so glad to see you again. How good that you're passing by just now. I'm having the damnedest time with this guy."

With all of this transpiring, it wasn't sad in that house, at that table, in that bathroom. Touching, yes. And moving. And immensely human and funny too. For Henry was a man at peace with himself. He had acted out and lived his beliefs. And when the by now rare "don't you know" crossed his lips, it was a burst of sunlight bringing tears to the eyes and a clutch of joy to the heart. One evening as he was being rolled off to bed, he noticed my skirt, which was bright red. Reaching forward, blind as he was, he gathered up the hem, stroking the material with his other hand, exclaiming how wonderful it was that I always wore such beautiful clothes.

In May of 1980, one month before Henry died, the Rumanian-born playwright Eugene Ionesco was visiting Los Angeles. I was doing an interview with him for National Public Radio, and in the course of our meetings I mentioned that I knew Miller. Ionesco, eager to meet Henry for whom he had great admiration, asked if I could arrange it.

No two men could have been more different. Ionesco all doubt and despair, fixed on the contradictions, consumed by anguish; Miller, all accepting, preaching surrender, abdication, and a self-created paradise, pure light. Yet they shared a reciprocal esteem for each other's work. Their starting point was similar; their roads different.

The meeting never occurred. Henry demurred, saying, "Oh, I don't want him to see me like this, how I am now." Adding a few minutes later, "If Ionesco could see me now, that's something he could write a play about." Instead I took a set of books inscribed to Ionesco from Miller.

When the end came it wasn't awful, it wasn't ignominious. It all happened very simply and was just short of a "going to sleep." Henry died at home in his own bed in the arms of Bill Pickerill on a Saturday afternoon.

I end this memoir with Miller's own words, words written about Auguste, his clown, in *The Smile at the Foot of the Ladder*: "Perhaps I have not limned his portrait too clearly. But he exists, if only for the reason that I imagined him to be. He came from the blue and returns to the blue. He has not perished, he is not lost. Neither will he be forgotten."

Prophet against God
William Empson (1906-84)

GEORGE WATSON

A little less than middle height, he spoke in an accent that sounded clipped and archaic, and his movements were as darting and unpredictable as his mind. It was natural to be startled by the presence of William Empson, however glad you might be to know that he was there. Of all the beings I have ever known, he was the most utterly alive, and you felt at once quickened and nervous in his company. When we first met, in a college room in Oxford in 1952, he struck me as someone peculiar to himself and wholly out of sequence, whether of time or place; and it was only with the passing years that his views and behavior began to cohere in themselves or to relate to anything much in the world at large. In 1952 I had never met anyone like him, and never did again.

 He had left England in 1930, after Cambridge and London, to teach English in the Far East, following his Cambridge teacher I. A. Richards. Brought up among the Yorkshire fox-hunting gentry after the First World War, he maintained to the end a style that never quite lost contact with that remote and forgotten world. "The literary tastes of the twenties," he once remarked, "are still encapsulated within me," and his turn of phrase often reminded you of some twenties novelist like Aldous Huxley or P. G. Wodehouse. Words like "ripping" and "plucky" came naturally to him. His manners could be impeccable, even elaborate, especially with ladies, when a gentlemanly upbringing and his Winchester school days came to the fore; but he could also be irascible, especially when bored. He believed that he had a duty to entertain, and that others did too.

His appearance broke the rules of any age there has ever been, especially in his middle years, when an abundant beard flowed out prophet-like from around and beneath his chin, which was shaved in front; in his last years it was removed, leaving only a white moustache. His movements too were disconcerting. Walking with me and his wife once in a Cambridge college garden, he suddenly shot ahead and disappeared down a side path, reappearing in front of us as if from nowhere—something he had done in a West African jungle, she told me uncomplainingly, leaving her with two small children for two hours in tropical heat. A bohemian gentleman, he governed his marriage by the rules, or rather the anarchy, of a world poised between the aristocratic values of an old ruling class and the literary bars and restaurants of a great city, living out his last years in London even when his teaching post was in his native Yorkshire. Divorce would have seemed middle class to him, in his lofty way; but his marriage remained till his death in 1984 a model of domestic affection, and it was at his kitchen table in Hampstead, in north London, that he seemed most at his ease. He drank seriously, at times too seriously, and adored quick-fire conversation, witty contention and Chinese food. Such, at least, was the being I thought I knew. But to the end of his days I was never sure if I knew him at all.

That, no doubt, was because in thirty years and more of acquaintance, I was always at least slightly afraid of William Empson. He did not suffer fools or dullards gladly, if at all. His intelligence to the end was iconoclastic, his hatred of convention implacable. He was also a genius, perhaps the only genius in academic English in this century, which is to say at any time, since the subject is new. An uncomfortable genius, he made admirers rather than disciples. There is no school of Empson and never was, as there was once a school of I. A. Richards and a school of F. R. Leavis, of Lionel Trilling and of Northrop Frye, though a cult of multiple poetic meanings began with his first book,

Seven Types of Ambiguity (1930), and lingered on in schools and colleges for years. But then he hardly stayed long enough in any one place to found a school or said the same sort of thing often enough to start a system; and as with other English critics of his generation—C. S. Lewis, for example—his theories never somehow entitled him to the title of a theorist. Talk about ambiguity, he would say in his later years, made him feel like Satan confronted with Sin and Death.

On the other hand, Empson was perhaps the only literary critic of the century to have invented what might, in an embarrassed sort of way, be called a philosophy of history. It arose out of his fierce and undying hatred of monotheism, whether Judaic, Christian, or Islamic; it figures most amply in his greatest and most radical polemic, *Milton's God* (1961);[1] and it informs, though not self-evidently, most of what he wrote in prose or in verse, early or late. In summary it goes like this. Since about 480 BC, when Buddha, Confucius, Pythagoras and the second Isaiah died, mankind has been dragged down against their better advice into intolerance, persecution, and religious wars by harsh dogmas of a single universal ruler, of divine rewards and punishments in an afterlife. Religion, as the Middle Ages and the modern age have known it, has made mankind worse; and what Ireland, the Balkans, and the Middle East illustrate in our times is the abiding peril of imagining that there is only one God and that you know what He wants and means. Bohemian morals are not only more agreeable, then, than those of a church congregation, but more elevating too. It is your duty to have fun. The licentious seventeenth-century poet Lord Rochester, he once remarked in a 1953 review of a new edition of his poems, "praises pleasure as a philosopher, whose serious opinion is that it makes people kind to each other," adding that there is "enough truth in this, especially after wars of religion, to have a startling moral weight."

Empson's moral weight lies there. The odd thing is that some of his readers notice it hardly at all, and there are even those who imagine

---

1. See also "The Satan of Milton," *The Hudson Review*, vol. 13, no. 1 (Spring 1960): 33–59.

it is not seriously meant. Empson is still seen as above all a prophet of ambiguity and as a wayward, untidy master of verbal analysis. His views of divine providence, which mattered to him vastly more than practical criticism, never entered much in his lifetime into theological or even moral debate, and he was not much preached against, if at all, though he deserved to be and probably wanted to be. Perhaps he was preached against so little because he was felt to want it. Or perhaps the modern clergy does not take its own doctrines seriously enough to want to defend them in any literal way. We are living in an age in which you have to be a skeptic to take scripture at its face value, and the devout, it is often to be noticed, care more about the euphony of new versions of the Bible than about their accuracy. Empson was a skeptic who took scripture seriously and attacked it head on, and that is why he deserves to be immortal.

The room in Oxford where we first met in 1952, though small, was rather cold, and the group that had come to hear him was not large. Many in Empson's audience were uncertain whether they were meant to laugh or not: a doubt, or anxiety, he was much given to creating, and one he may have enjoyed. His lecturing style might charitably be called grotesque. It was rather as if Buster Keaton had decided, after many years as a silent comic, to open his mouth and deliver a solemn parody of an academic lecture. His voice, rapid and soft, would descend momentarily into a slurred mumble when the intensity of his convictions appeared to embarrass him; at such moments, on a platform, he would close his eyes in an intense, beatific expression that was not quite a smile and not quite a grimace. Behind the whimsy, one often felt, lay a certainty almost too deep to bear, and to hear him read aloud from one of his own poems was to realize that he was less a Neo-Metaphysical poet in the school of Donne than a Neo-Romantic in the school of Swinburne.

Even in private Empson was not always audible or coherent, though he had a devastating wit. On a platform his notes, such as they were, were not always under his physical control. A sheet of paper in his hands could suddenly acquire a life of its own. Lost for a name, he would lift one sheet above his head, then another, and rotate them with a desperate upward glance, until by some magic they would appear to grow larger and threaten to engulf him. There would be a moment of near-panic, shared by his audience; finally he would get them back onto the desk, in a struggle that had plainly cost him something, where they quietened down a little in chaotic heaps, their secrets still untold. "I expect you know the name already," he would confide hopefully to his audience. Perhaps some of them did. But the contrast with the confident, extrovert lecturing style of his old mentor I. A. Richards could not have been larger, and Richards' own bafflement with Empson, in their long years of estrangement, was memorable. "I wish him articulacy," he once told me, with the air of one who preferred not to say more. Richards, who adored lecturing, left an audience happy, if not always enlightened. Empson was as unpredictable as an unexploded bomb.

Sometimes there was no explosion at all. Sometimes, when he took a platform, nothing happened, or nothing you could fathom. At other times, whether in classroom or in private conversation, he would explode, and the force could be shattering. In the 1930s, at a dinner in Hanoi in French Indo-China, as it then was, he remarked to Graham Hough, an old friend, shortly after the death of D. H. Lawrence: "You know, I think I see what Lawrence's novels are about. They are about *coming* at the same time," adding even more disconcertingly, "I have once or twice managed it myself." No doubt that refers to Birkin's complaints in *Women in Love* (1920) about Ursula's sexual appetite and his disappointment at not achieving a simultaneous climax. That was a private conversation, but Empson could be alarming, too, on highly formal occasions. A widow who had rashly given her consent to his delivering a pulpit address at her husband's funeral must have been more than shaken, along with a large and respectable congregation, to hear him remark casually of the deceased, "I first met him in a brothel—he took a very sporting attitude to brothels."

The first talk I ever heard, then, was a fitting prelude. It included short poems passionately uttered, some of them his own; an unscripted revelation that he had recently had his ears cleaned by a doctor who had wondered how he had managed to hear anything for years; and an insistence, highly unusual in the last months of Stalin's dictatorship, that people nowadays were inclined not to take his own youthful Leftism seriously enough. In that age, it will be remembered, a lot of aging men of letters were busy arguing in a desperate sort of way that they had never really believed in communism at all. Empson, alone in his generation, seemed to be worried about the reverse, as if his gaiety of manner might have led people to think him uncommitted; in fact, the title of one of his volumes of poems, *The Gathering Storm* (1940), had meant to him what it later meant to Winston Churchill who (he claimed) had borrowed it from him for a collection of anti-appeasement speeches.

But somehow, though a radical to his dying day, Empson never convinced you that he had ever quite belonged to the Left in its conventional sense, or indeed anywhere. *Some Versions of Pastoral* (1935), written just before Mussolini's seizure of Ethiopia and the outbreak of the Spanish Civil War, is a critique of Marxism, or at least of the notion of a Marxist literature, appearing at a moment when Marxist ideas were rapidly becoming fashionable; and the sheer churchiness of the Left—its easy disposition to form into congregations of the faithful and to accept direction from a priestly caste of commissars—must always have seemed repulsive to him, though like Richards he welcomed the Communist victory in China in 1949. "I quite saw why they would want to do it," I recall his remarking, telling how he had witnessed the Communist entry into Beijing in that year, led by a woman riding a horse—an event little noticed by the local inhabitants, he reported, who were well used to being conquered by then and saw nothing epoch-making about it. Empson's fellow traveling was always decidedly more detached than Richards'—"I'm a great admirer of his," Richards would say during Mao's dictatorship, in no doubt about which side he was on. Empson was on no side, and it is a question whether any political cause would have known what to do with him. He walked alone.

If there was a defining theme to his Oxford talk in 1952, it was anti-Modernism. This was the first time I ever heard a considered case made against T. S. Eliot and Paul Valéry by anyone who was not an old (or young) fogey, and the experience was memorable. Empson had first met Eliot as a Cambridge undergraduate in 1926, while Eliot was giving the Clark lectures there on the school of Donne. Empson did not attend the lectures, on the single and simple ground that he went to none at all. But he had been impressed, in the year before Eliot announced his adherence to Anglicanism, by his serious air in conversation with much younger men, and by his ability to listen to questions and to answer them. Deprived soon after of a fellowship at Magdalene College for sexual activities which today would excite little or no remark, Empson moved to London to finish *Seven Types* and renewed his acquaintance with Eliot there, horrified by his religious conversion but too deeply indebted to his critical mind ever to allow himself to speak or write against him.

He could speak against obscurity, however, especially obscurity of a wilful kind, and a consistent failure to make a point. The trouble with Eliot and Valéry, he told his Oxford audience, not to mention Ezra Pound, was that in the years in and around the First World War they had devised a poetic language in which it is all but impossible to say anything. "I have just been to south-west France," he explained, finding himself on the very coast that was the theme of Valéry's *Le Cimetière marin* (1922). "In fact it's quite an interesting place—there is no fresh water there, and a ship-wrecked sailor could die of thirst." Then he looked contemptuous. "That's why it's called the sea cemetery—but you could read and re-read Valéry's poem and never know." The point was characteristically radical, and an Oxford literary audience brought up to revere Eliot and Valéry shifted uneasily in their seats. Empson had let off his little bomb.

The attack on Modernism has since become associated with the names of Philip Larkin and Kingsley Amis, and it is curious to reflect that Empson got there first. It was rather like him to get there first and to persevere longest, and beneath the mask of whimsy his commitments were passionate. "People are wrong," he once said when I asked why he kept on writing, "and they need to be told it." Even his political radicalism, though inconstant in detail, was constant in its intensity. He did not mellow with age, though aware that some of the ideals of his youth, like state welfare, had become tarnished with misuse. He was derisive, for example, about tramps who moved into a National Health Service hospital near his home in north London, camping there for weeks and accepting free meals in bed at the hands of charitable ladies, but it was not clear that nonsense like that caused him to give up the notion of universal welfare. He was rather against ratting, as he called the abandonment of ideals. Old friends at school and college, he would recall with some bitterness, had often ratted. He had been a boy at Winchester College, for example, with John Sparrow, known to later generations as a pillar of the conservative establishment and warden of All Souls College in Oxford, and it was amazing to hear him talk of Sparrow as a youthful radical. Once, I recall his telling, at a speech-day at Winchester, the boy Sparrow had turned to him and asked him to stand up and look around at a large assembly of parents. Empson wonderingly did as he was told. "Now, Empson," said Sparrow, "when in years to come you are asked to appoint a Wykehamist or to overlook a fault in one, just remember what you have seen today." But now, Empson went on savagely, Sparrow after a life in Oxford had turned into "the trusted family butler—and that is just the matter with Oxford: it turns people into trusted family butlers."

His view of the contemporary world could be equally startling. In February 1974 there was a British general election at the height of the oil crisis, coinciding with his Clark lectures in Cambridge, and on the day before the vote I asked him who was going to win. "The Shah of Persia," he replied promptly. Then he added, "I hope enough Liberals are elected to keep both bulls in the china shop from behaving too badly."

His world of belief had been a series of leaps and bounds—if not into moderation, at least into searching and at times uncomfortable doubt. I wish I had known him when he was young. At Winchester he was the epitome of the witty, inky schoolboy, so a contemporary once told me, rushing past in a flying gown, and he once electrified the school in a performance of Marlowe's *Doctor Faustus*, where he played a minor devil, by suddenly and without rehearsal turning a cartwheel on stage. He was always a master of outrage and admired it in others. Sitting a scholarship examination at Trinity College, Cambridge, he once told me, he had been vastly impressed, after his well-regulated school life, to find that someone had been sick in his college room. I. A. Richards, who corrected his undergraduate punctuation in red pencil, had no doubt he was a genius, and was happy to encourage him to write the experiments in the verbal analysis of poetry that emerged, after he moved to London, as his first book, *Seven Types of Ambiguity*. His undergraduate powers of concentration were so great, Richards once told me, that friends would bang two volumes of the big *Oxford English Dictionary* against each other behind his head as he read on a garden seat, and he would notice nothing and read happily on. He must have been an oddly abstracted youth. A contemporary of his once told me that when he handed in some original poems to be read by the examiners of Cambridge English, who were chaired by Richards, they found them baffling and exercised the exceptional right of calling the candidate in for questioning. That was a great excitement to his friends, who waited anxiously for him in a neighboring bar. After the interview, Empson arrived, calmly ordered a drink and sat down. "What did they say?" his friends asked eagerly. "They asked me what they were about, you know." "And what did you tell them?" "Beauty, you know, beauty."

    His life of conviction was a mixture of constancy and flux, though it was the constancy, even the intransigence, that impressed. His second book, *Some Versions of Pastoral* (1935), is difficult to characterize in ideological terms, like everything he wrote. Only an admirer of Freud and Marx could have written it, but it leaves the reader subtly skeptical of both. *The Structure of Complex Words* (1951) was dedicated to I. A. Richards as "the source of all ideas in this book, even the minor ones arrived at by disagreeing with him," but that is amiable rather than convincing, since the book is based on lexical sources—most notably the Oxford dictionary that had failed to distract him from his reading in youth—and it has nothing much to do with Richards or his views. The grandiose ambition of Basic English to show that everything can be said in 800-odd words must have lapsed in his mind at about the time the book appeared, and it is subject to one overriding and insoluble disability: that whatever its uses as a second language, no native speaker of English is likely to remember in conversation which words he is allowed, in talking Basic, to use.

It was a game that did not work. When I visited Ronald Crane in Chicago in 1957, he told me that Empson had been there several years before, on his way home from China.

> He sat where you are sitting now and told me he had been teaching Basic English to the Chinese. "Do you mean to tell me," I said, "that you believe everything can be said in less than a thousand words?" Empson said he did. "I challenge you to pick a book off that shelf at random, open it and translate it into Basic English."

Empson put out a hand blindly and, as chance had it, pulled out Coleridge's *Biographia Literaria*. He opened it at a venture and read silently for a minute or two. Then he raised his eyes. "Of course," he said humbly, "it does rather make nonsense of Coleridge."

The great enemy, however, was Christianity, which he hated with an intensity that never waned. That intensity lay at the heart of his theory of history. The eighteenth-century Enlightenment had doubted miracles; Victorian "honest doubt" had accepted only the humanity of Christ. Empson went further and rejected the Christian ethic. To worship an act of torture like the crucifixion, to believe in an afterlife of eternal punishment, can only make people worse. Religion was far more deeply flawed for him than the Enlightenment or the Victorians had ever supposed. There could be no compromise with that view, which governed his sense of individuals as well as his sense of the human past. "She's a dangerous serpent," he once remarked of Helen Gardner, whose Anglicanism deeply shocked him, "but she doesn't do as much harm as she would like." For all his whimsy, there could be no joking about issues like that. For two millennia and more, he believed, monotheism had been the scourge of mankind, and modern tragedies like Ireland and the Middle East showed that the curse of superstition was at best dormant but never dead. Bosnia, had he lived to see it, would have confirmed his worst fears. It is the task and duty of a teacher of literature, as he saw it, to promote infidelity, to cause young minds to doubt—to make them see, as Milton partly saw in *Paradise Lost* and as Shelley saw altogether, that a world driven by the idea of a retributive God is a world riding to its own destruction. Not many teachers of literature believe, in their hearts, that they are doing anything that much affects what people think and do, and critical theory has recently encouraged the view that fiction and poetry teach nothing and change nothing. Empson thought otherwise. He believed that one could make a difference to the world, and no doubt he did.

What survives in memory, however, is less a prophet than a figure given to causing endless shock and surprise. "I've known you for a long time, Bill," I recall a contemporary of his remarking when they were both in their seventies, referring to the half-century that had elapsed since their student days, "and I still don't feel I really know you." Empson merely grunted. It was because he remained unknowable that he was a constant source of surprise. When it fell to me to tell the same friend of Empson's death in 1984, he summed up the sense of irreparable loss that many felt. "The death of William," he said after a silent moment, "leaves such a vacancy in the world."

He is one of the few, the very few, from the Age of Criticism that reached its climax in the 1950s whose works are still read, and read for the purpose for which they were written. *Argufying* (1987), which appeared three years after his death and collected his essays and reviews from as far back as 1928, is perhaps the liveliest gathering of critical prose in English in its century, and his prose, like his verse, lives as far more than a curiosity of time and place. He had a gift for seeing a point and summarizing a view more rapidly than anyone I have ever known. Intellection was seemingly effortless to him: he saw things in a flash. Once, on my remarking that I had just come from a seminar on music, he summed up the history of European music in its tonal phase in a sentence or two, noting the extreme brevity of that tradition compared with a literature that stretches back to Homer.

His writings are briskly intuitive in a similar way. In the first winter of the war, which he spent mostly in Boston, he noticed something about America that strikes an instant chord of recognition: the fondness of its public figures to utter the words "I believe" in a tone and in a context suggesting that to want something is to have it. That was in an article called "Passing through USA," which he wrote for Cyril Connolly's *Horizon* in June 1940. Americans, he remarked, "easily feel that belief produces its object," which is why they think advertising a good thing even when it tells lies, since it helps the economy. If never exactly pro-American, he was contemptuous of that state of mind, surprisingly common among European and Asian intellectuals, that thinks anti-Americanism an adequate substitute for political judgement. "An Indian lady came to see me last week," he once told me, "and talked for two hours about the wickedness of the whites, and how the Americans are trying to starve India, and how they have castrated three-quarters of the male population of Puerto Rico." Then he paused to take breath, but only for an instant. "All I can say is the other quarter must be working like horses."

He was not a sage, in fact or in pretension, and had no ambition to appear a saint. He was a bohemian gentleman who, after an early training in mathematics, had entered literary studies as an amateur, and he kept the freedom of the amateur to the end of his days, worrying, with some reason, that an unquenchable propensity to be flippant might persuade the world that he did not mean what he said or that what he said might not be worth attending to. His sense of fun sometimes betrayed him, as he knew. Perhaps there is a paradox there that speaks for the British genius in our age. If people are wrong, as he put it, they need to be told it. On the other hand, there is a social demand not to be a scold or a bore, and the long revisions that delayed his last collections of essays till after his death were largely induced by his attempts to lighten the mass of his critical writing and to entertain as well as instruct. After 1961 he never saw a book through the press. Revision claimed him. He had to revise until his prose ceased to bore even him. "I still have to put in the careless ease," he once remarked, sitting by the pond in his Hampstead garden, when I reproached him gently for not collecting his essays. "The careless ease always goes in last." It is as good a remark as you will hear about the art of exposition.

It is also a British remark. Most national traditions do not demand or even expect careless ease in their academic writers, and the ironic flippancy he loved, though often a joy, can also be a trap. It is the English vice, and when the French, in speaking of *le vice anglais*, mean masochism and cold baths they miss the point. The real English vice is whimsy. Empson was a master of whimsy, or perhaps whimsy was the master of him. It was there early and late. In the earliest surviving review he ever wrote, collected in *Argufying* as "Curds and Whey" from an undergraduate journal of May 1928, he wrote that poetry is "written with the sort of joke you find in hymns," which is at once marvelously funny and marvelously iconoclastic. There are no jokes in hymns, however funny they may unintentionally be. Empson's mind was devastating, and it devastated at high speed. To read him, to listen to him, was like standing by the roadside and watching a racing car go by and out of sight in an instant.

His sophistication was breathtaking. Those who love to shock do not always trouble to say what they think or think what they say, but with Empson the distinction did not arise. His beliefs were genuinely shocking. Nietzsche thought God was dead; Empson thought He was evil, and that it made you evil to believe in Him. That is easily more radical than Nietzsche, and I remember shocking some radicals in Berkeley, California, in the 1960s, who cheerfully wore "God is dead" buttons and thought nothing to the Left alien to them by expounding his views. They found it hard to think that anyone could seriously believe such things, which was Empson's problem throughout his life. Because he was endlessly funny, not everyone thought he was serious. Can one prophesy against God, or anything, in a style that moves the reader to giggle, to gasp, or to guffaw? I merely ask, being uncertain of the answer. In a land where conversation is one of the performative arts, Empson saw it as his unceasing duty to amuse, and did. Other prophets in history, such as Jeremiah and his own favorite Old Testament author, the second Isaiah, behaved otherwise, and only time will show which lasts better.

Who's Afraid of Virginia Woolf?
A Memoir

RICHARD HORNBY

In 1962 I graduated from university, begat a child, stage managed eleven plays, directed three including an original musical that I had co-written, and acted in six. I joined Actors' Equity, moved to New York, and never again made any money from acting. Much to the dismay of my pregnant wife, I turned down an offer of a well-paying job out of town in the nascent space program and continued to eke out a living in Manhattan by tutoring wealthy young dunces in mathematics. (The theatre world was divided into two places, Manhattan and "out of town," a.k.a. nowhere.) It was better than waiting on tables, and infinitely better than leaving the theatre, even though I was just barely in it. Neil Armstrong went on to take a giant leap for mankind without my assistance. The giant leap I was hoping for was onto the American stage.

Those were exciting days in the American theatre. The off-Broadway movement was breaking the commercial death grip of Broadway, while decentralization was generating major regional theatres in almost every state of the Union. European theatres, recovered from the destruction of World War II, were blossoming; suddenly everybody was babbling about Brecht, Sartre, Beckett, Ionesco, Pinter. After half a century of arguing the pros and cons of a subsidized national theatre, England suddenly had two; surely we would follow its lead. The Actors

Studio was still in its heyday in New York; although its limitations were becoming more and more apparent, surely it would expand from its introspective naturalistic style to include something lighter, more physical and more verbal, more fun. We even had a playwright who was the equal of those trendy European dramatists: Edward Albee.

Albee's *Who's Afraid of Virginia Woolf?* shocked the American theatre establishment the way that Sputnik had recently shocked the scientific establishment, forcing everyone to reexamine premises and rethink beliefs. It was intellectual yet vulgar, shocking yet hilarious, familiar yet frightening. Its stage set resembled that of a TV sitcom with the usual cozy living room, but the dialog began with the lead female shouting "Jesus H. Christ" and went downhill from there. It even had that staple of psychological realism onstage, a suppressed secret (the fictitious child that George and Martha have invented), but when that secret came out it explained nothing and only added to the confusion. Theatre audiences came away feeling that they had been sandbagged. Nevertheless, *Who's Afraid* won just about every prize for best play that season, including the Tony and the Drama Critics' Circle awards, but the Pulitzer Advisory Board (the trustees of Columbia University), shocked by the profane and obscene language, overruled the unanimous recommendation of its own drama jury and made no award that year. Members of the jury, including the distinguished drama critic John Gassner, resigned in protest.

Soon after the play opened, my father-in-law and two associates came down to New York from Massachusetts on business. As usual when on such trips, they wanted to take in a Broadway show. Of course, they invited my wife and me along. What could we recommend? "*Who's Afraid of Virginia Woolf?* is supposed to be good," we slyly replied, with a surreptitious nudge and wink. In the event, my father-in-law, an unsophisticated but intelligent man whom I liked very much, enjoyed the play immensely, but the two associates were literally pale and trembling. "Are there really people like that?" one of them asked. Well, no, probably not, although one of the great strengths of the play is Albee's ability to present imaginatively the faculty life in a small New England college with all the pettiness, anxiety, territoriality, and backbiting that go with it. Albee's only experience of academia consisted of getting kicked out of Trinity College in Connecticut in 1947, but in his play he depicts the place perfectly; among many other things, *Who's Afraid of Virginia Woolf?* is the best satire of American academic life ever written. Oddly, however, there are no students among the characters, nor none ever mentioned; the play can be seen as revenge on his Trinity faculty, but Albee himself is not in it, even in disguise, unless it is as George and Martha's imaginary child.

If Albee hated his professors, professors generally have loved Albee. Although the play, his first to be done on Broadway, came as a shock to traditionally-oriented theatre professionals and theatregoers at that time, Albee was already well known off-Broadway and in universities. Three of the four one-act plays he wrote before *Who's Afraid* were quickly recognized as masterpieces in the Theatre of the Absurd tradition with a realistic surface barely covering an outrageous line of action. I had directed all three while still an undergraduate. We were thus eagerly awaiting his first full-length play, whose opening scenes we had seen performed on public television several months before the play opened on Broadway.

Years later, in 2000, the Royal National Theatre in London polled its audiences to choose the best hundred plays of the twentieth century. *Who's Afraid of Virginia Woolf?* easily made the list, though not in the top spot, which went to *Waiting for Godot*. Two plays that had once been seen as outrageous had become standard classics! The RNT held panel discussions on every one of the exalted hundred; at the one for *Who's Afraid*, I was amazed at how the play seemed to have become cut and dried. Bliss was it in that dawn to be alive, but to be young forty years later was to be blasé. Although all the young panelists had been born after 1962, they proceeded to judge the original production in some detail, in particular trashing the performance of Uta Hagen as Martha, which I had found wonderful. I thought back to that businessman who had reacted to the play in near terror; he was naïve, but unlike these British highbrows, he had been awake and sensitive. My recollection was a reminder that every masterpiece begins as a risky, dubious, even disgusting event. Only after they have become masterpieces do they become commonplace. The members of the Pulitzer committee who went out of their way to reject *Who's Afraid* were obviously narrow minded, but at least they were not condescending. They knew they were dealing with a shocker.

Last fall, with the play now half a century old and Albee himself eighty-four, a commemorative production of *Who's Afraid* opened on Broadway on October 13, fifty years to the day since the original opening. The circumstances surrounding the production were evidence of how much our theatre has changed since those heady times. Instead of a trio of adventuresome producers (led by Billy Rose, a two-bit Ziegfeld, leaving us with the only masterwork of his career) there was a consortium of nineteen individuals and organizations, including the Steppenwolf Company of Chicago. Instead of a top ticket price of $7.50, tickets ran up to $127, seventeen times higher (about twice the general rate of inflation), which does not even include "premium seating," where producers can now extort even more from audiences for the best seats in the house. But perhaps the most telling difference between then and now is the fact that just about every Broadway play running when *Who's Afraid* opened was brand new, including many that are still well known—*A Funny Thing Happened on the Way to the Forum*, *How to Succeed in Business Without Really Trying*, *A Thousand Clowns*—while today almost all the Broadway plays and even a majority of those off-Broadway are old, including *Annie*, *Glengarry Glen Ross* (the second Broadway revival), *Golden Boy*, *Cat on a Hot Tin Roof* (revived many times), *Picnic*, and of course *Who's Afraid of Virginia Woolf?*, only seven years after its previous Broadway reincarnation. Revivals used to mean disaster on Broadway, so that only a big star would dare try one even with a Shakespeare play, but now with huge costs leading to alarming ticket prices, audiences only want a brand name they recognize. If *Who's Afraid* were an unknown play today, there would be no Billy Rose to produce it—especially if it meant having to find eighteen others to go in with him—but even if there were, it would take a very generous father-in-law to fork over $635 for five orchestra seats for a play named after a Bloomsbury intellectual who died in 1941. Virginia *who*?

The 1950s had seen the rise of the off-Broadway movement in New York, to be followed by off-off-Broadway in the 1960s. Venues like the Circle in the Square, the Theatre de Lys, La MaMa E.T.C., Caffe Cino, and the Living Theatre made deals with the theatrical unions that made it possible to put on plays of a more experimental nature than was then possible on Broadway. (We should not forget, however, that through much of the twentieth century many of the best American plays had been done on Broadway, including works by Eugene O'Neill, Arthur Miller, and Tennessee Williams.) Albee's early one-acts should be seen as part of the off-Broadway movement, with *Who's Afraid* as their full-length culmination. Three of these stunningly crafted pieces—*The Zoo Story*, *The American Dream*, and *The Sandbox*—are among the finest plays ever written for the American stage, outranked by *Who's Afraid* only because of its greater length. They bear all the earmarks of Albee's brilliance—exuberant energy, shocking dialog, and a wicked sense of humor combined with a genuine concern, and even love, for his characters. (A fourth early one-act, *The Death of Bessie Smith*, has some of these same qualities, but fails because it is set in the American South, about which Albee knew nothing.) Here is a sample from *The American Dream*, in which three of the principal characters are known only as Mommy, Daddy, and Grandma:

> MOMMY. Grandma, go get Mrs. Barker a glass of water.
> GRANDMA. Go get it yourself. I quit.
> MOMMY. Grandma loves to do little things around the house; it gives her a false sense of security.

As with *Who's Afraid of Virginia Woolf?*, the first impression is one of a normal American household, but the archetypal characters and wacky dialog soon destroy any sense of normality. Despite being written about a dysfunctional family, the play defies any kind of psychological interpretation. On the other hand, nothing is really missing; three short lines here vivify two extraordinary characters who are unlike any other being written for the American stage of the time.

Everyone else was trying to create individuals like Blanche Dubois or Willy Loman, realistic, psychological, deep. Albee's characters were surreal, dream-like, inexplicable, and all on the surface—but what a surface!

The Actors Studio, under its artistic director and teaching guru Lee Strasberg when Albee was writing, was devoted to the idea of personal history. Actors were even supposed to write biographies for their characters, with the histories always providing the reason—the "motivation"—for the individuals' behavior; but instead of being shaped by past traumas, Albee's characters do not even seem to have a past. They are like some of the great characters in American silent comic films, played by Buster Keaton or Charlie Chaplin, who simply are what they are. We do not know how or why Charlie's tramp became a tramp, and do not care because he doesn't.

In fact there is a good deal of exposition in *The American Dream*, but it is impossible to take it seriously. Grandma, for example, has a lot to say about the past, eventually telling Mrs. Barker a long rambling story of how Mommy and Daddy adopted a child (like the imaginary child in *Who's Afraid*), but the story may not even be true—in fact it had better *not* be true, since Grandma says they mutilated it, removing the hands and genitals! Near the end of the play a handsome young man—"the American Dream"—relates to Grandma his recollections of life in his mother's womb with his identical twin, a poignant story that, like the previous violent one, could not be true; even if he had a twin, no one can remember life before birth. Some of our greatest actors came out of the Actors Studio, but they were limited to psychological realism; an ahistorical absurdism was not only beyond their abilities, it was beyond their comprehension.

Although Edward Albee is listed as among the "notable alumni" of the Studio, in fact his relation to it was always unhappy. At his first experience there, in 1959, a single workshop performance of *Zoo Story* (which Strasberg did not even attend) was met with silence from the Studio members, followed by desultory criticism, until Norman Mailer piped up, "I'm surprised no one has said what a marvelous play this is."[1] By 1961, with Albee better established via his off-Broadway success and the Studio attempting to become a producing organization for the first time, there was serious talk of using *Who's Afraid of Virginia Woolf?* to open the initial season. Again there was a good deal of lukewarm and negative response (Geraldine Page, for example, turned down the role of Martha) until Strasberg decisively squelched the idea.[2] Billy Rose and two partners ended up producing with two non-Studio actors playing George and Martha, Arthur Hill and Uta Hagen. It is significant that the former was Canadian, while the latter was German born and married to an Austrian-American actor and acting teacher with whom she ran a famous acting school in New York, HB Studios. Thus both Hill and Hagen were less likely than American actors to be intimidated by a play that requires acting not behind the lines or between the lines, but simply *on* the lines. Similarly, both actors in the movie version, Richard Burton and Elizabeth Taylor, were British. Their accents were impeccably American, but their style was from the other side of the Atlantic—just say your lines and don't bump into the furniture.

Since then, the Studio became reconciled to Albee, and some of its members have successfully performed in his plays, as have actors of many different nationalities and styles in many different countries. I have seen *Who's Afraid of Virginia Woolf?* with a half-dozen pairs of actors in the leads, and they were always high quality. The play is actually not all that hard to perform if you do not intellectualize it to death. You must focus not on the past, nor on some stylish philosophy like the existentialism that underlies the plays of Sartre, Camus, and others from that same postwar period, but on the other characters, especially on your partner. George and Martha define each other, locked in a relationship that expresses itself through put-downs and game playing that go on forever. This is the reason that the ending of

1. Mel Gussow, *Edward Albee: A Singular Journey* (London: Oberon Books Ltd., 1999), 129.
2. Ibid., 167.

the play, with George and Martha admitting to each other that their imaginary child has never existed, seems so lame, so tacked on. The child game, like all the other games the two are playing, can have no end because the contest is set up that way. Under the rules they seem to have developed long ago, an ending is impossible. Similarly, the game has no hidden explanatory past, no "motivation" beyond the game itself, which they play for the game's sake.

After all, in *Who's Afraid of Virginia Woolf?* nothing much really happens. *Death of a Salesman* and *A Streetcar Named Desire*, two Actors Studio-based plays written a little over a decade before, had been loaded with intense events—confrontations, recognitions, rape, suicide—but Albee's play, for all the controversy it evoked, depicts a long and rather dull evening, certainly nothing the participants would even remember: A middle-aged professor and his sharp-tongued intellectual wife living in a college town return home half-drunk from a party hosted by the wife's father, who is never seen but who turns out to be the president of the college. They have invited an ambitious young professor and his vapid wife to join them. The young pair shows up. All four proceed to drink alarming amounts of booze and to flirt halfheartedly. The older couple mocks each other when not shocking the younger couple with outrageous remarks. After the guests finally go home, the older pair reveals that the son they have fleetingly talked about is an invention, a revelation that for some reason frightens them. There is plenty of opportunity for psychological analysis of the characters in this narrative, but none occurs within the play itself; the audience has to make the best of an enigmatic chain of events. At the end of *Death of a Salesman*, the audience knows everything there is to know about Willy Loman, and at the end of *A Streetcar Named Desire* they know everything about Blanche Dubois, but at the end of *Who's Afraid of Virginia Woolf?* they have more questions than they had when this thought-provoking play began. "Are there really people like that?"

It was interesting to compare this commemorative Broadway production at the Booth Theater with the original at the Billy Rose

Theatre (now the Nederlander—it has had many names since its opening in 1921, and the irrepressible Billy could not resist naming it after himself). Though not designed by the same architect, they were built around the same time with similar layouts including large proscenium stages. For *Who's Afraid* both the 1963 designer William Ritman and the 2012 designer Todd Rosenthal provided realistic interiors of a living room, with the latter's looking shabbier, perhaps reflecting the fact that George is only an associate professor and Martha, in keeping with early 1960s practice for wives, does not have a job. Books were everywhere, not only on shelves, as in the original, but even piled in the unused fireplace! Martha's line near the beginning, "What a dump," was certainly apt.

There were few changes in dialog, as far as I could tell, but the changes were interesting: The "F" word, forbidden on Broadway in 1962 though not on off-Broadway, was now old hat. Thus Martha shouted "Fuck you!" at George just before the entrance of Nick and Honey, the guests. The moment was not as funny as when staged by the original director, Alan Schneider, however, who had Arthur Hill pull open the door at the exact moment Uta Hagen shouted "Screw you!" so that she seemed to be shouting at the guests, to their awkward discomfort. Pam MacKinnon, who directed this time, has strong directing credits in New York and many regionals, but in general her staging was not so precise as Schneider's, probably America's finest stage director by the 1960s, whose work with poetic dramatists like Samuel Beckett and Harold Pinter gave him the sense of timing and nuance that Albee requires.

Another change involved the joke in the title of the play, which Albee had seen scrawled on a men's room wall. He of course intended Martha to sing it to the tune of "Who's Afraid of the Big Bad Wolf?," but Disney demanded two hundred dollars a week in royalties. The savvy individuals who run Disney today would never be so stupid, but there was nothing to be done in 1962, so the producers substituted the tune of the nursery rhyme "Here We Go Round the Mulberry Bush," which was in the public domain. I remember the *New York*

Times had an article on this, reporting the incident with some awe at the producers' ingenuity, but when I heard it onstage, I thought the Mulberry Bush tune killed the joke. It was good to hear it revived, but isn't it strange that such a small thing could end up being such a big thing? God is in the details.

Tracy Letts (author of the recent, successful Broadway play *August: Osage County*) and Amy Morton, both from the Steppenwolf Company, at first seemed a rather tame and sexless George and Martha, especially in contrast to Hill and Hagen, but soon Albee's magic infected them as it did us, and they were off and running. Madison Dirks as Nick did not seem very professorial, but Carrie Coon as his wife Honey was the best I have ever seen in the role, which I had come to believe was underwritten. Coon gave new meaning to the concept of passive-aggressive and also exhibited a sly eroticism that I never dreamed was in the character.

After *Who's Afraid of Virginia Woolf?*, Albee went on to write a long list of plays, most of which were successful, and to compile a long list of honors, but he has never written anything else as overpowering as his first full-length play or the great one-acts that led up to it. When I directed a university production of *The American Dream* and *The Sandbox* in 1962, there was a public critique after the final performance. The response was as listless as that for *Zoo Story* at the Actors Studio a few years before. "Warmed-over Theatre of the Absurd" was the consensus; Albee was derivative if not an outright plagiarist. Then a man got up and said he had been Albee's roommate at Trinity College back in the 1940s, before he or anybody else had heard of Theatre of the Absurd, and he was writing scenes and plays in those college days about Mommy and Daddy and Grandma all the time. I had no idea who the outspoken fellow was, or if what he said was true, but it makes a good story. True or not, it is undeniable that Albee's early plays were written to combat the demons that were haunting him from childhood, the snooty rich adoptive parents who did not know how to love. With *Who's Afraid of Virginia Woolf?*, he succeeded in conquering the demons, which was good for him psychologically, but alas bad dramatically. The later plays seem, even at their best (and some are very good), literary and overly philosophical, lacking in the drive and outrageousness of these wonderful early plays. But if you can write something as good as *Who's Afraid of Virginia Woolf?*, that ought to be enough by itself.

Horatio Hornblower

IGOR WEBB

C. S. Forester published the first of the Horatio Hornblower books that I read, *Lieutenant Hornblower*, in 1952, the year that my family and I arrived in the United States (the first book of the saga Forester wrote, however—*Beat to Quarters*—came out in 1939). It is the first book I read in English, and it is the book that made me a reader. I came across it entirely by accident at the Inwood public library up on Broadway one block north of my junior high school, P.S. 52 Manhattan (Alberto Manguel, in his wonderful *A History of Reading*, says that "largely [his] encounters with books have been a matter of chance"[1]). Perhaps it was on display as a new release. I liked to hang around the library after school because as the only child of working parents I found our empty apartment in the late afternoons cold and lonely. I don't have any recollection of the physical appearance of the book, but it must have been a new hardback, for I picked it up shortly

---

The Hornblower saga includes these eleven books, published in paperback in 1999 by Bay Back Books, an imprint of Little, Brown and Company: *Mr. Midshipman Hornblower*; *Lieutenant Hornblower*; *Hornblower and the* Hotspur; *Hornblower During the Crisis*; *Hornblower and the Atropos*; *Beat to Quarters*; *Ship of the Line*; *Flying Colours*; *Commodore Hornblower*; *Lord Hornblower*; and *Admiral Hornblower in the West Indies*.

1. Alberto Manguel, *A History of Reading* (New York: Penguin Books, 1997), 20.

after it was published. In contrast the Hornblower books I now own are in the handsome eleven-volume Back Bay Books paperback set. The jacket illustrations of these books pose one of the first questions that seem to come up immediately about the books that have made readers readers: Is this a book for children or adults?

There is a whole intriguing subset of books written originally for adults, and that sits pretty high on everyone's list of great books, that nonetheless became—at any rate for a time—books for children. I am thinking of books like *Gulliver's Travels, Robinson Crusoe, Pride and Prejudice, Jane Eyre*, and some (or many) of Dickens' books or Jack London's. The Hornblower books, clearly, are not books of this sort. They are more like Wells's *The War of the Worlds* (a book Forester was extremely fond of, and that he had read before he was ten) or Robert Louis Stevenson's *Kidnapped*. I own the Penguin Classics edition of *Kidnapped*, and its cover has the same ambiguous qualities as do the covers of my Hornblower books. Like *Kidnapped*, the Hornblower books are set in one of the most romantic historical periods, at least for the purposes of historical fiction—the final defeat of the Jacobite cause in 1746, in the former case, and the Napoleonic wars, in the latter. And so we find men in strange dress (and especially strange headgear) wielding swords on the covers of both books. The rendering on the cover of *Kidnapped* is in faded colors and foggy detail, while the Hornblower illustrations are sharp and made to appear as etchings—but in both cases there's a swashbuckling tone to the whole thing that tells you these are books of action or adventure, popular books, books full of excitement, romance (in the broad sense of the term), and promise that might be read by children and/or by adults. The books that have made readers readers seem to inhabit this borderland or twilight zone, and I want to consider a little what this might mean.

The author of the only scholarly study of Forester, Sanford Sternlicht, says that there were two main heroes of twentieth-century "escapist fiction": Hornblower and James Bond. "Forester and Fleming," Sternlicht argues, "captured the hidden self-images of their times," Forester for the World War II generation and Fleming for the Cold War one.² Sternlicht seems to be saying that in the forties and fifties the public persona of Western culture—by implication dull, upstanding, conformist—masked a much more adventurous communal inner self. But on a little probing, Sternlicht's phrase "hidden self-images" becomes more puzzling. Can Sternlicht mean that most of us see ourselves secretly as Hornblower or Bond? I'd say that's extremely unlikely. But we may wish we were, or we may slip away from war or cold war into fantasies that we are.

In this sense—reading as escape—the archetypal young reader, to my mind, is Jane Eyre, hidden in her window seat behind the red moreen curtain, clasping her volume of Bewick, and traveling by force of dread or imagination to Nova Zembla (an island, it turns out, in Baffin Bay near Greenland) or exotic scenes of crime and mystery (later, though I find this hard to believe, she says she found the same thrills in *Pamela* and *Henry, Earl of Moreland*. In any event her reading was prophetic, for she *did* marry her master. Although Jane is maybe being a little bold here. Charles Lamb tells the story of reading *Pamela* one day on Primrose Hill when a friend—"a familiar damsel"—finds him and sits by him, wanting to read along. "There was nothing in the book," he says, "to make a man seriously ashamed at the exposure; but as she seated herself down by me, and seemed determined to read in company, I could have wished it had been—any other book." Soon enough his friend is embarrassed and leaves. "Gentle casuist, I leave it to thee to conjecture, whether the blush [for there was one between us] was the property of the nymph or the swain in this dilemma"³). Jane is driven to her nook by her position as outcast: this however is the position of every reader, isn't it, and in

---

2. Sanford Sternlicht, *C. S. Forester* (Boston: Twayne Publishers, 1981), preface.

3. The impulse to read *Pamela* in unexpected places, and outdoors, seems to have struck Virginia Woolf, too: "The only peaceful places in the whole city," she writes in an essay on "Abbeys and Cathedrals," "are perhaps those old graveyards which have become gardens and playgrounds. . . . Here one might sit and read *Pamela* from cover to cover." See Virginia Woolf, *The London Scene: Six Essays on London Life* (New York: HarperCollins, 1975), 50–51.

particular of every young reader (Manguel writes that "readers are bullied in schoolyards and in locker rooms as much as in government offices and prisons")? Jane is at once escaping from something she knows well and fears and despises, and escaping to a place in the mind that she doesn't really have adequate experience of but that all of her instincts tell her is the right place for her. Because this is about looking for home in all the wrong places, both movements have something of wickedness about them. The *OED* quotes Darwin's use of an allbut-lost meaning of "escape" as a blunder or peccadillo (especially in the sense of a "breach of chastity"): "Now you may quiz me," he is quoted as saying, "for so foolish an escape of mouth." Jane's hope to escape the cruelty of the Reed household is a blunder, as is her delight in her imaginary travels, for she is soon found out; the very object of her escape is flung at her head by John Reed, and draws blood. Now, however, in unaccustomed rebellion, she lets fly and flings back at the Reeds words that are truly foolish escapes of mouth. For the first time she tastes the narcotic high you get from wielding a sharp metaphorical knife. And the bitter aftertaste.

(Like Forester a century later, Charlotte Brontë—a more extreme case than her heroine of reading to escape—took liberties with Wellington's family, the Wellesleys, using the family name as a pen name for an early novel, *The Green Dwarf*, and naming the hero of her childhood epic, *Tales of Angria*, Arthur Augustus Adrian Wellesley, Duke of Zamorna. She loved Scott above all novelists, and the Duke of Wellington above all men. We have this information from Brontë's biographer, Elizabeth Gaskell, who tells us about her own early reading that because she was raised in the countryside at Knutsford by old people who only had old books in the house, she read as a girl and loved Henry Brooke's *The Fool of Quality*, which as it happens John Wesley abridged into the book that thrilled Jane Eyre under the title *Henry, Earl of Moreland*.)

I should perhaps pause at this point and, to fill in the backstory, say a few words about my own particular circumstances at the time I first picked up *Lieutenant Hornblower*. The most important thing to say is that I was born in Slovakia in 1941 to Jewish parents. More or less everything follows from that at once wholly accidental and yet fateful fact of origin. We lived in a small town around thirty miles north of the Slovak capital, Bratislava. It was an unremarkable backwoods town, with the Catholic church on one side of the town square and the synagogue on the other. The only person of note in the town's history was Franz Liszt's father, who was born there. Through luck, the goodwill and occasionally the reckless bravery of others, and my father's indefatigable resourcefulness, we (my mother, father, and I) survived the Holocaust—first living right on the town's main street (my father was a "Jew Necessary to the Economy"), and then, for about nine months, in a hamlet and bunkers in the Little Carpathian Mountains.[4] More or less everyone else from the town who was Jewish, and who had not had the foresight or good fortune to have fled, perished. Among the dead were all but one of my father's seven siblings, his mother (his father had abandoned the family and emigrated years earlier), my mother's one sister, and her parents. Today there are no Jews in my hometown; the synagogue is a "cultural center."

After the War we lived for five years in Quito, Ecuador, before finally arriving in the United States and settling in the very northern tip of Manhattan, in an apartment on West 205th Street, a stone's throw from the Harlem River. I missed out on the common—and as far as I can tell universally loved—experience of having had stories read to me as a child, and I did not read any children's literature. Perhaps the long traveling among strangers and strange languages made choosing books for me impossible for my parents. In any event it did not happen, and I first read for pleasure—and, in the way these things seem to happen, was wholly swallowed up by—C. S. Forester's Hornblower books.

The Gothic fascination that drew Jane Eyre to Bewick was not what drew me to Hornblower. Jane, trapped in her enclosure in the cold north of England, longing for escape, found comfort in Bewick's exotic locales, and the farther from her world, and the stranger the

---

4. See my memoir under the pen name Jiri Wyatt: *Against Capitulation* (London: Quartet Books, 1984).

scene, the greater her thrill. I had seen more than enough of exotic locales; I had no desire to wander. On the contrary, I wanted to settle and bring my time as an outcast to an end. At the same time, I too, like Jane (and Charlotte Brontë), was looking for home—and I found it more or less as she did. Ferndean, the house Jane at last settles in with the blasted Rochester, and where she begins a family with him, is really a locale out of the Bewick Jane loved as a girl: the novel ends in a place very much like the place where it begins. Ferndean is best thought of as a reading nook, for it is not a house in anything you might call a neighborhood, a place with actual neighbors and dinners with company and that sort of reassuring, homely routine, but rather, more or less in every sense of the term, an escape, a place in the middle of the wood, the sort of place where Dante seeks Beatrice, a place in the mind.

And so, reading the Hornblower stories now, I can immediately see both how they appealed to me, and then how they offered me many things I didn't know to ask for. And let me say how lucky I was not to have picked up *Casino Royale* instead, the first Bond novel, which appeared in 1953. Hornblower's naval universe is a great place to run to—it is an "escape" without being altogether a fantasy (whereas the Bond novels are obviously, and wildly, fantastic). Forester's method, which is to narrate as though he were reporting mere historical happenings, gives the Hornblower books, once you grant their premises and volunteer a suspension of disbelief, a certain substance, a form of reality, and for a boy part of the unexpected qualities of this reality are the moral ones. Here, for example, is the first paragraph of *Lieutenant Hornblower*:

> Lieutenant William Bush came on board H.M.S. *Renown* as she lay at anchor in the Hamoaze and reported himself to the officer of the watch, who was a tall and rather gangling individual with hollow-cheeks and a melancholy cast of countenance, whose uniform looked as if it had been put on in the dark and not readjusted since.

This gangling, melancholy individual is Hornblower. Now the boy I am trying to conjure up, the Slovak boy lately come to Manhattan from South America, with his failing knowledge of Slovak and small knowledge of Spanish and English, and with his nonexistent knowledge of the greater world, this boy was a neat dresser, the only tidy thing about him, because his mother was a seamstress, and very particular. He will have noticed, with a mixture of emotions, Hornblower's ramshackle appearance, just as he must have been baffled by most of the rest of the paragraph, beginning with "H.M.S." (yes, it's a ship, but what can the letters stand for?) and the odd-looking "Hamoaze" (which I bet, dear reader, you too know nothing about), but continuing to "gangling" and "melancholy" (which perhaps by now, if you're anyplace near my age, is an old friend?).

The narrative perspective at the opening—and then at the close—of *Lieutenant Hornblower* is unusual, for almost always Forester narrates his stories in the indirect first person, sitting on Hornblower's shoulder from a sort of omniscient distance. But here, luckily for the Slovak boy first reading the book, Forester lets us look at Hornblower through someone else's eyes, and for a time the reader sees him and everything else from Bush's reliable, stolid, but downright mundane point of view. (First-time readers would not know that in every book Bush is to Hornblower as Watson is to Holmes.) Fleming also narrates in the indirect first person. But there the similarities end. Forester's English is the great plain style of the public schoolboy of the early twentieth century and is the same English you find in the writing of Bertrand Russell and Leonard Woolf and John Maynard Keynes and Graham Greene. It's an English grown up along exercises in Latin, of a certain structural rigor and rhythmic muscle, and in that sense athletic, no-nonsense, with an exact but never fancy vocabulary, and an air of inherited authority appropriate to inherited wealth (even when the writer has no wealth and is a Socialist, like Leonard Woolf). And although Fleming went to Eton, he writes a debased version of this English; and whereas everything in Forester is credible, and in fact the beauty of his narratives is that you receive them as reports of actual events by a redoubtable observer, little in Fleming is credible, and for the most part what he tells us is silly when not ridiculous, and is only salvaged in the Bond movies, with their witty self-mockery. Here is a little philosophy from James Bond as he's about to take on the notorious Le Chiffre at baccarat:

> Above all, he liked it that [in gambling] everything was one's own fault. There was only oneself to praise or blame. Luck was a servant and not a master. Luck had to be accepted with a shrug or taken advantage of up to the hilt. But it had to be understood and recognized for what it was and not confused with a faulty appreciation of the odds, for, at gambling, the deadly sin is to mistake bad play for bad luck. And luck in all its moods had to be loved and not feared. Bond saw luck as a woman, to be softly wooed or brutally ravaged, never pandered to or pursued. But he was honest enough to admit that he had never yet been made to suffer by cards or by women. One day, and he accepted the fact, he would be brought to his knees by love or by luck. When that happened he knew that he too would be branded with the deadly question mark he recognized so often in others, the promise to pay before you have lost: the acceptance of fallibility.[5]

Although this is tawdry, it does reveal one of the main motives for reading, especially of those books that have made readers readers, and this is the desire for guidance. (There are more ways to serve your country in war and peace, Fleming demonstrates, than to serve as a foot soldier or to slave in factory or office.) It may be curious, a paradox, that you should go to escape fiction for guidance, but nevertheless that's the way it is. The point is perhaps more obvious in the case, say, of Jane Eyre, or me at age twelve, for to learn what we needed to we had only books to go to since there was no example in the adult world to follow, in Jane's case on account of the perverse morality of her various guardians, and in mine because my parents had even less purchase on the ins and outs of the New World than I. In this sense it is as if every young reader is Huck Finn, whose moral examples are his father the town drunk, on the one hand, and his

---

5. Ian Fleming, *Casino Royale* (New York: Penguin Group USA, 2002), 42.

hopelessly straitlaced guardians, on the other, and who therefore has to find his way on his own. At its most obvious, the guidance we want from books is about what "H.M.S." stands for, or on which side of the plate to put the forks, or how to address the Lord of the Manor, and more of the same. (The Hamoaze, incidentally, is a stretch of estuary that runs past the Devonport Dockyard, which belongs to the Royal Navy.) More broadly, and deeply, the guidance one seeks in books is about how to get on in the world, how to manage one's initiation or rite of passage, a process that obviously applies to the young person coming of age, but that can as well, in a more profound sense, have to do with becoming an adult, which is perhaps a process without an age limit (and so the books that end with a marriage, and the books that begin with a marriage).

What makes *Jane Eyre* a book that can be read happily by children is that on the novel's first page its heroine is a child of ten, and her trials and triumphs from that point on are equally bracing. If the novel has been abbreviated or otherwise edited, the power of the plot becomes all the more exciting and triumphant, but even unabridged the novel can electrify the young reader despite the fact that he or she may be unable to follow some of the book's conflicts, themes, or plot lines to their adult conclusions. Injustice, especially injustice wedded to hypocrisy, is a sure draw for the young reader (apparently we all feel hard done by as kids). Insofar as *Jane Eyre* can be a book for children, it is a book with a definite ending and unequivocal resolutions. The reason, however, that some things are not fit for children is not they are too violent or too raunchy but too ambivalent. The child who encounters too early the reality that things may or may not work out for the best is a child whose childhood has been blasted. The books *intended* for children build up to a definite ending, something like an enormous, dense wall. An adult finds in these books pretty much what a child does. Not only can these books not be open ended, they do not open out onto any vista; they are not about becoming but about being, being twelve, let's say, or thirteen. It may be that even if we open these books to escape, once we begin reading we encounter ourselves in ways we had not expected to (as Jane does in Bewick). Nevertheless the adult who reads *Jane Eyre* will read even as triumphant a book as this one, as he or she will read every great book, that is, with a sinking heart. The inescapably tragic qualities of human *being*, its rudimentary incompleteness, its curious, exasperating embodiment, its slavery to drives and instincts and passions, not to mention, as Helen Burns insists on mentioning, our mortality—all this forbids not necessarily a happy ending, but finality. There is something of Coleridge's Wedding Guest in every adult reader, and once the tale is told we return to our everyday world wiser, yes, and vivified by art, but also sadder.

Forester thought of the Hornblower books as books for adults; to him they are psychological studies of, as he puts it, "man alone." I don't know whether he cribbed this from Conrad, but if he did he misunderstood Conrad, who was interested in failure, and who (like Beckett after him) saw every human endeavor as a failure (*Heart of Darkness* has not been abridged for kids), whereas Forester, who writes after all as an entertainer, is interested in success. In Forester's books success means a successful course of action, problem solving in small and large ways, and leadership. He is in fact intensely interested in the details of action, an area of manliness that only enters Conrad's books on the level of philosophy: we know that Marlow believes he is distinguishable from Kurtz because he has things to do, a routine to keep, but in truth we never see him doing these things as we do Hornblower.

(Forester loves the accessories of the manly life, and his vocabulary is full of the relish of naming, a delight given extra spice by period detail. When Hornblower first appears on deck in the opening of *Beat to Quarters*, we learn that "Brown, the captain's coxswain, had seen to it that the weather side of the quarterdeck had been holystoned and sanded at the first peep of daylight." The deck is sanded because Hornblower takes his daily walk there. "On one hand his walk was limited by the slides of the quarterdeck carronades; on the other by the row of ringbolts in the deck for the attachment of the carronade train tackles. . . ." And there's plenty more of the same in every book and on practically every page of the Hornblower saga. In Patrick O'Brian's Aubrey and Maturin books there's an occasional, half-hearted effort to provide the poor reader with some help in grasping the names of things, so that, for example, several volumes in the series contain a full-page drawing of "The sails of a square-rigged ship, hung out to dry in a calm," with each sail assigned a number and its name nicely laid out in an accompanying chart. Even so, just in this one chart, there are twenty-one sails to master: there's no mastering the welter of details about these ships without becoming a fanatic or a time traveler, titles that seem to apply pretty accurately both to Forester and to O'Brian. I want to say for the record that, whatever else might be said, O'Brian's prose is a sludgy compound compared to Forester's clean and elegant sentences.)

Hornblower's success, though, attractive as it is to the young reader, is hardly a one-dimensional matter. He's not made of wood, and he's not a cliché. When Bush first meets him, in the opening pages of *Lieutenant Hornblower*, Hornblower is fiercely berating the acting gunner, Hobbs, and his manner, at least momentarily, gives Bush a wrong impression.

> Bush was making a mental note that this Hornblower was a firebrand when he met his glance and saw to his surprise a ghost of a twinkle in their melancholy depths. In a flash of insight he realized that this fierce young lieutenant was not fierce at all, and that the intensity with which he spoke was entirely assumed—it was almost as if Hornblower had been exercising himself in a foreign language.

Not too much later we find Hornblower is green with seasickness, and in each of the books we learn too that he is squeamish about, and thoroughly uncomfortable with, corporal punishment. Now Hornblower, a great leader of men, is always in the company of others, his inferiors and his superiors, friends and enemies, women and men. Forester provides us, that is, with ample evidence of how others respond to exactly the same dilemmas, dangers, opportunities, triumphs, and defeats as Hornblower does. Bush's insight reveals that Hornblower's leadership is thoroughly self-conscious: what makes him a great leader, morally, is that he assumes as a matter of course that he *must* lead (rather than that he *can* lead; Hornblower's pervasive sense of responsibility would be much diminished if it all came to him naturally) and that he acts therefore as each situation demands. He can be self-effacing, or fierce, or obsequious all depending on what is necessary to get the job done. As it happens, Hornblower's many other gifts, including a formidable diligence, always beyond the call of duty, and a supple intelligence, make him a man others trust and lean on; but for the reader, especially the young reader, it's his moral qualities that are most engaging, and instructive.

Still, there's something upsetting about the thought that Hornblower, in telling Hobbs off, was practicing a foreign language. And perhaps the phrase says more about Forester than Hornblower. *Lieutenant Hornblower* was the seventh novel of the saga that Forester wrote (and maybe he hoped it would be the last: like Conan Doyle with Holmes, Forester was forced by public demand to keep on producing Hornblower stories to the bitter end), but its chronological place is near the beginning of Hornblower's career. A reader who had followed the stories from *Beat to Quarters* on would have been thoroughly familiar with Hornblower by the time he came to *Lieutenant Hornblower*, and would have known more or less everything there was to know about the man's character, abilities, and habits. Perhaps displaying Hornblower's leadership had grown tiresome to Forester. In any event, it's clear that to Forester a leader is a man who must always play his part, and who to succeed must know how to use his part to achieve victory. But the suggestion that the language of leadership is foreign to Hornblower clashes with what we know of him; in fact, although he is not a man of steel, or whatever would be the appropriate stereotype, he has an unusual gift for this language, and takes to it readily. That, after all, is what differentiates him from the other, frequently quite capable, characters in the novels, and from us.

At the same time, thinking of being a man as a language that can be learned is enormously reassuring as well as seductive, especially to the young reader (who I assume is likely to be male). The form of courage most often displayed in the novels is overcoming one's fears. In particular, Hornblower—unassuming, generous, tender-hearted— shows that the man alone, Forester's pedagogic model for how to be a man, is someone who does what he must, whether he likes it or not, and (of course) without complaint; if he must climb up a mast even though it makes him dizzy, he will do so without hesitation, just as he will exact punishment even though it makes him wince (inwardly), obey orders with grace even though he thinks them wrong, and drink fetid ship's water with relish, because to do otherwise would demoralize the men . . . When I started reading *Hornblower*, I was still waking most nights screaming from recurring nightmares caused by my memories of the terrorizing sound of weapons being fired. I was told by my mother—for I don't remember this—that when we were still living openly in our hometown in Slovakia, and she had taken me out in a carriage for a walk one day, planes appeared overhead. She says I said to her (I was three), "Don't let them kill me!" Some months later, when I was playing outside the second bunker in which we were hiding, now fairly deep in the Small Carpathians, a German soldier wandering through the woods spotted me and fired his rifle at me. Toward the end of our time in hiding, when we were living high in the mountains, in the fifth and most roomy of our hiding places, the final Russian assault passed directly over our cabin, an enormously loud barrage directed at the retreating German troops. My father refused to stay in the mountains until the Russian advance passed, and we left our hideout with me being pulled in a handcart in the midst of the half-wild Russian front-line soldiers, a bumpy, chaotic, and most of all fearfully noisy journey back to our hometown. These terrifying sounds of war have remained with me all my life, but only rarely after the age of fourteen or so did they blast me out of sleep. In the end I simply outgrew them, or perhaps I felt, finally, safe enough, and magically could no longer hear them. But in the meanwhile, I imagine it must have been very soothing to that uncertain Slovak boy to keep company with the upstanding Lieutenant Hornblower and *his* wartime terrors, and to believe too that not only were there things that even Horatio Hornblower was afraid of, but that these sorts of terrors, apparently common to us all, could be overcome.

    In *Lieutenant Hornblower*, Hornblower and Bush are junior officers on board H.M.S. *Renown*, whose commanding officer, Captain

Sawyer, is paranoid (actually paranoid), cruel, and, as the book establishes almost at once, unfit for command. I said earlier that injustice is a sure draw for the young reader, and Pip, in Dickens' *Great Expectations*, explains exactly why this is so. The way his sister raised him, he says, made him "sensitive. In the little world in which children have their existence whosoever brings them up, there is nothing so finely perceived and so finely felt, as injustice. It may be only a small injustice . . . but the child is small, and its world is small." In Pip's case injustice took the form of the "capricious and violent coercion" he suffered at the hands of his sister, that he suffered, as he puts it, "in a solitary and unprotected way," with the result that he "was morally timid and very sensitive."[6]

I too was morally timid and very sensitive. In my case the injustice—though I would not have used the word, or recognized it as applicable—was also capricious and violent. Capricious, violent, but impersonal, and for that reason liable to the most satisfying trouncing not in life but in art. In *Lieutenant Hornblower* Captain Sawyer's incapacity for command so exasperates his officers that they arrange a clandestine meeting to talk things over, the only time Hornblower is ever seen to be willing to plot against authority. But as it happens, on his way to uncover the plot in the dark lower decks, the captain stumbles down a hatchway and dies of his injuries. Hornblower is the first to find him, and we are lead to believe—or, in any event, we are not discouraged from thinking—that Hornblower might well have pushed the captain to his death.

Something I could never have done, and in the reading, as an adult, still find it hard to imagine fully. In *Lieutenant Hornblower* Captain Sawyer's death doesn't raise any moral issues or doubts. The only question is whether there will be a suspicion of mutiny when the incident is investigated, and in that case what such an outcome might augur for Hornblower and his fellow officers. But the idea that injustice can be overcome by murder seems in the book—and of course, the

---

6. Penguin Classics, 1996, 63.

Renown is a ship at war—to be a perfectly plausible course of action. Sawyer dies quite early in the book, and his death is followed by a series of adventures, as well as an uncharacteristic denouement (about which, more in a moment). Hornblower has no second thoughts, and we never learn what actually happened. Still, I don't think I could have done it, not then, when I first read the book, and I doubt I could do it now. I don't mean to suggest that the act was morally wrong, and I am repulsed by it; no, for there does not seem to be a standard to apply, let alone an absolute standard. Rather, the killing of the captain—if he *was* killed—brings you directly up against what might be called the Israeli dilemma. As the victim of caprice and violence, are you justified in using caprice and violence to prevent further caprice and violence?

In one of Tom Stoppard's brilliant short plays for TV, *Professional Foul* (1977), an Oxbridge professor travels to Prague, ostensibly to attend a linguistics conference but actually to catch a soccer game in the European Cup (one source for the title). A former student, Hollar, searches him out and asks him to smuggle his thesis on ethics to the West. The professor, a worldly and clever Oxbridge type, is uncertain, and in conversation with Hollar debates the rights and wrongs of doing what his student asks. Hollar tells him that when he is unsure of what's right and wrong he has a simple way of settling the matter: he asks his eight-year-old son. And indeed his thesis is based on the idea of "a sense of right and wrong that precedes utterance," a sense of "natural justice."

As a child, you believe—I believed—in this sense of natural justice. In childhood, when, as Dickens so poignantly puts it, the child is small and his world is small, injustice takes the form of, say, being cheated, or, as so often in Pip's life, of being accused of crimes you have not only not committed but could not have committed (such as having willed your birth to plague the adults). One's sense of being wronged is visceral and immediate—and we know it to be justified. But Magwitch, Miss Havisham, and Estella confuse things. In his encounters with these compelling but morally ambiguous persons, Pip feels . . . guilty. He is not so much guilty about anything in particular as he is afflicted with a Kafkaesque sense of guilt, one that is existential and, in the end, beyond any apparent cause. By doing the wrong thing for the right reasons—as when he steals food for Magwitch—Pip encounters a new kind of injustice. He is not being cheated, nor is he being falsely accused. In fact he accuses himself, or rather feels the emotion of self-accusation—guilt—at the same time that he loses his sense of natural justice, loses, that is, his bearings. The injustice is no longer something external, happening *to* him. Instead, the injustice seems to arise directly out of the circumstance of being Pip, that is, of being human. Pip's sadness, as an adult, is the residue of his guilt and comes from his knowing that there is no natural justice, and worse, that once you have set off for Vanity Fair, as we all do and as we all must, there is no sure way to find your bearings.

A child of the Holocaust, if I am at all a fair example, is a child who knows two powerful truths: that without a sense of natural justice the world is mean, and life a soiled thing; and that survival requires capricious and violent coercion. As a boy, though, I was wholly incapable of capricious and violent coercion. I hated the idea that being a man meant throwing around your fists, and I resisted all assertions that the world is a shithole and I'd better start looking out for Number One, now! But my incapacity troubled me. It is obvious to every boy that the field of meaning is the playing field, which strictly obeys the rules of Darwinian natural selection and whose only morality is: survival of the fittest. It was salving to escape this tangle by living vicariously through Horatio Hornblower, who was steady, wily, tough-minded, but nonetheless good.

At least while he was out on the seas. On land however—and we find Hornblower on land infrequently—he is awkward, diminished, vulnerable, although still recognizably Hornblower. On land, his decisions are not always reliable, and he is, I guess I should say "of course," especially bad at relationships with women. In the closing sections of *Lieutenant Hornblower*, after a lot of daring and ingenious triumphs that earn Hornblower promotion to commander, we find him in poverty in a wintry Portsmouth. Peace with Napoleon has been signed, the great Royal Navy has been beached, its ships returned to port or worse, and its officers put on half pay. We now discover that Hornblower's promotion was never confirmed because peace broke out first, and he has therefore had to live without any regular income at all while he pays back the difference between his lieutenant's wages and the captain's pay he earned during his few months in command. Only then, still five months into the future at the time we meet him at Portsmouth, will he finally receive even half pay. In the meantime he lives without an overcoat or much to eat, lodges in a cheap boarding house where he is behind on the rent, and keeps body and soul together through his earnings from games of whist at the Long Rooms, a military club in the port.

What might make others bitter, and might without exaggeration be taken as injustice, is accepted by Hornblower with stoicism, grace, and ingenuity. His ordeal is made a bit easier by the practical help and emotional solace he receives from Maria, the faintly dowdy daughter of his gorgon of a landlady. She mends and brightens his threadbare clothes, feeds him, and even slips money into his pockets, all of which is just about beyond bearing for the proud Hornblower. At the very end of the novel, when war is once more declared, and Hornblower is called again to command, poor Maria is crushed. She can't hold back, sobs that she wishes she were dead, and—this is the word Forester uses—wails in grief. Bush, who is witness to all this, voices our reaction: "'Oh, for God's sake,'" he says, "in disgust." But Hornblower is incapable of being disgusted by another's grief, especially as he sees himself to be the cause of it, and especially if the grief is a woman's . . . and so, naturally, he marries her.

We know he marries her because of the coy pleasure Forester very clearly derives from this, the book's final paragraph:

> She gazed up at Hornblower with adoration shining in her face, and he looked down at her with infinite kindness. And already there was something a little proprietorial about the adoration, and perhaps there was something wistful about the kindness.

Which is not how Hornblower feels about Lady Barbara Wellesley, Wellington's sister. In *Beat to Quarters*, where Hornblower battles the

Spanish off the coast of Central America, he is ordered to carry her, and her maid, home to England from Panama on his thirty-six-gun warship, the *Lydia*. Hornblower has little occasion, as a seaman, to encounter women, but when he does it is almost always on shore. He meets Lady Barbara, uniquely, on board his ship. At first he is irritated to have to care for her; she is a distraction and he is at war. Before returning to England he has to take on the much bigger *Natividad*, which has fifty guns. In *Beat to Quarters*, the barbarity of battles at sea, in wooden boats that can barely protect the men, without adequate medicines or medical knowledge or even for that matter adequate ventilation—all this, with its brutality, bodily anguish, and loss of life, is baldly displayed. Hornblower expects the aristocratic Lady Barbara to be squeamish and spoiled, but she is neither, proves to be a compassionate but steely and martial companion, as well as an especially able nurse of the many ghoulishly wounded. They fall in love. But as the prospect of arrival at Portsmouth sinks in as an imminent reality, Hornblower finds that

> . . . the image of Maria had been much before his eyes of late; Maria, short and tubby, with a tendency to spots in her complexion, with the black silk parasol which she affected . . .

He thinks prudently, moreover, that the "Wellesley family could blast him at their whim. . . . To meddle with Lady Barbara would mean risking utter ruin." But "then all these cold blooded considerations were swept away to nothing again in a white hot wave of passion as he thought of her, slim and lovely . . . He was trembling with passion, the hot blood running under his skin. . . ." Finally: "it was coincidence that his hand should brush against her bare arm as they stood cramped between the table and the locker . . . She was in his arms then, and they kissed, and kissed again." She tells him his hands are beautiful and that she has loved them ever since she boarded the ship. Hornblower, however, is for once paralyzed. "'What are we to do?' he [asks] feebly [!]." He tells her, "I am a married man," and she replies, "I know that. Are you going to allow that to interfere with—us?" Hornblower hesitates. "She saw the look in his face, and rose abruptly.

Her blood and lineage were outraged at this. However veiled her offer had been, it had been refused. She was in a cold rage now."

The setting is 1808; the publication date is 1939—dates that I bring up because, unlike James Bond, Hornblower is a virtuous figure. There's never any doubt about his virtue (and virtues) so long as he is strictly in the company of men. In the company of women, though, he is not just uncertain but frequently conflicted, and often enough wayward. Now the Hornblower books were enormously popular, and so I think it's safe to say that Forester's treatment of relations between the sexes, and of sex, reflects the outlook of the time. There is something of the suggestion, here and there in the books when women appear, that the time in question is the Napoleonic era, and that, say, the sexual forthrightness of Lady Barbara can be attributed to her "lineage" as an aristocrat in an aristocratic age (but then Charles Lamb's embarrassment at reading *Pamela* in the company of a woman suggests something different). One of my first surprises, on rereading the books, was to find not only that Hornblower had a wife but that his emotional and sexual passions are so directly and explicitly on show. Even more, who knew that women could be so straightforward about sex? Upon returning to the novels, I discovered that I didn't remember anything about the women in the saga. From the point of view of guidance, though, the picture here is nothing like as clear as with Hornblower the leader of men. At sea, Hornblower is always in command; but even at sea, his relation with Lady Barbara turns the tables of power. He is nonplussed; he is unsure of himself; he speaks *feebly*—all of these unthinkable under any other circumstance. It is as if the boy's fantasy of adventure can be persuasively turned adult in the theater of war, where human relations are molded by the fierce rules of necessity that every organization devoted to war rigidly imposes on all its members. The common sailors are kidnapped and then brutally schooled into becoming able-bodied seamen (and killers); the officers are strapped into a code of conduct even more rigid than that imposed on the sailors. Once a week the captain reads out loud to the assembled ship's company the Articles of War, with their merciless warnings against mutiny (even Hornblower worries about the possibilities of mutiny on his ships). The code of conduct that governs relations between men and women seems, in contrast, wholly inadequate. The military code tells you exactly how to behave; but it seems entirely unclear how you're supposed to behave when a woman presses her leg against yours under the table. Hornblower mainly blushes and obliges. For the young reader all of this must be pretty confusing and, if the reader is a boy, must confirm the troublesome credo that feelings should be kept at a distance, or better, hidden or suppressed, and that whatever happens with women is unfathomable and anyway an exception to the lucid, rule-bound, repressed and repressive world of men. Be a wiseguy, but don't be a sissy.

On the other hand, or alongside this worldly moral, the Hornblower books—like all novels—appeal to an unworldly judgment, the judgment of a figure you might call the eternal reader. Hornblower's example is different for us as readers than it is for the characters in the novels because we know what's behind the façade. When he overcomes fears, or aversions, we know while those other fictional beings living with him don't know. This is the point not only of omniscience but of all narrative: we know the characters of fiction as we can never know another human being, and as others can never know us. Virtue, in fiction, is sanctioned, then, not along the lines of the usual rules of human relations, which depend upon society (and in this case upon society very much in the sense that Rousseau attributes to it, the society of willing consent and de facto total participation). Nor is virtue in fiction sanctioned by religion, by the Christian, Jewish, Islamic, Hindu . . . God, except by analogy or metaphoric reference. No, instead judgment—implicit but palpable and definitive—is rendered by the collective reader, a divinity present only in the act of reading but in whom the living and the dead, the readers who inhabit the very pages of the books they are reading, equally thrive. This collective conscience frowns upon, or in any event scrupulously examines, the ethos of the playing field: Charlotte Brontë was voicing its credo when she defended *Jane Eyre* against the religious literary journals of her own time by saying, "Conventionality is not morality." This collective conscience, the eternal reader, favors the sensitive and morally rigorous over the unreflective doers, insists that truth is beauty and beauty truth (without bothering to declare just what this might mean), and holds the human heart to be most beautiful of all. The eternal reader does not insist on marrying for love but rather on being true to one's self, which is one version of its faith and is what D. H. Lawrence was talking about when he said, famously, that you have to be so religious to be a novelist.

(The boy Eugene Gant, in Thomas Wolfe's *Look Homeward, Angel*, his soul bruised by the roughness of his schoolfellows, a devotee, provides a—fulsome, I think is the right word—apologia for the young reader's agonized faith in literature's eternal judgment: "His faith was above conviction. Disillusion had come so often that it had awakened in him a strain of bitter suspicion, an occasional mockery, virulent, coarse, cruel, and subtle, which was all the more scalding because of his own pain. Unknowingly, he had begun to build up in himself a vast mythology for which he cared all the more deeply because he realized its untruth. Brokenly, obscurely, he was beginning to feel that it was not truth that men live for—the creative men—but for falsehood. At times his devouring, unsated brain seemed to be beyond his governance: it was a frightful bird whose beak was in his heart, whose talons tore unceasingly at his bowels. And this unsleeping demon wheeled, plunged, revolved about an object, returning suddenly, after it had flown away, with victorious malice, leaving stripped, mean, and common all that he had clothed with wonder.")

After a time Maria dies and Hornblower marries Lady Barbara. *Commodore Hornblower* opens with Hornblower—now Captain Sir Horatio Hornblower—in his bath being made ready to receive the ceremonial welcome of the villagers of his new estate, Smallbridge. "Park and orchard and church were all his; he was the squire, a landed gentleman, owner of many acres, being welcomed by his tenantry. . . . This was the climax of a man's ambition. Fame, wealth, security, love, a child [Richard, his one surviving child by Maria]—he had all that heart could desire. Hornblower, standing at the head of the steps as the parson droned on, was puzzled to find that he was still not happy. . . . [H]e was contemplating the future with faint dismay;

dismay at the thought of living on here, and positive distaste at the thought of spending the fashionable season in London. . . ."

Just at the end of the ceremony a letter arrives from the Admiralty: he is to be made Commodore and to report immediately for instructions. He is giddy with excitement: "this life here in Smallbridge or in Bond Street need not continue." He orders his best uniform and sword, the horses and the chariot . . . before he notices that Barbara has all the while been standing next to him. "God, he had forgotten all about her in his excitement, and she was aware of it." But she puts a brave face on it (of course), and tells him, "And you will come back to me." "Of course I will," he responds.

Okay, so this sort of thing goes back to Penelope and Odysseus. Domesticity is the harbor from which the hero sails out into the great world, and to which he returns. Adventure and domesticity are inextricable, and although this is obvious in the books of adventure, it's essential too to the main tradition of the novel in English, which reverses the center and the periphery, or better the canvas and the frame, making domesticity primary and adventure something out there. At the same time, adventure can be incorporated into the domestic, though this can be dangerous and unsettling (as in *Wuthering Heights* or *The Sound and the Fury*). In the Hornblower books, though, not to get distracted, Forester lets us down softly from our visions of escape. Life in Smallbridge and Bond Street may seem miserable to Hornblower, who loves nothing better than to be risking his neck out at sea, but even the Slovak boy who read Forester's novels with utter unreflective absorption knew that life at sea was not for him. He didn't want to kill anybody, and knew he'd have to settle . . . well, but to settle where? to settle how?

PART FOUR

Facing the Text

Nell and I

JOYCE ZONANA

In West Philadelphia's Clark Park, a shabby collection of trees and benches in a once-grand neighborhood—and across the street from a city public health clinic—looms a life-sized bronze statue of Charles Dickens, comfortably seated in a large armchair atop a five-foot red granite base. Below the author is another figure, a just-adolescent girl who steadfastly looks up at him, one arm resting on his pedestal, the other at her side. The girl is "Little Nell," the celebrated heroine of Dickens' 1840–41 serial novel, *The Old Curiosity Shop*. She is gracefully poised on delicate feet, with long hair, a sturdy body, a simple dress, and a face expressing calm devotion to the writer who looks serenely down at her. For nine years in the seventies and eighties, I lived just a few blocks from *Dickens and Little Nell*, taking daily walks along or in Clark Park. Yet in all that time I never paused to look carefully at either the girl or her creator.

For most of those years, "Little Nell" was just a name to me, a vague and somewhat distasteful name, evoking images of saccharine sweetness and sentimentality. I didn't know her story and, I told myself, I didn't want to know it—though I remembered having heard that readers loved her so much that church bells rang throughout England when the installment detailing her death was published. In New York, the dock had been crowded with readers waiting for the latest number: "Is Nell dead?" they clamored. Although I was a passionate student of nineteenth-century British literature, Nell was one cultural icon I wanted to ignore. The oddity of a statue representing an author and his character as equally tangible mortal beings merely served to underscore the naiveté of the Victorians. Resolutely, I turned away.

Now, more than a decade after having left Philadelphia, I find myself yearning for that statue in its obscure corner on South Forty-third Street. Now, I'd like to get up close to it, study it well, perhaps even touch it. Nell figures in my dreams and meditations, my conversations and my teaching. I want to understand her, to know how and why she captured the imagination of her time, to know what it was about this fictional child that made grown men weep at her fictional death. I want to know why she was so popular in her day and why she has been so forgotten in ours; I want to know what Dickens was doing in this novel and what happened to the people who read it. Nell's story is suddenly important to me because I know now that she has always been important to me. I've discovered that she has been lodged in my unconscious for nearly forty years, and thus to know her is to know a central aspect of myself. And, because I'm convinced that the outline if not the detail of my own story is not unique, I suspect that Nell—or someone very like her—figures in the imaginations of many other readers as well.

When I was ten, living with my parents, my younger brother, and my paternal grandmother in a two-bedroom apartment in Brooklyn, I had an experience of reading that has resonated ever since as my most complete immersion in a fictional world. Although for many years I could recall neither the characters nor the plot of the novel that gave me this experience, I remembered with hallucinatory intensity finding the book at the Bath Beach Branch of the Brooklyn Public Library. I discovered it wedged on a shelf in the lower-left corner of the adult fiction section. At ten or so, was I already allowed to check out adult books? Or was the librarian, knowing my love for reading, letting me pass? I can't say. The book was illustrated with old engravings, I know that, and the volume I took home was thick and yellowed, with well-rubbed, velvety-soft pages bound in a nubby hard cover.

What happened when I began to read was something that had never happened before, and that hasn't happened in quite the same way since: I was possessed, entering the book without reserve and allowing it to enter me. It was as if the novel provided a seamless, completely unselfconsious passage into its world; I left my ordinary reality behind and lived utterly in that of its characters. I was both lost and found in its pages, alive with an intensity unavailable in my day-to-day life, safe in the sure progress of its narration. I read without stopping, transported, absorbed.

For years afterward, I was haunted by this memory of passionate, deep reading. I told myself I wanted to read the book again, but because I knew neither author nor title, I also told myself it would be impossible to find. I never went back to the little library on Bath Avenue to discover what books were shelved in the lower-left-hand section. Nor did I reason that the author's last name must start with a letter at the beginning of the alphabet. I simply dreamed, and occasionally picked up a book with old engravings, looking for a picture of an antiques store. I remembered that much: the book had something to do with an antiques store. I also vaguely remembered a girl and gambling. Yet for all my desire to re-experience the novel, I never asked anyone if they knew of such a book, nor did I engage in any systematic exploration.

I realize now that in fact I was quite happy to keep the identity of my great book a mystery, a numinous archetype of reading, mythic and unattainable. For what would I have done if I had found *The Old Curiosity Shop* too soon, how would I have come to terms with its intensity of emotion? Even today, I am often in tears as I write this essay, my breath suddenly stopped as I realize one and then another way in which Nell's story is mine. What would I have done if I had found her too soon?

Laughed at her, probably, as in fact I did when, in graduate school, I deduced that *The Old Curiosity Shop* must be the book that haunted me. I had been reading about Dickens while taking a course in nineteenth-century British fiction. Some description of the novel struck me—I recognized the young girl, an old man, the antiques store—and I realized that this must be the book that had so deeply affected me as a child. I borrowed a copy from the Van Pelt Library at the University of Pennsylvania and took a look. What I found, to my dismay, was a vapidly sentimental and mawkish tale. Yes, this was the book of my childhood, and what a pathetic book it was. What an absurd plot! What an idealized, victimized heroine! Scornfully, with all the superiority of a Ph.D. candidate, I dismissed the novel—and my child-self.

Ten years passed, bringing me to New Orleans, a city as dark as Dickens' London, as crammed with curiosities as the shop that is Nell's home. Talking one afternoon with a therapist, I recalled the book that had offered the most complete escape from the pain of my childhood home. "Going away" was what I called my propensity to abandon reality for the consolations of an ideal realm of dream and fantasy. "Dissociation," Eileen said to me, "splitting." We were talking about when and how this tendency began and what I might do now to counteract it. And I remembered *The Old Curiosity Shop*. "So," Eileen asked, "have you read it lately?" "I read it a few years ago," I muttered, "and it's really dumb." "Well," she blandly replied, "I guess you need to read it again." And she insisted that, this time, I buy myself a copy. Two days later I purchased the illustrated paperback that in its turn is now well-worn and tattered.

The Old Curiosity Shop is a classic early Dickens novel, featuring an innocent orphan, grotesque and predatory adults, a frightening city, an idyllic countryside, and a variety of wildly comic incidents that flesh out a grandly tragic story. Little Nell, the heroine, is introduced as a "pretty little girl," a "child" of indeterminate age who lives alone in London with her grandfather. In the second chapter, readers learn that Nell "will be a woman soon" and that an "elderly" dwarf of "remarkably hard features and forbidding aspect" hopes to make her his "little cherry-cheeked, red-lipped wife." In the seventh chapter, it is at last revealed that Nell is "nearly fourteen"—a "fine girl of her age, but small"—though she continues to be called a child throughout the novel.

From the first, Nell is a focus for other people's fantasies—most of which center around her status as an attractive virgin who will inherit her grandfather's supposed wealth. Poised on the verge of an adulthood she will never reach, Nell evokes the pecuniary and sexual desires of men who visualize her as simultaneously younger and older than she is. Nell will "become the sole inheritor of the wealth of this rich old hunks" affirms her brother Fred to the friend he hopes will marry her and split the wealth with him. "Such a fresh, blooming, modest little bud," leers the dwarf Quilp, "such a chubby, rosy, cosy, little Nell."

Even Nell's grandfather, her guardian, sees her only through the lens of his own desire. Wanting her to become a "fine lady," safe from the "rough mercies of the world," he spends his nights feverishly gambling, compulsively borrowing money from Quilp in the hope of winning a fortune for his granddaughter. "She shall be rich one of these days, and a fine lady," he insists, even as he slips more completely into Quilp's eager grasp.

Very late in the novel, the grandfather's younger brother reveals the background of the old man's destructive obsession. In their youth, the two brothers loved the same woman. The younger brother, feeling beholden to the elder, left town without revealing his feelings so that the elder might marry. This he did, but his wife died shortly after bearing a daughter. Raised by him, this child in whom "the mother lived again," grows up to marry an abusive and shiftless man; after his early death, she dies as well, leaving two orphaned children—the infant Nell, who resembles her mother and grandmother, and her brother Fred. When Fred gets into financial trouble and goes to sea, his grandfather becomes haunted by fears of "poverty and want" for Nell. He decides that he can make a fortune gambling, and so he becomes obsessed, increasingly out of touch with everything else—including the child he purports to love.

When the elderly narrator of *The Old Curiosity Shop* first meets Nell at the beginning of the novel, he is walking through London late at night. She is returning from Quilp's house, where she has been sent by her grandfather to borrow more money. Before describing their encounter, the narrator analyzes his habit of solitary nocturnal walks. He then evokes the desolation of Covent Garden Market at dawn, a place notorious in mid-Victorian London for prostitution, and he laments the exploitation of young women, "shrinking from the hot hands of drunken purchasers." When Nell approaches him, he is struck by her exposure and vulnerability. His "curiosity" aroused, he accompanies her home instead of simply giving directions. As he does so, he tells himself that his intentions are honorable, though he suggests the possibility that they might not be. "As I had felt pleased at first by her confidence," he asserts, "I determined to deserve it."

The narrator is horrified to find where Nell lives—"one of those receptacles for old and curious things which seem to crouch in odd corners of this town." A jumble of "fantastic carvings" and "distorted figures," it houses "strange furniture that might have been designed in dreams." The narrator's description of the shop is an apt description of the novel itself: it is a book designed in dreams and apprehended by the reader's dream-consciousness. Perhaps this is why I could remember so little of it from my first reading: "designed in dreams," the book entered directly into my own, passing through my conscious self with little evident trace.

Disturbed to learn that Nell lives alone in the curiosity shop with her "haggard" grandfather, the narrator becomes haunted by images of the "old dark murky rooms—the gaunt suits of mail with their ghostly silent air—the faces all awry, grinning from wood and stone." Fearing that some harm will come to the child, but unable to intervene, he returns to his own cozy fireside, where he dreams all night of "the beautiful child" sleeping in such an "uncongenial place."

The first illustration in the novel, of Nell asleep in her tiny room at the shop, perfectly figures forth what many have taken to be the allegorical shape of this novel: of youthful feminine innocence threatened by decaying masculine corruption. It is the determining image, the central picture I retained without knowing it during the years when I remembered nothing of the novel's plot or characters. "A girl and an antiques shop," I knew that—and when, finally, I held the book in my hands again, it was by this picture that I knew it.

In the drawing by Samuel Williams, one of four illustrators of the first edition, Nell sleeps peacefully on a high bedstead in a small room crowded with misshapen and mismatched objects: a crucifix, a suit of armor, leering masks, contorted statues, clocks, broken columns, pictures, architectural fragments, a huge candlestick, a mirror. Nell is at the center of a threatening vortex: many of the objects appear to be alive, focusing their malevolent energy against her. The engraving is dark, composed of closely spaced fine lines; much of it is simply black. The only clear space is Nell's face and pillow and the wall just above her head.

From age seven to fourteen, I shared a room with my father's mother, my grandmother known to us as "Nona"—a personage as grotesque to me then as any of the curiosities in Nell's life. Born in Aleppo in a large Jewish family and raised in Cairo, Nona had married young and borne three boys to her merchant husband. (Her second child had been a girl, dead in infancy.) When her husband died suddenly during a typhoid epidemic, she was emotionally and financially devastated. She went to live with her mother-in-law and devoted herself to raising the children who must have reminded her of her dead spouse. When these sons grew up, the elder and the younger moved away: Isaac to work in a bank in Upper Egypt, Ezra to found a kibbutz in Israel. Felix, the middle son, remained at home in Cairo, taking a civil service post in the court system.

When Felix—the man who would become my father—married at thirty, Nona accompanied him and my mother on their honeymoon, demanding that she be given a trousseau to match the young bride's. When the couple set up housekeeping, Nona moved in with them, possessively guarding her son. My mother, taught by her mother that she must accept her fate with good grace, acquiesced in what was to become an increasingly destructive arrangement. I have been told that in the early months of my parents' marriage, Nona would sit every night on the floor outside their bedroom door and moan, crying that she had been abandoned by her two other sons, that she was desolate. She would continue until my father opened the door and came out to console her. When my mother—against all odds—became pregnant with me and had to spend the pregnancy off her feet, Nona tormented her with foods she knew she did not like.

In 1951, afraid of increasing anti-Semitism, my parents immigrated to the U.S., leaving Nona behind in Cairo with Isaac and his family. In 1956, the rest of the family arrived in the States; Felix once again took Nona in, and with my parents she remained until one year before her death in 1976.

The room that Nona and I shared was small. Our single beds were no more than four feet apart, and the only window looked out on a brick wall. During those years Nona was in her late sixties and early seventies, a pale, ungainly woman who never left the house alone. Every day she would sit on the living room couch and weep to the accompaniment of Middle Eastern music, lamenting the losses she had endured: her husband, her two sons, her daughter, her homeland. When she wasn't crying, she would sit, steadily and silently watching the activity around her. I grew to fear her eyes, to feel them on me wherever I went and no matter what I did. Because I was a girl and not a boy, because I resembled my mother and not my father, because I was filled with the excitement of growing up in America, I was anathema to this immobile, angry woman, who longed for a past to which she could not return.

Yet even as I cringed from Nona's disapproving and angry gaze, I also found myself fascinated and horrified by what I saw of her—unable to turn my eyes away. Every night, before sleep, she removed a flesh-colored foam pad she had stuffed into the left side of her large brassiere. The pad covered the flat surface where her breast had been; on the other side, a loose breast sagged. Next, she would take from her mouth a set of false teeth, dropping them into a dented metal cup filled with water and placed on a shaky folding table beside her bed. The teeth would clatter against the metal, then come to rest, glistening an eerie pink and white beneath the water. These were her nightly rituals, performed always when I was in the room; in the morning, transfixed, I would watch again as the parts were returned to their places.

During these years, I had one frequently recurring dream:

> I am being pursued by a lion across a wide, barren plain. I come to the plain's edge; it is as if this were the edge of the world, for there is only a vertical drop of terrifying height. I can see no bottom. And I am confronted with a choice: either stop and be mauled by the lion or jump and meet my death. I am paralyzed with fear, unable to choose.

Most nights I would wake in the midst of a fall: I never faced the lion.

In a painted wooden toy chest on my side of the room, I kept a rubber witch's mask, green and wrinkled, with a long nose and curly black hair. This witch's face terrorized me: I would cry when I saw it, cowering in fear. I tried to keep it buried beneath my other toys—board games and building blocks—but occasionally it would surface, grinning at me grotesquely from the top of the pile. My brother would often tease me with the mask, pulling it out to shake in my face. Once, he put it on and chased me around the apartment; he had to be stopped by my parents while I cried uncontrollably. Yet despite my horror of it, I never threw this mask away. It served as a necessary focus for my fears—an objective correlative that allowed me to cry. If I could not run shrieking from Nona, I could at least run from my mask. Every day I shuddered to remember it lying in wait for me within the toy chest—even as I strove not to think about the false breast, the false teeth, and the grotesque, decaying body on the other side of the room from me.

Nell too is a child surrounded by fears, simultaneously frightened of and fascinated by a grotesquely menacing world. Although the idealizing narrator imagines that she has "light and sunny dreams" amidst the "fantastic things huddled together" in the curiosity shop, Nell's reality is quite different. Looking out her window at dusk, she fancies "ugly faces that were frowning over at her and trying to peer into the room"; these "hideous faces" mingle "with her dreams," and she lives in constant dread of some dark catastrophe. Quilp is "a perpetual nightmare" to Nell, who is "constantly haunted by a vision of his ugly face and stunted figure." Thinking about her grandfather, whom she sees sinking into the "despondent madness" caused by his gambling and indebtedness, she wonders:

> If he were to die—if sudden illness had happened to him, and he were never to come home again, alive—if, one night, he should come home, and kiss and bless her as usual, and after she had gone to bed and had fallen asleep and was perhaps dreaming pleasantly, and smiling in her sleep, he should kill himself and his blood come creeping, creeping on the ground to her own bed-room door—

The catastrophe Nell anticipates appears to come when Quilp takes possession of the shop, "coil[s] himself" into Nell's "little bed," and evicts her and her grandfather. Yet this is not the disaster it seems. "Let us wander barefoot through the world, rather than linger here," Nell urges, and the old man, reduced to a state of childish dependency, agrees. Departing London without plan or provision, the "two poor adventurers" set forth, determined to escape Quilp. Once on the road, they encounter living curiosities more intriguing than those in the shop, and sometimes more menacing. This, the picaresque and largely comic segment of the novel, serves as a necessary, albeit brief, counterpoint to the nightmarish scenes in London, providing images of a resourceful, hopeful, even cheerful Nell. Dickens' imagination has full play here, as he conjures up characters and incidents that make life on the road seductively appealing. Eventually, Nell and her grandfather come upon the "comfortable" Mrs. Jarley, the proud possessor of Jarley's Wax-Work Show. This accommodating "lady of the caravan" employs them in the wax-work exhibition—he dusting the figures at night, Nell advertising the show by day. For a time they thrive, until one evening during a relaxed walk in the country, they enter an inn to take shelter from a storm.

To Nell's dismay, a game of cards is in progress, and the grandfather feverishly joins in. After he has lost the contents of Nell's "little purse" ("A very pretty little purse. Rather a light purse . . . but enough to amuse a gentleman for half an hour or so," leers one of his companions), Nell reasons that she can use her reserve—a gold piece she had sewn into her dress before leaving London—to pay for supper and two rooms, for the storm is still raging. "If I had only known of it a few minutes ago!" complains the old man when Nell says she has a little more money. Nell ignores him and privately conducts her transaction with the innkeeper, taking the gold coin from its hiding place and changing it to pay for their lodging. She has the sense that she is being watched, but decides it is her imagination.

Alone in her room, Nell fears that one of the rough men downstairs might come to rob or murder her. She sleeps fitfully only to dream of "falling from high towers," then wakes suddenly to find a "figure in the room":

> A figure was there. Yes, . . . there, between the foot of the bed and the dark casement, it crouched and slunk along, groping its way with noiseless hands, and stealing round the bed. She had no voice to cry for help, no power to move, but lay still, watching it.

Moving "silently and stealthily," the figure, with "wandering hands," takes Nell's clothes from the bed and searches through them. Once it has the money, it replaces the clothes and "drop[s] upon its hands and knees and crawl[s] away."

In silent shock and terror, Nell's first impulse after the figure leaves her room is "not to be alone," to "have somebody by," so that her "power of speech would be restored." She rises and goes to the door, following the figure down the stairs, hoping to reach safety in her grandfather's room. When the figure stops at her grandfather's door, she fears for the old man. When it goes in, she is dumbfounded. Resolved to "preserve" her grandfather or "be killed" herself, she "stagger[s]" to the door and discovers "the old man himself . . . counting the money of which his hands had robbed her."

Nell's response, once she is back in her room, is one of complete devastation. "No strange robber," she thinks, "could have awakened in her bosom half the dread which the recognition of her silent visitor inspired." The reality of the "grey-headed old man . . . acting the thief while he supposed her fast asleep, then bearing off his prize and hanging over it with . . . ghastly exultation" is "worse—immeasurably worse, and far more dreadful, for the moment, to reflect upon—than anything her wildest fancy could have suggested." She fears her grandfather's return and imagines a footstep on the stairs, the opening of her door:

> It was but imagination, yet imagination had all the terrors of reality; nay, it was worse, for the reality would have come and gone, and there an end, but in imagination it was always coming, and never went away.

When I first reread this passage a few years ago, I was as paralyzed and dumbstruck to discover it as Nell is to discover her grandfather counting her money. I understood, in an instant, why the novel would have meant so much to me at the age of ten—and also why I would so thoroughly have repressed it. For although I was never physically harmed by my grandmother, I was subjected nightly to a palpable "robbery" of my spirit—what Leonard Shengold[1] chillingly calls "soul-murder." It was an experience magnified by my imagination and made greater because it could never be named. Yet here, in this novel discovered by chance at the local library, I found a scene setting forth an image of my own life—a girl violated by a grandparent. No wonder I experienced the book as a refuge, reading it with hunger and abandon.

Dickens' description of the robbery is vivid and precise, an example of his writing at its best. Yet very few critics have analyzed or called attention to this pivotal moment in the novel, the scene that epitomizes its plot and theme. In an extensive survey of the criticism, I have found only one article, by Gareth Cordery,[2] that uses it as a central part of its argument. Cordery, in a provocative Freudian reading, calls

---

1. Leonard Shengold, *Soul Murder: The Effects of Childhood Abuse and Deprivation* (New Haven: Yale University Press, 1989).

2. Gareth Cordery, "The Gambling Grandfather in *The Old Curiosity Shop*," *Literature and Psychology*, 33, no. 1 (1987): 43–61.

the theft a "symbolic rape," a "symbolic violation," diagnosing the grandfather as a "compulsive or pathological gambler whose repressed sexual desires for Nell . . . manifest themselves in gambling."

While Cordery's interpretation is more classically Freudian than the text seems to warrant, Dickens certainly suggests that the grandfather's feeling for Nell reenacts his feeling for his wife. Described in terms that evoke a specifically sexual attack, the robbery may be as close as Dickens, writing for a Victorian family audience, could come in depicting an actual rape. Given his emphasis on Nell's vulnerable sexuality early in the novel, it is hard to believe he did not want adult readers to understand the scene as having overtones of violation and exploitation.

Just as arresting as the sexuality of the scene is its violence. If, as many feminists have argued, the essence of rape is not sex but power, then Dickens has, in another sense, written a terrifying rape scene. More than desire for his granddaughter, the robbery enacts his rage against the women (his wife and daughter) who abandoned him in death—and perhaps even before death. I think again of my grandmother, at what must have been her rage after her daughter's death, and then at her husband's sudden death from typhoid fever. And I know that my mother and I became the focus for that rage. While agreeing with Cordery, then, I would go further: this "symbolic rape" is an actual assault; the violation of a child need not be sexual, or even physical, to be devastating.

While Dickens' portrayal of the old man's violation of Nell seems unmistakable, critics have usually focused on Quilp, that "gargoyle perversion of cruelty" whom Edgar Johnson[3] calls "the supreme grotesque creation of the book," and whom Paul Schlicke[4] describes as the "embodiment" of the "frightening and hostile world" in which Nell finds herself. To Schlicke, Quilp is an "archetypal image," the

---

3. Edgar Johnson, *Charles Dickens: His Tragedy and Triumph* (New York: Simon & Schuster, 1952), volume 1.

4. Paul Schlicke, "The True Pathos of *The Old Curiosity Shop*," *Dickens Quarterly*, 7, no. 1 (March 1990): 189–99.

"fantastic projection of all of Nell's fears," giving "anxiety a mythic dimension." Yet because Dickens creates such a powerful symbol in Quilp, readers are likely to forget that the immediate threat to Nell comes not from him but from her grandfather.

I too have succumbed to the fascination with the "archetypal image." Not long after my recent rereading of the novel, and when I had already begun to plan this essay, I dreamt that I killed Quilp:

> I am spending the day in a large library, in a city that is a cross between New York and New Orleans. I have been working late, absorbed in my reading. I leave to go home and turn down a street, intending to catch a bus. Suddenly I have entered a nightmare city: the street is dark and deserted; and although I know that I am just around the corner from familiarity and safety, the way back appears long and dangerous. Now I sense a man coming towards me from behind; I feel that he wants to harm me, and I think he is about to begin chasing me. Because I know that he is faster than I am, I realize that my only hope is to face and confront him. So I turn, seeing in him a vision of concentrated ugliness, of deliberate evil, of the desire to annihilate me. He is across the street, coming steadily towards me. There is no one else around, and my only choice is either to fight or be killed. Instead of letting him get to me, I kill him. I use what is at hand, a folding shopping cart I find on the street, which I hook over his head, twist, and use to break his neck. I am extraordinarily pleased with myself, delighted to have survived intact.

I woke thinking "I just killed Quilp" and feeling an enormous sense of triumph.

But now I wonder about my triumph in killing Quilp. For Quilp is a dramatic displacement, a distraction from the central source of danger to Nell. Like the mask in my toy chest, the lion in my dream, he is a safe focus for Nell's and the reader's anxieties. In creating such a richly symbolic figure, Dickens colludes with his readers' desires to deny the dark message embedded in his novel: that the greatest damage children sustain comes not from external predators but from the adults with whom they live. Today I long for a dream in which I turn to face, not Quilp or a lion or a witch's mask, but my grandmother herself.

For Nell, the inability to confront her violator proves deadly. Her first response to the discovery that her grandfather has robbed her is the classic response of the rape victim and particularly of the child victim of incest. She is silent, terrified, immobilized—and ashamed. In a scene set on the morning after the theft, Dickens uncannily externalizes Nell's sense of humiliation. She has been sent by Mrs. Jarley to advertise the wax-works at "Miss Monflathers' Boarding and Day Establishment." Nell arrives at the door just as Miss Monflathers and her "young ladies" are leaving, and Miss Monflathers seizes the occasion to chastise Nell, the "wax-work child" for being "a very wicked little child," "naughty and unfeminine," because she is not engaged in productive work. Bursting into tears, Nell feels herself the center of attention and cannot speak. When one of the girls picks up and gives back to Nell the handkerchief she has dropped in her distress, Miss Monflathers reprimands *her* for being "vulgar-minded" and indecorous.

In the days that follow, Nell keeps her terrible secret, unable to confront her grandfather or to tell anyone else. She withdraws completely into herself, coming to live in a devastating isolation:

> the colour forsook her cheek, her eye grew dim, and her heart was oppressed and heavy. All her old sorrows had come back upon her, augmented by new fears and doubts; by day they were ever present to her mind; by night they hovered round her pillow, and haunted her in dreams.

She takes to following the girl who had picked up her handkerchief. This girl shares a warm relationship with a sister. As Nell watches the two from a distance, she imagines having a friend to whom she might tell her troubles. Yet she is too timid to approach the girl.

When, a few weeks later, Nell overhears her grandfather plotting to rob Mrs. Jarley, she insists that they must leave—claiming to have had dreams of an old man who robs his friends while they sleep. Back on the road, they spend a miserable day in the rain, then arrive at a dark, polluted, and depressed industrial city. Nell suffers from "cold, wet, hunger, want of rest," becoming "ill in body, and sick to death at heart." Although the desperate pair are rescued by a kindly schoolmaster whom they had befriended earlier, it is too late for Nell. Brought to a peaceful village where she is at last safe and surrounded by genuine love and care, she gives herself over to death—tending flowers in a graveyard and dreaming of being welcomed into heaven. Her saintly dying occupies the final 200 pages of this nearly 700-page novel.

And it is this death, drawn out and apparently savored by Dickens, that has prompted the most extreme reactions to *The Old Curiosity Shop*—from the tears of the Victorian men who broke down and cried when they came to the novel's concluding pages, to the guffaws of succeeding generations who affirmed with Oscar Wilde that "One must have a heart of stone to read the death of Little Nell without laughing." For 150 years, critical opinion about the novel has swerved between these two extremes. The high charge associated with the novel, either for praise or blame, suggests that it touches a territory of taboo. *The Old Curiosity Shop* causes us to laugh or to cry but rarely to look steadily at the phenomenon at its center: the neglect and abuse of children.

In a recent article, Robert Polhemus[5] argues that Nell functions as a "Protestant, Victorian version of the Virgin Mary," a sacrificial Madonna/Christ who could "focus and purge cultural, collective, and personal guilt—particularly conscious and unconscious male guilt towards girls and women." Polhemus' is one of the few essays I know that gets at what appears to have been a major function of *The Old Curiosity Shop* for its nineteenth-century audience, accounting for both the tears and the laughter, and not flinching from an examination of the pain at the novel's core. Yet Polhemus' focus is on adult

---

5. Robert M. Polhemus, "Comic and Erotic Faith Meet in the Child: Charles Dickens's *The Old Curiosity Shop* ('The Old Cupiosity Shape')," *Critical Reconstructions: The Relationship of Fiction and Life*, ed. Robert M. Polhemus and Roger B. Henkle (Stanford: Stanford University Press, 1994), 71–89.

male readers who need Nell's sacrificial death in order to "revive the spiritual potency of the old dying patriarchal faith." But what if one wants not to shore up old ruins but to create a vital new religion? What if the reader is, not an adult male, but a female child?

The final illustration of *The Old Curiosity Shop* shows Nell being lifted up to heaven by angels; it is an image that echoes Renaissance portrayals of the Assumption of Mary. This Nell is an embodied female divinity who dies to save a fallen world, a goddess who provides her age and ours with a figure of redemptive feminine power in a culture that has, until recently, forgotten the goddesses that warmed the ancient world. Yet Nell is a divinity without sexuality—a child-goddess who never achieves adulthood, who is never in full possession of herself. Polhemus argues that Nell dies a virgin, and that this is essential to her apotheosis. I am not so sure, for if the robbery represents a rape, then Nell—in Victorian terms—is a fallen woman (and thus also destined to die). But in either case, untouched virgin or rape victim, Nell dies a child. Despite her grandfather's lament that she "would be a woman soon," Nell turns away from her own womanhood, and Dickens' unorthodox goddess suffers from—and inculcates—the same deprivations as does Christianity's orthodox female icon, the Virgin Mary.

Dickens retreats from the radical potential of his devastating analysis of abuse and exploitation into a sentimentalized version of sacrifice and redemption. This is why Oscar Wilde was right in laughing at the novel's conclusion. Dickens' vision of the dying child ultimately betrays her and the truth his novel has so carefully unfolded. That the novelist could imagine other endings to his story is evident in his portrayal of the Marchioness in this novel—a horribly abused girl who manages, through wit and perseverance and luck, to triumph quite nicely over adverse circumstances. Nell remains, however, the center of *The Old Curiosity Shop*, the suffering and silent victim whose death became a Victorian media event.

Reading and rereading *The Old Curiosity Shop* today and recognizing the extent to which I identified with Nell as a child, I know that it is time to let her go—even though I cannot now imagine what my childhood would have been like if I had not found her. She was my witness, my alter ego, the self who existed in language and gave me a home there as well. Nell dies, it is true, but not before she has been given the kind of attention abused or neglected children rarely receive; with a fervor born of his own early pain, Dickens lavishes on Nell the care all children deserve. That I felt safe in Dickens' world but not my own is hardly surprising: for, in its acknowledgment of Nell's vulnerability, the narrative itself gives Nell the love she needs. While reading *The Old Curiosity Shop*, I could relax into the shelter of its printed words, words that took seriously my own circumstances, that gave shape to my own fantasies and fears. If the domain of written language became, then, my primary place of survival, it is no wonder. It is where I live most truly still today, and where, after all these years, I have sought to resurrect this lonely child of dream and vision.

Yet as I bring Nell into consciousness, I can see her as the construction of a culture that has glorified its innocent victims to purge its guilt even while it continues to commit its crimes. I also see her as a construction of my own dreaming self, seeking vindication rather than transformation. For Nell is the sacrificed child in all of us, the uncorrupted embodiment of innocence destroyed, the fantasized redemption we all seek in our lost Edens. Giving up identification with her involves giving up a schematized vision of good and evil, victims and perpetrators: I come to see my grandmother not as a witch but as a broken woman, my parents as themselves bewildered children trying to balance their loyalties and responsibilities. I can, in this moment, forgive them—not with the forgiveness of perfect self-sacrifice that Nell embodies, but with the forgiveness of a troubled and incomplete compassion. For I too am both good and evil, victim and perpetrator, caught in the same tangled web of circumstance. Saying good-bye to Nell, the child who sustained me for so long, I can at last begin to live—in the world of reality as well as dreams.

That statue of *Dickens and Little Nell* in Clark Park makes sense to me now in a way I could never have anticipated during those years when I was busy earning my Ph.D. Completed by Frank Edwin Elwell in 1890, it was commissioned by Washington newspaper publisher Stilson Hutchins. When Hutchins failed to pay for it, Elwell took his sculpture to England hoping to find it a home—and learned that in his will, Dickens had requested that no "monument, memorial or testimonial whatever" be constructed. The British honored Dickens' request. Back in the States, Elwell exhibited *Dickens and Little Nell* at the 1893 Chicago World's Fair, where it won two gold medals and attracted the interest of the Fairmount Park Art Association, which purchased it in 1900.

Over the years, *Dickens and Little Nell* has become a favorite haunt of neighborhood children. Annually on Dickens' birthday, the Philadelphia chapter of the Dickens Fellowship lays a wreath of holly at Nell's feet; periodically, neighborhood associations rouse themselves against efforts to move the statue to a more prominent location in Center City Philadelphia. In November 1989, vandals damaged the statue, ripping Nell from the base and leaving her face down on the ground. "Terrible news: Little Nell has been ravaged," wrote Martha Rosso of the Dickens Fellowship to London headquarters. A series of articles in the *Philadelphia Inquirer* decried the desecration; Charles Dickens' great-grandson in London was notified; and the Friends of Clark Park launched a campaign to raise funds to restore the statue. By October 1990, one hundred years after its completion, $6,500 had been raised and the statue was restored and rededicated. Today Nell is again a powerful presence in Clark Park. On my next trip to Philadelphia, I intend not merely to pause before this remarkable tribute to a fictional character and her creator, but to bring this wreath of my own.

My Roommate Lord Byron

THOMAS M. DISCH

> In my youth's summer I did sing of One,
> The wandering outlaw of his own dark mind. . . .
> —*Childe Harold's Pilgrimage*, Canto the Third

It would have pleased Lord Byron to know that, having been the most renowned, imitated, and execrated of the Major Romantic Poets, he is now, almost two centuries later, the least honored, the most ignored and deplored of that select few. For he thrived on giving offense. He was a sexy, swaggering contrarian whose wisecrack answer to the earnest inquiry of Concerned Virtue, "What are you rebelling *against*?," would have been the same as Marlon Brando's: "What have ya got?"

As with Brando, behind the mask of the rebel shaking his fist at prim respectability was the furrowed brow of a sensitive guy not afraid to cry, a misunderstood teenage werewolf or, better yet, a vampire—a possibility he darkly hinted at in his letters.[1] Byron pictured himself (under the alias of Childe Harold) wandering about the Alps at midnight alternately exulting in thunderstorms and crying tears of secret melancholy. Generations of readers have thrilled with

---

1. Recently that hint has been taken up by the novelist Tom Holland, who has portrayed Byron as a vampire in three of his novels, *Lord of the Dead*, *Slave of My Thirst*, and *Deliver Us from Evil*.

a sympathetic vibration to that particular passage (*Childe Harold*, Canto 3, stanzas xcii–xcvii). But the storm passes and the poet moves to other scenes, other feelings, other roles. He roars at the ocean— a splendid roar (Canto 4, stanza clxxix); he luxuriates among the odalisques of his harem or runs off with someone else's begum, then addresses songs to her, such songs! lyrics of irresistible seductiveness; following which he joins his gentlemen friends for brandy and cigars and brags to them of his exploits on the tilting grounds of love, a perfect cad.

Those who prize sincerity in poets and would hold them to their word, as to a marriage vow, cannot but take exception to such will-o'-the-wisp fickleness of purpose. That was the Prosecution's chief charge against Lord Byron back when; that is its charge now. And now it is a graver charge, for the one sin a poet cannot be forgiven in our age is lying in the confessional of his poetry. Read any of his poems titled "Stanzas for Music"; for instance, the one that begins:

> I speak not, I trace not, I breathe not thy name,
> There is grief in the sound, there is guilt in the fame:
> But the tear which now burns on my cheek may impart
> The deep thoughts that dwell in that silence of heart.

The sound is so smooth that the comma-spliced phrases glide by almost without making sense. Indeed, some of his best-loved lyrics don't bear thinking about at all. "She walks in Beauty, like the Night / Of cloudless climes and starry skies." What or who is being likened to the Night, She or Beauty?

To ask such a question is to be deaf to the poem. As well ask the meaning of the viola's recurring theme in Berlioz's *Harold in Italy*, or of a kiss. Byron's love lyrics are pure blarney, part of the apparatus of seduction of the nineteenth century's most accomplished make-out artist. One doesn't ask for good sense from such entertainers but rather intoxication, which together with love is one of the favorite themes of their songs. "Oh, Believe Me If All Those Endearing Young Charms," an internationally popular song of Byron's time, was written by Thomas Moore, his best friend, professional rival, biographer, and literary executor, and it was the beau ideal and bull's-eye of poetic aspiration: a "parlor song" of lilting melody, elegant diction, sweet sentimentality, and unexceptionable good taste. Moore, who was also an accomplished performer, was the most successful purveyor of such goods in the early Romantic era, but Byron wrote a couple of dozen almost as endearing and enduring, including one addressed to Moore himself, which he wrote, drunk, on a Carnival night in Venice:

> So we'll go no more a-roving
>   So late into the night,
> Though the heart be still as loving,
>   And the moon be still as bright.
>
> For the sword outwears its sheath,
>   And the soul wears out the breast,
> And the heart must pause to breathe,
>   And Love itself have rest.
>
> Though the night was made for loving,
>   And the day returns too soon,
> Yet we'll go no more a-roving
>   By the light of the moon.

"Ode to a Nightingale" it's not. Indeed, it comes close to the doggerel of greeting card verse, and an academic critic isn't given much of substance to "interrogate," but the three stanzas approach the platonic condition of lyric utterance and engrave themselves on memory at a first reading.

It was Byron's knack to speak in marble, as it was for only a few other poets—Shakespeare, Ben Jonson, Pope, Keats, Tennyson, Yeats. Auden was the last, since when; though there have been a few poets who've earned two or three citations in Bartlett's, there are none who have been so unfailing a source of plums and one-liners as Byron.

If Byron's poetry were limited to his various "Stanzas for Music" and poems of love, loss, and ineffable self-pity, it would need no more by way of an introduction than Enjoy! But that would leave the main continent unexplored. For Byron was much more than another crooner of old sweet songs. He had ambitions that could only be satisfied on the scale of the big players—Shakespeare, Dante, Tasso, Goethe; accordingly he wrote a goodly number of long narrative poems, sustained meditations, and verse dramas. However, in none of these ventures—excepting the picaresque verse-novel *Don Juan*—has Byron won friends among today's critics. Indeed, a major vein of his work, the many Oriental Tales, such as "The Bride of Abydos" or "The Giaour," have become the *bêtes noires* of an entire school of criticism, Post-Colonial Theory, as exemplified in the work of Edward Said, author of *Orientalism*. These critics are concerned to show that the machinery of such romances—the harems and their doe-eyed odalisques, the sighs, the pirates, the derring-do—are all not simply beneath the notice of mature readers, but bad for us, because they trivialize foreign cultures and fail to do justice to their diversity. In short, Byron is politically incorrect, and not only with respect to his Orientalism, but in the way his art embodies the Male Gaze. Breathes there a sophomore who would not bring a charge of harassment against the professor who required her to read such verses as these?

> Her eye's dark charm 'twere vain to tell,
> But gaze on that of the Gazelle,
> It will assist thy fancy well;
> As large, as languishingly dark,
> But Soul beam'd forth in every spark
> That darted from beneath the lid,
> Bright as the jewel of Giamschid.
> Yea, *Soul*, and should our prophet say
> That form was nought but breathing clay,
> By Alla! I would answer nay. . . .
> "The Giaour," ll. 473–82

This is the territory not of Apollo and his Muses but *Xena: Warrior Princess*. Indeed, if poets have left off catering to such needs, it is only because movies and television do the job so much better. Byron's Oriental Tales must be read in the same spirit as one watches

Valentino as *The Sheik* or Hedy Lamarr as DeMille's Delilah—a spirit not of camp in the snickering, Sontagean sense but rather of a happy surrender to one's own inner twelve-year-old and sheer bad taste.

Byron can be thought of as one of the inventors of Hollywood, but so too can Sir Walter Scott—and such composers as Verdi and Berlioz, such painters as Delacroix and J. M. W. Turner. I mention these four in particular because each found inspiration for major work in Byron's verse tales and dramas. As have myriad others. There have been six operas based on "The Bride of Abydos," another six taken from "The Corsair," and eight from "Sardanapalus" (not to mention the songs set to his lyrics: seventy-three just for "She Walks in Beauty"). Such posthumous creativity is a surer testimony to the merit of a poet's work than any amount of critical "interrogation." The poet who inflamed the imaginations of Verdi, Mascagni, Schoenberg, Gounod, Hindemith, and Busoni certainly had to have been doing something right.

And still we have not touched on Byron's greatest works, the four cantos of *Childe Harold's Pilgrimage*, and the unending epic impromptu, *Don Juan*. The latter is a book-length work and would need an introduction all its own. The Byron who wrote it was another poet than the one who wrote the other narrative poems, with the exception of "Beppo," a short story told in ninety-nine stanzas of ottava rima, the same verse form employed in *Don Juan*, in which Byron found, for perhaps the first time in all poetry, the cadences of his own voice. Not the voice of The Poet, in its bardic or lyric vein, but the voice of the funny, flirty, snobbish, bawdy, brawling celebrity, rock superstar and aristocrat that was George Gordon, aka Lord Byron.

Of course, it may simply be a mask, a persona, but the illusion that one is meeting a real person who has been transformed into ottava rima is still compelling two centuries later, and once your ear is tuned to that voice the entire oeuvre begins to resonate.

For that reason Byron may be the most living of all the Dead White Males who wrote poetry. Keats will shiver your soul to a deeper depth, and Wordsworth elevate it to a higher altitude, but if you simply want to spend the night with your best friend, Byron's the man.

Begin with *Childe Harold*. That's how his own world got to know him first, and it's still the best entrée. Here is the Byron who became the first matinee idol poet. He sets his wit aside and fixes his gaze on you and pours his heart out in a nonstop monologue about Napoleon and all the brave soldiers who died at Waterloo; about the most spine-tingling of Alpine thunderstorms, and the sheer genius of Jean Jacques Rousseau; and oh yes, his half-sister Augusta, whom he too dearly loved, and the daughter separated from him by an ocean; he will open the door to his soul, and to yours, too—though with Byron it is sometimes hard to get a word in edgewise, but that's the problem of having a genius for a friend. *Childe Harold* is the ultimate all-night bull session, and to read it is to be twenty-four again and know you'll live forever.

Flannery O'Connor Resurrected

SUSAN BALÉE

April 1994

Flannery O'Connor had some advice about trips to Atlanta: "Get in, get it over with and get out." I can only imagine how she would feel about the Atlanta International Airport in 1994. You can get in, all right, but getting out requires some doing, including a long ride on a computerized monorail, à la Disney World. Passengers separated from their luggage must worry about it, concourse after concourse, until the train finally deposits them at Baggage Claim. I try to picture Flannery negotiating all this on crutches, her hips disintegrated by lupus. "The lame shall enter first," she once observed wryly, "because the lame will be able to knock everyone else aside with their crutches!"

But Flannery O'Connor died before Atlanta—and its airport—grew to monstrous size. In fact, she's been dead since 1964, and it is the scholars, writers, and artists who have come to commemorate the thirty-year anniversary of her death who scuttle through these terminals in mid-April 1994, en route to Milledgeville, Georgia. Flannery's alma mater, Georgia College (once Georgia College for Women), is hosting "The Habit of Art," a four-day interdisciplinary tribute to Milledgeville's resident genius. Over five hundred people have paid $125 for the "full ticket" of events, and I am one of them.

My biography of Flannery O'Connor is due out from Chelsea House in August 1994. It will be the first biography of this Southern author ever published, and its audience will consist of young adults—an irony that would have made Flannery chuckle. She never intended any of her stories for young people and couldn't figure out why so much was made of Harper Lee's *To Kill a Mockingbird*, which she deemed "a nice book for children." Flannery, who also hooted with laughter when Gene Kelly was selected to play Mr. Shiftlet in the TV dramatization of her story "The Life You Save May Be Your Own," would probably bust a gut if she could see who introduces her first biography: Jerry Lewis. Lewis, as chairman of the Muscular Dystrophy Association, has written an introduction that appears in all the books in Chelsea House's series, "Great Achievers: Lives of the Physically Challenged." Flannery's co-celebrities in the Great Achievers series include athletes, Roman emperors, rock stars, painters, and scientists; *Flannery O'Connor* will wedge neatly between *Mary Tyler Moore* and *Itzhak Perlman* on library shelves.

Although I wrote this biography for money, I also wrote it with love. I've known Flannery O'Connor's work for a long time, at least since my ninth-grade English class in Jacksonville, Florida. Like Flannery, I knew how it felt to grow up Catholic in the Baptist South. And like Flannery, I grew up reading the tales of Edgar Allan Poe. For me, Faulkner, Eudora Welty, Katherine Anne Porter, Walker Percy, and Flannery O'Connor herself eventually followed. Southern literature not only gave me words for my own experiences, it ultimately helped me find a profession.

Therefore, when the chance came to write the biography, I thought it would be a cinch. Because I knew Flannery O'Connor's work, I thought I knew her as well. But I didn't. By the time I finished writing, I had more questions than answers about Flannery O'Connor's life. But the sources that could tell me what I longed to know more about—her relationship with her mother, her love life, her honest views on Southern race relations—were not and are not in the public domain. During my research in the summer of 1993, however, I found out who possesses the unpublished personal letters and the journal that I suspect exists (for I have known of very few writers who didn't keep one). The personal documents I lacked reside with two people: Sally Fitzgerald, the authorized biographer, and Regina O'Connor, Flannery's ninety-eight-year-old mother.

Mrs. Fitzgerald has not yet brought forth her biography, though its arrival has been anticipated for over twenty years. Last summer, Frederick Asals, an eminent O'Connor scholar, wrote to me, "I have been expecting Sally Fitzgerald's biography for so long that I have stopped expecting." Meanwhile, Mrs. O'Connor carries on, heading for her own centennial and our millennium and remaining of sound mind and firm will. I think it is not too much to assume that there is a connection between Sally Fitzgerald's unborn biography and Regina O'Connor's unfinished life. I wonder if I will have the nerve to ask Sally Fitzgerald about that, or if she would even tell me. At any rate, we are scheduled to meet, and I am eager to interview this woman who was once Flannery's dearest friend.

But first I have to get to Milledgeville, a place I've written about but never seen, and a famous historic town in this state. Milledgeville was Georgia's capital until 1868, but a few years after The War Between the States—or "The Late Unpleasantness" as it's known down here—the capital moved to Atlanta. Nevertheless, in 1961, Flannery's letters record the (white) townsfolk merrily celebrating the centennial of "Secession" with parties and parades. Flannery herself hoisted a glass to Jefferson Davis. The conference begins on April 13, and the date strikes me—it was on April 12, 1861, that the Confederates fired on Fort Sumter and the Civil War began.

Another April, another spring, and I walk out of the airport into a high, hot blue day. It's been so long since I've been in the South, and for a moment I forget the forced weaning of my five-month-old son and simply inhale the bright air. I remember something Flannery wrote to a friend. "It's perhaps good and necessary to get away from [the South] physically for a while, but this is by no means to escape it. I stayed away from the time I was 20 until I was 25 with the notion that the life of my writing depended on my staying away. I would certainly have persisted in that delusion had I not got very ill and had to come home. The best of my writing has been done here." I realize that I have not come here for the academic part of this conference; I have no interest in putting on my scholar's cap and contributing to deconstructionist or new historicist readings of Flannery's work. Instead, I have come to immerse myself in Flannery's home country—to see what she saw, to talk to the friends whom she knew—to grasp somehow, finally, the truth of her life.

Here, in North Georgia, the median strips and trees are still light green and fresh leaved. Spring is yet young, but by June's beating heat, all the deciduous plants will have darkened or withered. But it hasn't happened yet, so I'm glad to accept the cone-green convertible Chrysler LeBaron that Thrifty Rent-a-Car offers me for the same price as a stodgy compact. I'm glad, at least, until I get the shiny beast up to full speed on I-285. At that point, I remember how much Flannery O'Connor always hated cars; she saw them as the quintessential American symbol of evil, and in *The Violent Bear It Away*, the devil appears driving a fancy sedan. Meanwhile, I am undergoing my own Purgatory trying to keep my linen blazer from blowing out of the car, my long hair from whipping my eyes, and the sun from frying my scalp. A worse nuisance, however, soon overtakes me. Every unreconstructed male on the highway finds it necessary to pull up beside me, and then to ogle, honk, wave, and hoot. I had forgotten: a big-bosomed, long-haired blonde with her car top down is more than their manhood can endure in silence. After an hour of this, I pull off and, in the parking lot of a Piggly Wiggly, I put the top up.

A little while later, when I turn onto U.S. 441 South, the two-lane highway to Milledgeville, the landscape of unbroken piney woods—shades of the murderous Misfit—gives way to domesticated fields. Orchards of pecans and peaches line the road. Red clay gashes the green fields, and cows graze in the pastures. Indeed, a sign welcomes me to "Georgia's Dairy Capital." Andalusia, the farm where Flannery moved with her mother in 1951, was a working dairy farm—Regina worked it with no husband to help her. Vidalia onions and boiled peanuts are "4-Sale," as are the ubiquitous peaches and pecans. Christ is available everywhere and for free—at the Trinity Baptist Church, the Harmony Baptist Church, the Fountain of Praise Fellowship, the Morgan County Church of Christ, and several Bethany Baptist churches. I am in the "Christ-haunted South," as Flannery called this place. I am in her homeland.

Besides Christ, the Civil War still haunts the South. A sign tells me that I'm on the "Antebellum Trail," but I haven't yet seen anything ante about 1950. Trailers, permanently moored, seem the dwelling of choice. A few tin-roofed shacks hang back from the road behind sagging fences; rusty tractors and balers stand useless beside weather-beaten barns. The occasional farmer in overalls graces the landscape, along with the occasional store—"Pettigrew's Beer, Ice, Groceries," "Brantley's Marina & Guns"; restaurants appear here and there—"Hug's," the "Br'er Rabbit Tavern," the "Blue Crab Seafood," which has a life-sized Angus steer inexplicably adorning the roof. The Oconee National Forest blooms beside the highway for a few miles; dogwoods appear suddenly in a cloud of white blossoms amid the new-leaved deciduous trees; a fallow field of yellow wildflowers crops up between the farms and the forest.

I pass the Kountry Kollectibles store in Eatonton, and I am in Alice Walker's hometown, a short hop from Milledgeville. Alice Walker said of Flannery O'Connor, "Her stories are about grace, not race," but I wonder. On Friday afternoon, according to my program, a panel called "O'Connor and Race" will convene in the Russell Auditorium of Georgia College. Four theologians—one of them black—will attempt to determine whether Flannery O'Connor was a racist. The South is not merely Christ-haunted, it is race-haunted too. I pass the Southern Boys Barbecue, and then I'm in town. The relative sophistication of the town over the country immediately strikes me when I read a sign wheeled up to the highway. It says, "The harvest is plentiful, the reapers are few." I look behind it for a Baptist church and see instead a real estate office.

The motel where I'm staying is newish but run-down. Gum stains the carpet, grout grips the mold in the bathroom, the shower head nearly flies out of the wall the first time I turn it on. Nevertheless, I struggle into fresh clothes, climb back in the Chrysler, and drive downtown. Sally Fitzgerald told me that she would be staying in an historic house across from "the old Cline place"—Regina's family home, where Flannery spent her high school and college years—and that I should look her up for an interview. I decide to try to find Sally before the "Celebration Mass" at 8 p.m. (Clyde Tipton's musical composition in honor of Flannery will be the first big event of the conference.)

Dusk finds me wandering aimlessly down Greene Street. I pass the Old Governor's Mansion and recognize a site I wrote about but have never seen with my own eyes. Adjacent to the governor's gardens stands the house where Flannery spent so many years; a picture of it will be published in my biography. I have seen the picture and read Robert Fitzgerald's description of this antebellum mansion with its columns and porticos, but I am unprepared for the reality of what time has done to this edifice. I stop on the sidewalk before a decrepit house; its paint is peeling and its porch sags. A chain extends across the entrance to the porch with a sign warning off trespassers. I feel like I'm looking at Boo Radley's house, not Flannery's, and I am unutterably depressed.

A curtain flicks in a window upstairs, and I know better than to keep loitering where visitors are not welcome. I turn on Liberty Street and wander past a dozen beautiful Georgian mansions; azaleas bloom against their white walls, and almost every house has an historic plaque commemorating it. But I'm lost, and I don't remember which house Sally said she'd be staying in. I think she mentioned the "Bearden-Montgomery House," but I ring that doorbell and no one is home. Luckily, a middle-aged woman in a jogging suit appears on the sidewalk and, with Southern friendliness, asks me whom I'm looking for. I tell her, and she quickly sums up the possibilities. "If she's here for the conference, she's probably staying at Mara's Tara," she tells me. I have no idea what or where that is, but the woman offers to take me. We walk back past the ruined Cline mansion, and my companion shakes her head. "It's a shame," she tells me, "but the Historic Society can't do a thing about private property. Some people say that Regina is just too old to see how bad the house looks, so she doesn't care about fixing it up."

"Is she living there?" I ask.

"She's there all right. Sick, though. Ailing. But sure, she lives in the house." She points to a dark car that's pulled up in front of the Cline house. "Those are Pinkerton guards," she says. "They're here for the conference. Regina doesn't want to be bothered by any visiting scholars or tourists."

She leads me up the steps of another large Georgian mansion, this one in mint condition. A sprightly woman in her late sixties is sitting on the porch having a drink and a smoke.

The friendly jogger introduces me and departs, and Rowena Mara and I begin to talk about Flannery O'Connor, Milledgeville, and other topics of related interest. I instantly realize that I'm in the presence of a master storyteller, and in about twenty minutes I know more about the history of Rowena's aristocratic ancestry than I would ever have thought possible. And she's as witty as can be—deadpan, as often as not. She keeps calling me "Miss Bidet," though I've told her it's *Balée* at least five times. At last she laughs, "The first time I saw a bidet in Paris I wondered what in tarnation it was. A footbath, I figured." Her eyes twinkle. "What's your name, again?"

"Here's Sally now," Rowena says at last, and I stand up. I'm not prepared for the woman who mounts the steps to Rowena Mara's bed and breakfast. Even though I know that over thirty years have passed since the letters collected in *The Habit of Being* were written, it is the Sally Fitzgerald of those letters whom I know. A Sally still in her thirties, with her cluster of babes around her, her marriage to Robert Fitzgerald still happy, intact. Time hasn't done to her what it's done to the Cline-O'Connor house, but it has altered Sally from the energetic young mother of the 1950s and early 1960s to a thin, grey woman in her seventies. Nevertheless, her voice thrills me with its clear melody, and a youthful vitality still shimmers out from her slender frame. I clasp her hand and am surprised by its dry strength.

Unfortunately for me, Sally has a dinner date with someone else and suggests that we meet the next day. Rowena then invites me to a restaurant with her, and I'm delighted to accept. I hear more about her father, and her husband, Colonel Mara, both of whom were fine military men. In fact, Colonel Mara was graduated from Georgia

Military Institute, right down the street from where we're having dinner. Rowena loves the military and particularly the Southern military hero—*the* Southern hero since the Civil War. I mention Sherman's visit to Milledgeville before he marched across Georgia, destroying everything in his path. "Honey, it wasn't Sherman done that damage," Rowena tells me. "He was an officer, and I never knew an officer who wasn't a gentleman. Those vandals were foot soldiers. With a large army, you're gonna have the ragtag types—there's nothing you can do about it. People blame Sherman for burning Atlanta and tearing up the rest of the state, but *he* didn't do it. It was some of his soldiers, the dregs of the army."

By the time I've drained my iced tea to the dregs, it's time to gallop to Russell Auditorium for Clyde Tipton's "Celebration Mass." The place is packed, but I find a seat, and the performance begins. It's a strange event—snippets of an actual Catholic mass mingled with music and narration by William Morgan, a Presbyterian minister (priests are obviously as hard to find in Milledgeville now as they were in Flannery's day). Julie Morgan (I wonder if she's related to the preacher) is the featured soprano, and she's good. She sings excerpts from writers and philosophers who influenced Flannery; I hear passages from T. S. Eliot's "Four Quartets," Teilhard de Chardin's "Hymn of the Universe," and part of a letter about the Holy Spirit that O'Connor wrote to T. R. Spivey. The Georgia College Concert Choir sings with the soprano on the refrains, and some of them also ring bells at regular intervals.

At one point, Clyde Tipton—who has the long hair and white beard of an Old Testament prophet—snaps up a violin and does a little fiddling. All I can think is, "Would Flannery O'Connor enjoy this?" I remember something she wrote to a friend: "I have the Original Tin Ear, that is to say, the First and Prime Tin Ear. So I like music that is guaranteed good because I have no way of finding out for myself. Old stuff like Haydn that there is positively no doubt about. On my own I wouldn't know it from Music to Clean Up By." So I guess she'd be pretty amused by this performance in her honor, but I think she'd like it too.

I slip out a bit before the end and head down Clark Street towards Greene, where my car is parked. Night-blooming honeysuckle perfumes the air, and I wonder what Sally Fitzgerald will tell me tomorrow about Flannery's love life. Gay Studies, ever on the lookout for new authors to induct, has been gazing recently at Flannery O'Connor. *Could she have been?* If so, she would join the ranks of Willa Cather and Elizabeth Bishop; she could become A Lesbian to Look Up To for young writers and scholars. My thought is, she *could* have been, but she wasn't. She had that intense correspondence with "A."—who gave Sally Fitzgerald her cache of letters on the condition that she remain anonymous—and I think A. may have been bisexual, but I don't think Flannery was worldly enough to recognize that kind of love. And in the end, it was not *eros* but *agape* that she knew best.

Driving back up 441 to the motel, I realize I have to buy other shoes—the new ones I bought for the conference are martyring my feet. A Wal-Mart catches my eye, and I park between two pickups outside its main entrance. It's 9 p.m. on a Wednesday night in Milledgeville, but the Wal-Mart is hopping. All of a sudden, I realize that *this* is Flannery O'Connor's Georgia. If she were alive and writing in 1994, this is where she'd be researching her characters. You want evangelists? Check out the Jehovah's Witnesses handing out copies of *The Watch Tower* by the front door. Looking for a tattooed man? Here's a shirtless one buying an electric drill. An enormous woman rifling through a rack of denim shorts directs me back to the Shoe Department. On the way there, I see both blacks and whites browsing among the clothes and accessories. In the shoe section, a mother and her teenage daughter are pulling out boxes, looking for "something in white." The teenage daughter is obviously pregnant and, from their conversation, I realize that she is trying to find shoes to go with her wedding gown.

On Thursday morning, I make it down to Georgia College in time to hear Lee Smith read an excerpt from a new novel, tentatively titled "Paradise." The novel, about a snake-handling Christian sect in the Deep South, is absolutely hilarious. Smith has all of us laughing for an hour, and I rush to the conference bookshop to buy one of her books.

In the afternoon, I skip the scholarly panel and wander around the campus instead. I study the O'Connor-inspired art in Blackbridge Hall and lust after the $200 copy of Barry Moser's woodcut of Flannery's face. It's on all the conference paraphernalia, and it really captures her essence. But I don't have $200. In fact, I hardly have $100 left, and it's possible I could spend all that on food for three days. I wander away and sit in the governor's gardens for a while. The back of Regina Cline O'Connor's house doesn't look as bad as the front. An old Cadillac sits back there—hers, no doubt.

Numerous Georgia College students troop by, in various states of undress. It's hot, and the kids are wearing shorts and T-shirts. They're a happy-looking bunch, and many of them are black. Times have changed since Flannery's day. She saw the first black students enter the college during the civil rights movement, but those were dark days in Georgia's history, and many such students were harassed. These students look at ease. I left the South to go to graduate school in New York back in 1983, and there was still a great deal of unreconstructed racism among the white middle class. I hope it's changed, and maybe—if these perky students are any indication—it has.

At 5:00 p.m., the time Sally Fitzgerald has given me for our meeting, I go back to Mara's Tara. On the porch, I meet Cecil Dawkins, an old friend of Flannery. She has a square, amiable face, short steel-grey hair, and an easy manner. She reminds me of an old athlete, still comfortable with her body. She's wearing loose-fitting cotton clothes, and though she left Alabama forty years ago (and now lives in New Mexico), she's still sporting a Birmingham accent. We begin to talk about Flannery and about writing, and I'm struck by the intelligence of her remarks. I regret that I couldn't find any of her books in print, for she obviously knows the craft she's speaking of. And she's also obviously tired of having her work linked to her friendship with O'Connor. She is an important correspondent in *The Habit of Being*, and she did show Flannery many of her stories. "But I'd already written *three* stories before she ever saw my work," she tells me. "She was a great reader—none better—but I only sent her stories that I'd finished. She didn't revise them for me." I can understand why Cecil is irked. Most people nowadays know her primarily as a friend of O'Connor. It's not fair, but there it is.

Soon, Barry Moser and Louise "Molly" Westling, an important O'Connor scholar, join us on the porch. I tell Barry how much I loved the Flannery woodcut but that I couldn't afford a copy. "Oh," he says, "I'll give you one." Wonderful man—he leaps up, heads upstairs, and comes back with a copy signed to me. "What color were Flannery's eyes?" someone asks. "I think they were blue," Barry says, "although I only saw black-and-white photos of her. But she was Irish, so . . ." Cecil Dawkins shakes her head. "Her eyes were brown," she tells us. I look closely at Cecil; *her* eyes are brown. "Oh well," Barry says, "the print I did is black-and-white so it doesn't really matter." Molly Westling and I discover we're both from Jacksonville, Florida, and as we reminisce about the old town, Sally arrives home. Molly gives her a chair, and I turn on my tape recorder.

I ask her about the men in Flannery's life. Sally had dropped tantalizing hints of love affairs in her Chronology in the Library of America edition of the collected works, and I want to know. "Oh, Flannery had many boyfriends," she tells us. "She was a charming woman—certainly not the lonely wallflower that they were making her out to be at that scholarly session today. I knew her, she was lovely. She loved people." Cecil nods in agreement. "A. asked her if she'd ever known love," Sally went on, "and Flannery told her that she had known it *many* times." A small crease appears briefly between Cecil's eyes. "Men were just crazy about her," Sally continues. "John Sullivan here, Robie Macauley at Iowa."

"But Macauley was engaged, wasn't he?" I ask.

"Yes," she answers, "he was. But he admitted in his letters that he was dating her then. I have tracked down all of these people," she tells me. "I have met them, talked to them." She leans toward me. "But Flannery was a Catholic, and she knew she had lupus. She could never marry, for to bear children would kill her. She couldn't have done that, not with lupus. So that kind of a relationship with a man was not an option for her."

I begin to see Sally Fitzgerald's image of Flannery—a Catholic wedded to words, and through words, to Christ. A kind of literary nun, almost. I'm not sure I believe it. Flannery didn't find out she had lupus until she was well into her twenties; most girls of her age and station married much earlier than that.

I ask Sally about her six children, and she names them off for me and what they're doing. Two are translators, one is a movie producer, one writes screenplays, another is a fiction writer. I can't keep track of them all, but it's lovely to see how proud Sally is of her successful brood. She begins to reminisce about the making of *Wise Blood*. One of her sons wrote the screenplay, another produced the film, and John Huston directed it. Sally herself was the costume designer, and she found most of what she needed in Macon, Georgia, thrift shops. We all agree that it was a great movie.

We drift back in time to their days in Ridgefield, Connecticut, when Flannery was a boarder, and Sally remembers literary arguments over the dinner table. "Sometimes I would disagree with their interpretation of a story, but then Robert and Flannery would gang up on me. Oh, it used to make me mad!" But she laughs. I am utterly charmed by Sally Fitzgerald, even if she is beatifying Flannery O'Connor. After all, worse things could happen to a dead writer. "I can still hear your Southern accent on some words," I tell her. And I can; beneath the dignified Bostonian accent the Texan peeps out: she still pronounces ruin "rue-een," and children "chirren."

I have many more questions to ask, but it's time to go to a reception at the town library down the street. Cecil drives Sally and me over to the Mary Vinson Memorial Library. Upstairs, on the main floor of the library, a friend calls Sally over, and Cecil and I are left to fill our plates together. We spear a few appetizers and let the servers spoon dollops of chicken casserole on our plates, and then we lean against a counter to talk and eat. "I don't think I agree with what Sally said about Flannery's love life," Cecil tells me. "I don't think Flannery had all those boyfriends. I don't think she knew anything about men, or about sex either. She just didn't know about things like that. She was a Catholic, and she'd lived a sheltered life. And she lived with Regina."

"What was Regina like?" I ask. I've been dying to know, and no one has ever really said. Flannery's contemporaries keep describing Regina as "full of energy," which may be true but also sounds like a euphemism for something else.

"Regina was full of energy," Cecil tells me.

Another friend of Flannery overhears and comments: "Regina's personality was just like the mother in the stories. Just like those mothers."

I think of Hulga's mother and of all the other tough-minded single mothers in Flannery's stories. They are materialistic women, those characters; they are frequently spiritually blind as well as annoyingly self-righteous. They aren't often admirable characters, but they ring true. When I wrote the biography, I had the idea that those women were modelled on Regina, but I couldn't comment on what I didn't know for sure. And no one has ever really described Flannery's mother in print. Regina O'Connor is, after all, still alive. I wonder if Sally Fitzgerald's biography will render an accurate portrait of that mother/daughter relationship, and I wonder if that's the real reason she has never published it? She doesn't want to hurt Regina. Sally's sense of delicacy struck me during our brief interview; she has no desire to wound anyone, only to protect.

Cecil changes the subject. "I think it's ridiculous that people are so interested in writers' sex lives. Who cares about their sex lives? It's their work that matters."

"But people do care," I say. "They want to know. I think that Sally is trying to defend Flannery from the recent contention that she might have been a lesbian."

Cecil snorts. "She wasn't a lesbian," she says. "She just didn't know a thing about sex. She didn't know *what* she was."

I think that most people have a pretty good idea of "what they are" by the time they're in their teens, but I also believe that Flannery was innocent in many ways. Not naïve, just innocent. When I read *The Habit of Being*, I thought that A. might have been prodding Flannery toward some deeper articulation of her sexuality, but it's impossible to tell from just Flannery's half of the correspondence. I mention something like this to Cecil.

"A. is a manic-depressive," she tells me. "I wish she would have gotten on lithium a long time ago—I think it would have helped her. She used to get crushes on writers, and she did write brilliant letters. She had a crush on Flannery, one on Iris Murdoch, and later she got one on me."

"Do you still correspond?" I ask, surprised.

"Oh, no," Cecil laughs. "Her letters got too strange. When she told me she was writing poems about her father's penis, I figured it was time to end the correspondence. But she was very smart, in her way. And her letters were absolutely brilliant."

Two women come up to talk to Cecil; they know and love her books—*The Quiet Enemy*, *The Live Goat*, etc.—and I feel stupid again that I haven't read any of them. I have made mental notes of all the titles, though; I'll find them in the used bookstores back in Philadelphia.

I leave the reception early and walk back up the street to the Georgia College campus. That night, I attend the Leo Kottke concert. He says of his link to Flannery, "It was the barbed wire that kept me going." Hazel Motes, the evangelist hero of *Wise Blood*, wraps himself in barbed wire as penance for his sins.

The next morning, I am at the Russell Auditorium hunting for Stan Lindberg, the editor of the *Georgia Review*. We have a lunch date, and he is also going to introduce me to Louise Erdrich, a featured speaker and one of my favorite novelists. She is, many people think, the heiress of Flannery's style—another writer who merges humor and tragedy and comes up with "the grotesque." In return for the introduction, Stan has asked me to identify Erdrich in my article on the conference as "an Advisory and Contributing Editor to *The Georgia Review*, which—not surprisingly, given its status in American letters—has published several of her finest pieces." I have agreed to use his exact words. I finally find him, and he is as good as his pledge: he introduces me to Louise Erdrich, and I think she must be one of the most beautiful women I have ever seen, better looking in person than on her book jackets. She too reads an excellent portion of a new novel, and after an hour-long book signing session, a number of us head out to lunch at the Southern Café. It's Southern all right—a cafeteria-style place serving collard greens, chicken and dumplings, biscuits, and fat sausages. Not the kind of place I would think to take a visiting writer, but Erdrich doesn't seem to mind.

After lunch, I hurry to the session on "O'Connor and Race." As I had suspected, it turns out to be the most revealing of all the conference sessions. Ralph Wood, the theologian whose paper opens the session, describes a new collection of O'Connor letters recently donated to Georgia College. These are more letters from Maryat Lee, the sister of the former college president, and Flannery's good friend. The letters, according to Wood, reveal that Flannery was in fact a racist. In the letters, Flannery wrangles with Maryat—a confirmed liberal—over race relations. When Maryat requests that Flannery write a public letter on the race question, the Milledgeville prophet snorts. Then she says that though she believes in integration as "a moral ideal," she doesn't really like black people, particularly not "the new kind." Wood laments this but says that her personal opinions never contaminated her art—she portrays blacks fairly in her stories and often ennobles them far above the white characters. Three theologians respond to Wood's paper, and one of them is Willie Jennings, a black Doctor of Divinity. Indeed, Jennings is the *only* black person at the conference—a fact that may say more about Flannery's work and its reception than any of the words being thrown about by the participants.

Jennings, like all the others, must conclude that Flannery was indeed a racist, but he wisely notes that such a question is too simplistic; "racism" is too narrow a category. "She was not stronger than the Jim Crow South," he notes, "but she was not chained to it." Another theologian, Henry Russell, observes that "Flannery will be vilified as her views are made better known," but he wonders why we must bandy about terms that damn authors, terms like "racism," "homophobia." What's the point? he asks. "It's disturbing to hear that

Flannery doesn't like black people," he says, "but it's obvious that she didn't much like white people either."

The session runs way too long, but I have been mesmerized by it. Afterwards, I'm amazed to hear people speaking angrily about that panel, about how the theologians tried to make Flannery out to be a racist, to ruin her reputation. I had not thought that at all; I felt they all tried to say that Flannery could not rise above her cultural milieu, her time and place. For it's true that if we turn politically correct eyes on white Southern writers of thirty and more years ago, not one of them will measure up. That session, for me, remains the most important part of the conference.

That night I listen to Joyce Carol Oates read a story from *Heat*, but I skip the book-signing line and go instead to the Governor's Mansion to see Flannery's paintings on display. Because I also draw and paint, I have been looking forward all week to this exhibit. But the paintings are roped off from the visitors, signs warn us not to take photos, and dark-suited men stand around ominously. You would think we were looking at the Mona Lisa, but we're not. And I am disappointed in Flannery's paintings—they are amateurish renderings of birds, for the most part, and the years have muddied the colors. Thank God for the books, I think. Time cannot muddy those fine sentences, those striking metaphors. Flannery wanted to be a painter, but she was really a writer. And as a writer, she wanted to be a novelist, but she was really a first-rate short-story writer. Sally Fitzgerald would not agree with that, but Cecil Dawkins would.

On Saturday morning, I finally hear Cecil Dawkins read, and her story is the best one out of all the famous authors who have graced the conference. I am stunned by how good "The Quiet Enemy" is—and by the fact that Cecil's writing owes nothing to Flannery O'Connor. I recognize no similarity between them other than brilliance. The audience claps long and appreciatively when her tale is done, and I rush down the aisle to shake her hand before she's swamped by fans. Her brown eyes gleam triumphantly; she's good and she knows it, and now we know it too.

The last event I attend is Sally Fitzgerald's talk about Flannery's friendships. She is candid about herself, notes that she is aging but still "viable," and then she raps the knuckles of scholars (I think of the theologians) who "venture opinions on the letters without knowing everything about them," for they "will come up with wrong answers." No doubt she's right, but that's all the more reason why she should bring out her biography and set the record straight. Sally's talk focuses again on Flannery's many relationships with men, but this version of Flannery is that of the unrequited lover. She "endured" being in love, again and again, but was not loved in return. Flannery emerges from this treatment as a kind of martyr to love—ennobled by loss. She turned to words, and her loss became our gain.

The conference is almost over, and I am thinking of the flight home to my husband and children. Claire Shepard, a Milledgeville English teacher who has become my boon companion for the last two days of the conference, takes me to the Memory Hill Cemetery. I want to visit Flannery's grave; I want to get closure on her life, and that is where her life closed. Her grave is marked by a flat tombstone surrounded by gravel; it's near a steel fence, at the edge of the cemetery that gives onto Franklin Street. There's nothing romantic about her grave, but here it is. Claire and I sit beside it, and I make a sketch of the stone, of her name and dates and parentage.

Two blocks away, Regina O'Connor rests in her crumbling house on Greene Street. Her tombstone is yet uncarved, for she has outlived her daughter by thirty years. A twist on the natural order of things. Our children are the seeds we plant for the future, to flower after we are gone. I feel suddenly sorry for Regina, this iron-willed woman whom I will never meet. Claire likes my drawing and asks if she can have a copy of it. "Sure," I tell her, though it's not even an accurate rendering of the stone—I've made the writing too big for the rectangle. But I guess it's my version of reality, and that's all we're ever left with anyway. For if I have learned anything at this Flannery O'Connor conference, I have learned that there are many versions of the truth. And each one rings true to the teller.

The Pleasures of Reading

JOSEPH EPSTEIN

Five or six years ago, I was informed by my literary agent that two of my books were to be recorded by a firm called Books on Tape. Although the advance was not such as to earn me an honorable discharge from the financial wars, this was nonetheless pleasing news. Five or six months later, two smallish boxes arrived with the actual tapes. Ah, thought I, now here is a scrumptious little snack for the ego. I shall play these tapes in my car as I drive around Chicago, or on the Indiana Tollway, or up the Pacific Coast Highway. How soothing, how delicious the prospect, driving along and listening to that most amusing of people, oneself, or at least one's own thoughts. Wasn't it Philip Larkin who said that sex was altogether too good to share with anyone else? Listening to oneself on tape seemed the literary equivalent of Larkin's sentiment. Onan, I'm phonin', dear boy, to say you don't know the half of it. Or so I had supposed.

When I slipped my first tape into the tape player in my car, waiting for the lush cascade of words—my words, every last darling one among them—I was aquiver with anticipation. Cutting now directly to the chase, allow me to tell you that I didn't end up wrapped round a telephone pole, a silly grin of ecstasy on my face. No, I never made it through the first tape—I never made it, in fact, through even the first five minutes of the first tape. As it turned out, the man assigned to record my books had an odd, slightly twerpy accent; his rhythms were not mine; and listening to him rattle on, rolling obliviously over my careful punctuation—all this was more than I felt I could take.

I have since had four other of my books recorded on Books on Tape. The most recent of these has been a book of short stories, which contains ten or twelve Yiddish words that the (I assume underemployed) actor hired by Books on Tape, in his conscientiousness, actually called to get official pronunciations of such words as: *mishagoss, nurishkeit, mishpacha*. But I found I could not listen to these tapes, either. I didn't even open the boxes in which they arrived. What is going on here? I know lots of intelligent people who listen to books on tape with intellectual profit and simple amusement. Why can't I?

Before getting round to an answer, let me go on to a further confession: I cannot read detective or spy fiction. It is not that, along with Edmund Wilson, I don't care who killed Roger Ackroyd—though I guess, deep down, I really don't care all that much—but that I just don't care to read about it. It is not my immitigable highbrowism, for my highbrowism turns out to be pretty easily mitigated. I don't in the least mind watching detective or spy stories in the movies or on television. Some of the best Hollywood movies—*Double Indemnity, The Maltese Falcon, Farewell, My Lovely, The Day of the Jackal*—have been detective and spy stories, with the rest probably westerns; and while I wouldn't think to read a Tom Clancy novel, at my regular evening post as couch potato, I find I am able to watch VCR versions of his movies and feel, as is nowadays said, hey, no pain whatsoever. I just can't bear to read the stuff.

The problem for me is that reading is I won't say a sacred but nevertheless a pretty serious act. A very sensual act it is, too. I take account of the look, feel, even smell of a book. I like, or feel uncomfortable with, its heft in my hand. In reading, pace means a great deal, and one of the good things about a book, as opposed to a tape, is that you can read it at your own pace: flying on by, stopping, rereading, even nodding, nodding more frequently, till—*ka-boom*—the book drops from your hand.

I read, for the most part, very slowly. The very notion of speed-reading is repugnant to me. ("Read *Anna Karenina* last night," an old joke about speed-reading has it. "A book set in Russia, isn't it?") The better the book, the more slowly I tend to read it. The older I get, also the more slowly I read—not so much because my mental faculties begin to break down, which I'm sure they do, but because I am no longer so confident, as when younger I was, that I have a respectable chance of returning to reread the book in my hand. Besides, the notion of speed-reading is doubly repugnant for speeding up a pleasure. If speed-reading were really to catch on, can speed-eating be far behind? Let us not speak of other pleasurable activities.

In a brief piece in the *New Yorker* of this past spring, Benjamin Cheever, a great devotee of listening to books on tape, recounts that he not only listens to books on a tape player in his car but walks around the house wearing a Walkman "so that I can listen to a book while I run, rinse the dishes, make coffee, or shave." I myself rarely leave the house without a book, and I have been known to read a few paragraphs in the elevator in our building, or possibly finish a page or two while in line at the bank, and even catch a quick paragraph in my car at a longish stoplight. But whenever, or wherever I read, I need a pencil nearby to make my inevitable sideline of something I consider important, or plan to return to, or need to look up. I sometimes copy out things from books I am reading in a commonplace book I keep. I cannot depart from a book until I have a distinct sense of my place and usually prefer not to cease reading until I arrive at the beginning of the first full paragraph on the left-hand page. You may think me very anal, but I need to observe all these little idiosyncrasies. ("Anality!" a character in an English novel exclaims when accused of it. "Anality—my ass!")

Being a writer also makes me a slower reader. Anyone—and I exclude only Ludwig Wittgenstein from this proposition—who reads a sentence has to make the following little check on it: 1. Is it clear? 2. Is it (grammatically, semantically, logically) correct? 3. Is it interesting? 4. Is it true? 5. Is it (charming bonus) beautiful? And then, if he or she is a writer, three further questions arise: 1. How was it made? 2. Could it be improved? and 3. What, for my own writing, can I steal from it? I have never met a good writer who wasn't also a penetrating reader; and every good writer, with varying degrees of consciousness and subtlety, is also a plagiarist.

Shocking to report, closing in on sixty, I still do not know all the words in the English language. The other morning I was reading Owen Chadwick's fine book *Britain and the Vatican during the Second World War* and came upon Chadwick's description of Myron Taylor, President Roosevelt's personal envoy to Pope Pius XII, as "Rhadamanthine." It bugs me not to know a word. I am content not to know the meaning of the universe, or why God sent sin or suffering into the world, but not to know what a word means is beyond my tolerance. I trust you will think me on this matter altogether too Rhadamanthine, which is to say, severe, or strict, coming from the judge Rhadamanthus in Hades in Greek mythology. But there it is, a tic, and I am stuck with it.

I am also stuck, though at last becoming slowly unstuck, with the notion of finishing any book I begin and of reading every blasted word of it. I was pleased, some years ago, to discover that Justice Holmes, a wonderfully penetrating reader of excellent taste, suffered the same affliction until the age of seventy-five. Behind this was Holmes's worry that, at the gates of heaven, St. Peter would quiz him about his reading, and he didn't want to be caught saying he had read a book that he hadn't really finished. I read this in one of the collections of Justice Holmes's letters, of all of which, take my word on it, I have read every word.

I have at long last arrived at the age of skimming, which I still don't do with an altogether clear conscience. But why, I now tell myself, should I suffer painful *longueurs* in novels, too-lengthy plot summaries in biographies of novelists, long quotations from third-rate sources. I may be beautiful, as the blues song has it, but I'm goin' to die someday, and, I now say to myself, how 'bout some better readin', before I pass away.

The notion that, *mirabile dictu*, I am going to die someday, now all too realistic, makes me more cautious in what I choose to read. I am handed an eight-hundred-page biography and am now forced to consider that reading such a book entails at least two weeks out of my reading life. Do I wish to make the investment? Suddenly this has become a fairly serious question.

Gertrude Stein said that the happiest moment of her life was that moment in which she realized that she wouldn't be able to read all the books in the world. I suppose what made it happy for her was that it took off a fair amount of pressure. I have finally come to the realization that I shan't be able to read even all the good books in the world, and, far from making me happy, it leaves me, a naturally acquisitive fellow, a little sad. It does make rather more pressing, once one grants a world of limited possibilities, the question of which books one ought to read and which exclude.

The late Alexander Gerschenkron, an economic historian at Harvard, once took up the matter of how much one can read in a lifetime, and with rather depressing statistical consequences. Gerschenkron was then near seventy, and he estimated that, in his adult life, which he felt began at the age of twenty, he read roughly two books (outside of his professional reading) a week. This meant that, over fifty years of reading, one will have read only five thousand or so books. A piddling sum, when one realizes that something like fifty-five thousand books are published annually in the United States alone.

Given this daunting logistical problem, Gerschenkron, in an essay in *The American Scholar*, remarked that it is a shame to have read too many of the wrong books, and so set out to discover criteria for establishing which are the right—or best—books. He arrived at three criteria, and these are: 1. a book should be intrinsically interesting; 2. a book should be rereadable; and 3. a book should be memorable. These criteria are thoughtful, impeccable, and, as by now you may have noticed, utterly useless. How, after all, can one know if a book is interesting until one has read well into it, or rereadable until one has read it through a second time, or memorable until long after one has finished reading it? One can't.

Advice about books has always been plentiful. The more practical the better I like it. The *Wall Street Journal* columnist Irving Kristol used to tell students at the NYU Business School never to show up for a job interview carrying a novel, which seems to me very sound advice, unless you happen to be interviewing for the job of literary critic or novelist. The late Arnaldo Momigliano, the great historian of the ancient world, once told me, in his strong Piedmontese accent, "You know, the cheapest way to acquire a book remains to buy it." I puzzled over that for an hour or two, before figuring out that what Arnaldo meant was that if you bought a book, rather than have it given or lent to you, at least you weren't under any obligation to read the damn thing.

Perhaps in America, where cultural confidence has always been a bit shaky, advice about what one ought to read has also been especially plentiful. As early as 1771, a man named Robert Skipwith, who was to be Mrs. Jefferson's brother-in-law, asked the then twenty-eight-year-old Thomas Jefferson to draw up a list of books "suited to the capacity of a common reader who understands but little of the classicks and who has not leisure for any intricate or tedious study. Let them [these books] be improving and amusing." Jefferson obliged with a list of 148 books, mostly in the classics but with a few intensely practical works, among them a book on horse-hoeing husbandry and Nourse's *Compendium of Physic and Surgery.*

The flow of such advice since has never ceased. There was Harvard's once famous five-foot shelf of classics and, later, Encylopaedia Britannica's *Great Books of the Western World.* In the early 1980s, a book was published titled *The List of Books: A Library of Over 3,000 Works.* By the time it was published, of course, the list was dated, being filled with books of that day on politics and popular culture: instructing one on the importance of the novels of Kurt Vonnegut, the Vietnam history of Frances FitzGerald, Frantz Fanon's *The Wretched of the Earth,* and other books that one now turns away from at the asking price of 25 cents at garage sales.

No one, I fear, can offer much useful advice on what you ought to read, apart from making the important distinction between serious and unserious books. I once suggested in an essay that certain books were age specific—that is, that certain books ought or ought not to be read before or beyond certain ages: no Thomas Wolfe after eighteen; no F. Scott Fitzgerald beyond thirty, no Chekhov before thirty; no

Proust before forty; no James Joyce beyond fifty—that sort of thing. Perhaps the best and only worthwhile distinction is that made by a character in an R. K. Narayan novel, who divided his personal library into good books and bad. In mystical fact, books have a mysterious, unpatterned way of appearing when one needs them. Or so at least they have in my life.

I grew up in an almost entirely unbookish home. Although neither of my parents was an immigrant, and both were well-spoken, I don't remember there being an English dictionary in our apartment. Magazines and newspapers were around in plenty. Only two books were kept, these in many copies, and both were stored in the basement. These were books written by my grandfather, in Yiddish and Hebrew, published in Montreal, where he lived, and subsidized in good part by my father. Whenever someone visited us who read Hebrew or Yiddish, I was instructed to run down to the basement to supply him or her with one of my grandfather's seemingly never diminishing stock of books.

I mention all this even though it does a bit of damage to one of the more pleasing stereotypes about Jews—that they are all bookish, artistic, sensitive, intellectual, born with something I can only call a culture gene. I grew up in a mostly Jewish neighborhood in which this gene seems never to have shown up. None of my boyhood friends was a reader, and neither was I. None of us played the piano, and certainly not the violin, that Jewish instrument *par excellence*. What we played were American sports, and what we yearned to be was wise in the ways of the modern city. The sons of moderately successful businessmen, we were adolescent gamblers and artful dodgers who hoped to grow into savvy men over whose eyes no one could pull the wool (make that cashmere).

Lonely children, or at least lonely boys, read books, and I was never lonely. A story is told about Edmund Wilson, whose mother worried that her son spent altogether too much time with books, and so bought him a baseball uniform and glove—in which the young Wilson suited up and promptly sat under a tree in the family's yard in Red Bank, New Jersey, where he continued reading. If my mother, going in the opposite route from Mrs. Wilson, had given me a set of books, I should probably have used them as bases and to mark the foul lines.

When a boy I read a book or two—*Hans Brinker, or The Silver Skates, Black Beauty*—but for the most part my reading consisted of comic books and a publication still in circulation called *Sport Magazine*. When it came time to give book reports, I cheated by giving them from Classic Comics. When we were in, I believe, the fifth grade, a woman from the Chicago Public Library visited our school and, in a treacly accent, told us, "Boys and girls, *boooks* are your friends. They will take you to unknown shores and reveal to you hitherto hidden treasures. Yes, boys and girls, *boooks* truly are your friends, so you must never bend their backs or write in their margins or dog-ear their pages." This most impressive little talk put me off serious book reading for at least another full five years.

I have since come not only to agree with the library lady, to whom I owe an apology, but to go a step further with Marcel Proust, who in his essay "On Reading" claims, with some justification, that books, at least as company, are really superior to friends. One need engage in no small talk with a book, as Proust noted, no greetings in the hall, no expressions of gratitude, or excuses for delayed meetings. With books, unlike with friends, no sense of obligation exists. We are with them only because we absolutely wish to be with them. Nor do we have to laugh, politely, at their attempts at wit. As Proust says, "No more deference: we laugh at what Molière says only to the degree that we find him funny; when he bores us, we are not afraid to appear bored, and when we decidedly have had enough of being with him, we put him back in his place as bluntly as if he had neither genius nor fame."

We may even, in extreme conditions, and contra the library lady, break the back and dog-ear the hell out of a book, which we certainly cannot do to friends. Besides, as you cannot with a friend, you can deal with a book at the pace you prefer: maundering, skimming, or plowing straight through. You can argue with a book, or even curse it, and not have to worry about being put down by a superior mind.

(An Evanston bookseller once told me that he was much amused with a book that came into his shop that contained, in the margins of one of its pages, the remark, "C'mon, Ortega!")

The first book that really, that deeply, engaged my interest arrived when I was thirteen. It had a thick red cover, trimmed in black, and was titled *All-American*. It was written by a man named John R. Tunis, and was, as I had hoped it would be, about football—high-school football. It was illustrated by a man named Hans Walleen, had a protagonist named Meyer Goldman, a Jewish halfback (anti-Semitism was part of the story), and was so immensely readable that I lapped up its 250 fairly large-print pages in a single day. As we should say nowadays, it blew me away.

How to recover what Marcel Proust calls the original psychological act of reading? I am not sure I can do it justice. I remember being swept up in John R. Tunis' story. I remember pulling for characters— wanting them to win through. I remember wanting to rush to the end of the story, to make sure it ended in a victory for goodness, fairness, and decency (not to worry, it did). At the same time that I wanted to know how things worked out, I didn't really want the book to end and so to be ejected from this swell world that John R. Tunis had created.

All-American did something that not many other things I had thus far encountered in life were able to do—it took me out of myself and put me into a larger world. Not all that much larger, now that I come to think about it, but larger enough to stir my imagination. Even the details of reading the book return to me, forty-five years later. I read part of it in our living room, and finished it, supine, propped up on my bed, on top of the spread, leaning on my right elbow.

I can remember the conditions surrounding the reading of lots of books that had a strong effect on me as a boy. I remember sitting up all night, in the bed next to which my father slept in the Brown Hotel in Des Moines, Iowa, where at sixteen I had gone with him on business, to finish Willard Motley's *Knock on Any Door*; I remember sitting, legs crossed Indian style, reading John Dos Passos' *U.S.A.* in a park called Indian Boundary on the North Side of Chicago. I remember reading *Catcher in the Rye* on a train headed for Champaign, Illinois. Oddly,

I don't remember the conditions under which I read *The Grapes of Wrath*, another key book for me in my youth.

All of these books I read with no sense of their quality or place in the general hierarchy of critical importance, for these things, pleasant to report, had not yet any meaning for me; these books excited me because they seemed to take hold of life, and consequently they took hold of me.

Proust, that brilliant anatomist of passion, recalled everything about his own reading experience, about which he reports both in *Remembrance of Things Past* and in "On Reading." Characteristically, he laments the passing of the intense pleasure that his boyish reading gave him. Reporting on his emotions upon the completion of a book, he writes:

> Then, what? This book, it was nothing but that? Those beings [its characters] to whom one had given more of one's attention and tenderness than to people in real life, not always daring to admit how much one loved them, even when our parents found us reading and appeared to smile at our emotion, so that we closed the book with affected indifference or feigned ennui; those people, for whom one had panted and sobbed, one would never see again, one would no longer know anything about them.

"How do you manage to know so many things, Monsieur France?" Proust is supposed to have asked Anatole France, to which the older writer is said to have replied: "It's quite simple, my dear Marcel. When I was your age, I wasn't good-looking and popular like you. So instead of going into society I stayed at home and did nothing but read." Later in life, given a choice, would Marcel have preferred going to a party or staying home with a book? It would depend, I suppose he might have answered, on who was giving the party and whether certain duchesses would be there. And of course much later in life, he preferred to stay home to write a book that has kept many of us at home reading it for weeks on end.

I ought to have known that I was in danger of being seriously hooked on books and the pleasures of reading when, one sunny summer afternoon in my fourteenth year, I stayed home to read another John R. Tunis novel, this one about baseball. When I could as easily have been outside playing the game, I preferred at that moment to continue reading about it. A bookworm, clearly, was in the making.

Still, the hook took a while to sink in. I read scarcely at all in high school, and then mainly books about the slums. *The Amboy Dukes* by Irving Schulman, a novel about a bunch of thuggish kids in Brooklyn, was a much thumbed book in my high school. In print—in actual print in those happily prudish times—it used the word "jugs" to refer to a girl's breasts. I read other books in this general line of hoods in the slums books, including one actually called *The Hoods*, by a man named Harry Grey, from which, owing to the perverse games that memory chooses to play, I still recall the sentence, "Cockeyed Hymie at the wheel, the big boat pulled into the night and I thrilled to the sensation of the clutch."

Although I was never a good student, the University of Chicago did teach me which were the important books. I was, though, pleased to depart that exalted setting so that I might read, alongside all those great books, a number of merely good ones, of my own choosing and to be read in my own unsystematic way. My own unsystematic way included a few key motives, among them reading to discover what life was supposed to be like and how one was supposed to live it. "Genius," wrote Henry James, "is only the art of getting your experience fast, of stealing it, as it were." I hoped to steal a lot of experience from books and believe I may have done so. Then, too, the question implicit in reading every great writer, or so I began to sense, is, What would he or she have thought of me? Reading a serious book, it turns out, provides a way of reconsidering one's own life from the author's perspective.

I have never clocked myself here, but my guess is that rare is the day when I do not spend anywhere from three to five hours reading. Apart from ablutions and making coffee, reading is the first thing I do in the morning and generally the last thing I do at night. I once tried to go a day without reading and found it compared in difficulty of deprivation with going a day without smoking; and I speak as a former two-pack-a-day man. My children seem to recall the most repeated phrase from their growing up with me as their father being, "One moment: I'll be with you as soon as I finish this paragraph." Whenever I am abroad, in no matter how exotic the city—Athens, Constantinople, Jerusalem—at some point I yearn to stay the day in the hotel room and do nothing but read.

I am always amused to note, when the *New York Times* prints one of its Man or Woman in the News pieces, one of these men or women listing under hobbies such items as "Tennis, Travel, *Reading*." The notion of reading as a hobby to one for whom it is very nearly a way of life is comically absurd. With any luck at all, I shall never be the Man in the News, but if I am, I should as readily list under my hobbies, "Tennis, Travel, and *Breathing*." Hilton Kramer, another voracious reader, has more than once remarked of certain jobs—in government, as directors of large museums and other cultural institutions, as presidents of universities—that they are among those jobs "which never allow you to read another book." A poet, a Russian proverb has it, always cheats his boss. A really serious reader, a proverb I have invented for this occasion, is probably better off not being a boss.

I don't wish to make my own reading seem grim, a lonely quest for wisdom, a form of psychotherapy by other (and less expensive) means, onward ever onward, beating on, boats against the current, working in the dark, my passion my task . . . and the rest of it. On the contrary. My motives in reading are thoroughly mixed, but pure pleasure is always high among them. I read for aesthetic pleasure. If anything, with the passing of years, I have become sufficiently the aesthetic snob so that I can scarcely drag my eyes across the pages of a badly or even pedestrianly written book. I count myself one of Henry James's little band, "partakers of the same repose, who sit together in the shade of the tree, by the plash of the fountain, with the glare of the desert around us and no great vice that I know of but the habit perhaps of estimating people a little too much by what they think of a certain style." Along with the love of style, I read in the hope of laughter, exaltation, insight, enhanced consciousness, and dare I say it, *wisdom*; I read, finally, hoping to get a little smarter about the world.

Such are my hopes. But what, exactly, do I actually get out of this activity on which I spend three to five hours daily? What is the point? I explain to my students that I by now have probably forgotten more than they have read—a remark made not in a spirit of braggadocio but in literal truth and true regret. There are whole—and entirely serious—novels I have read about which I cannot recall a thing. One such is Dostoyevsky's *The Idiot*. All I can tell you about that thick book is that its protagonist is a man named Prince Myshkin, he is an epileptic, and, in ways I cannot recall, somehow wise in his innocence. Otherwise: total blank, nada, zilch. Read *The Idiot* roughly thirty years ago—a novel set in Russia, isn't it?

Plots do not stay all that long in my mind. I do not, as a previous generation did, memorize vast stretches of poetry. What I consciously take away from many of the books I read are scenes, oddments, bits and pieces. I am somehow less interested in the final meaning of T. S. Eliot's "The Love Song of J. Alfred Prufrock" than I am in the fact that so many of the phrases from that poem have stuck in my mind for more than forty years. From an Isaac Bashevis Singer story, I recall the earlock of a yeshiva student, flapping in the wind; I remember the little finger of Father Sergius, in Tolstoy's story of that name, twirling in the air after he has chopped it off in his struggle to hold sensuality at bay; I remember the hero of one of Henry Miller's novels—one of the *Tropic*s—making love standing up in a hallway in Paris when a coin drops from his companion's purse and the Miller narrator remarks to himself, "I made a mental note to pick it up later"; in Owen Chadwick's *Britain and the Vatican during the Second World War*, I already suspect that, in the years to come, I shall only recall the diary entry of the British envoy to the Vatican, D'Arcy Osborne, who, unable to leave the Vatican while Italy was at war with England, noted, "I reached the grave conclusion during the mass that I am nothing but a pencilled marginal note in the Book of Life. I am not in the main text at all."

Reading is always at its best for me when the writer makes of it a sheath of words with which to capture the rich, unpredictable, astonishing flow of life. The metaphor of the sheath comes from Willa

Cather, who in *The Song of the Lark* has her opera-singer-heroine Thea Kronborg, while standing in a stream in the pueblo country, reflect, ". . . what was any art but an effort to make a sheath, a mould in which to imprison for a moment the shining, elusive element which is life itself—life hurrying past us and running away, too strong to stop, too sweet to lose?"

Not only am I unclear about what the main text of the Book of Life is, but I am not always entirely sure what the main texts of actual books are. Am I, I wonder, insufficiently interested in such ideas as works of literature may be said to contain? There are those, and I am among them, who claim that, when it is going at its best, literature sails above the realm of ideas anyhow.

"He had a mind so fine no idea could violate it," said T. S. Eliot of Henry James. By that lovely rhythmic formulation I take Eliot to mean not that James was incapable of grasping or of functioning at the level of ideas, but instead that his true interest was elsewhere. James, Eliot is saying, was not interested in the knowledge contained in the various ideas or "isms" of literature, but in the truths known to the human heart and soul, the truths of sensibility-interested, that is, in what for the artist are the higher truths.

T. S. Eliot, at the age of thirty, writing to his friend Mary Hutchinson, allowed that there were two ways in which one ought to read: "1) because of particular and personal interest, which makes the thing one's own, regardless of what other people think of the book 2) *to a certain extent*, because it is something one 'ought to have read' but one must be quite clear that this is *why* one is reading." Eliot goes on to say that, apropos of reading, there are two kinds of intelligence: "the intellectual and the sensitive—the first can read a great deal because it schematises and theorises—the second not much, because it requires to get more out of a book than can immediately be put into words." He then adds that "*I* read very little—and *have* read much less than people think—at present I only read Tudor drama, Tudor prose, and Gibbon—over and over—when I have time to read at all. Of course I don't count the countless books I have had to skim for lectures etc."

Marguerite Yourcenar said that there were three sources of knowledge in the world: that knowledge which comes from observing fellow human beings, that knowledge which comes from looking into one's heart, and that knowledge which comes from books. Is there any point in ranking the three according to importance? I suspect not. Not to observe others is to put oneself in danger in the world, not to observe oneself is to lose the permanent use of that unnamed organ responsible for reflection, not to read is to risk barbarizing oneself—leave any one of the three out and you have a less than fully equipped human being.

I am not sure Marcel Proust would agree. He had strong notions about the limitations of reading. He thought reading especially useful to the indolent mind, which cannot think in solitude, but requires the lubrication of another, superior mind to set its own in thoughtful motion. My guess is that Proust thought his own a mind of this kind. I know my own is; if my thoughts are ever to catch fire, I need to rub them up against those of a finer-grained mind than my own.

Proust thought that the true point of reading was to waken us to the life of the spirit. The danger in reading, he felt, was when it tended to substitute itself for this life of the spirit—when, as he wrote, "truth no longer appears to us as an ideal we can realize only through the intimate progress of our thought and the effort of our heart, but as a material thing, deposited between the leaves of books like honey ready-made by others, and which we have only to take the trouble of reaching for on the shelves of libraries and then savouring passively in perfect repose of body and mind."

Yet this danger, of substituting books for intelligence, Proust thought, grew less as intelligence grew greater. Once we knew that we could "develop the power of our sensibility and our intelligence only within ourselves, in the depths of our spiritual life," books become, as Proust calls it, "the noblest of distractions, the most ennobling one of all, for only reading and knowledge produce the 'good manners' of the mind."

I suppose one can accept Proust's strictures on the limitation of books, with this one qualification: how does the flame of intelligence grow greater without the substantial kindling of books to ignite it? Sometimes, too, more than mere intelligence is ignited by reading.

Consider, for example, the following scene: a very nervous young black man, not long up from Mississippi, appears at the desk of a branch library in the city of Memphis, Tennessee. He has forged a note, asking the librarian to give him some of the books of H. L. Mencken, an author whose name he had come across in that morning's paper. (It is the late 1920s, and the reason the note has to be forged is that blacks are not allowed to use the Memphis public library.) After a very nervous-making exchange, the young black man, whose name happens to be Richard Wright, is given two Mencken titles: one of these is *A Book of Prefaces*. Wright, in *Black Boy*, his autobiography, provides an account of the effect of his reading H. L. Mencken for the first time:

> That night in my rented room, while letting the hot water run over my can of pork and beans in the sink, I opened *A Book of Prefaces* and began to read. I was jarred and shocked by the style, the clear, clean, sweeping sentences. Why did he write like that? And how did one write like that? I pictured the man as a raging demon, slashing with his pen, consumed with hate, denouncing everything American, extolling everything European or German, laughing at the weaknesses of people, mocking God, authority. What was this? I stood up, trying to realize what reality lay behind the meaning of the words . . . Yes, this man was fighting, fighting with words. He was using words as a weapon, using them as one would use a club. Could words be weapons? Well, yes, for here they were. Then, maybe, perhaps, I could use them as a weapon? No. It frightened me. I read on and what amazed me was not what he said, but how on earth anybody had the courage to say it.

Richard Wright continues:

> I ran across many words whose meanings I did not know, and I either looked them up in a dictionary or, before I had a chance to do that, encountered the word in a context that made its meaning

clear. But what strange world was this? I concluded the book with the conviction that I had somehow overlooked something terribly important in life. I had once tried to write, had once reveled in feeling, had let my crude imagination roam, but the impulse to dream had been slowly beaten out of me by experience. Now it surged up again and I hungered for books, new ways of looking and seeing. It was not a matter of believing or disbelieving what I read, but of feeling something new, of being affected by something that made the look of the world different.

Let me italicize Richard Wright's phrase *the impulse to dream*, which, he says, "had been beaten out of me." At times, much less brutally than in ways the young Richard Wright had to undergo I grant you, life beats it out of all of us. And books, "that noblest distraction," can replace it, sometimes in direct, sometimes in subtle ways.

Because I was born into a family with a strong practical cast, which I cannot shake off, nor want to, I have to ask myself what does all my reading mean? What does it come to? Again I ask: What is the point of spending so much time, on my duff, a book in my hand, reading vast quantities of lovely prose and poetry, much of which I shall probably forget?

I have asked this same question of my students. For the better part of four years, I say to them, you have read a mass of poems, plays, novels—what does it all come down to? Their answers, though not unintelligent, are a bit predictable. All this reading sharpens their minds, they say; it tends to put them in touch with noble ideals; it lets them experience things that, without books, they could never experience (the eighteenth century, for example). All these answers, though a mite platitudinous, are nevertheless correct. I have the advantage over them of at least making a living off all my reading. But does all their reading come together, does it add up to something at least philosophically if not commercially useful? Is there, in the impatient phrase of the day, a bottom line? Here, in searching for an answer, they stumble. I'm sure I couldn't have answered it myself at twenty or twenty-one, but I should like to attempt to do so now.

A fair amount of reading, of a belletristic kind, I have come to believe, confers on one—or at least ought to confer on one—what I think of as "the literary point of view." This point of view, which is taught not by any specific book or author, or even set of authors, teaches a worldly-wise skepticism, which comes through first in a distrust of general ideas. "As soon as one creates a concept," says Ortega, "reality leaves the room." (Right on, Ortega! I hope someone will write in the margin of this essay.) The literary point of view is distrustful of general ideas and above all of systems of ideas. It teaches, as Henry James advises, that you should "never say that you know the last word about any human heart." It teaches one to hold with Chekhov, who favored no sides or classes but wrote, "I believe in individuals, I see salvation in isolated personalities scattered here and there throughout Russia; whether they're intellectuals or peasants, they are our strength, few of them though there are."

The most complex lesson the literary point of view teaches—and it is not, to be sure, a lesson available to all, and is even difficult to keep in mind once acquired—is to allow the intellect to become subservient to the heart. What wide reading teaches is the richness, the complexity, the mystery of life. In the wider and longer view, I have come to believe, there is something deeply apolitical—something above politics—in literature, despite what feminist, Marxist, and other politicized literary critics may think. If at the end of a long life of reading the chief message you bring away is that women have had it lousy, or that capitalism stinks, or that attention must above all be paid to victims, then I'd say you just might have missed something crucial. Too bad, for there probably isn't time to go back to reread your lifetime's allotment of 5,000 or so books.

People who have read with love and respect understand that the larger message behind all books, great and good and even some not so good as they might be, is, finally, cultivate your sensibility so that you may trust your heart. The charmingly ironic point of vast reading, at least as I have come to understand it, is to distrust much of one's education. Unfortunately, the only way to know this is first to become educated, just as the only way properly to despise success is first to achieve it.

Let me return and give all but the last word to Marcel Proust, who wrote:

> Our intellect is not the most subtle, the most powerful, the most appropriate, instrument for revealing the truth. It is life that, little by little, example by example, permits us to see that what is most important to our heart, or to our mind, is learned not by reasoning but through other agencies. Then it is that the intellect, observing their superiority, abdicates its control to them upon reasoned grounds and agrees to become their collaborator and lackey.

That seems to me impressively subtle, immensely smart, very wise. I came upon it, you may not be astonished to learn, in a book.

Copyrights and Credits

Notes on Contributors

Copyrights and Credits

Susan Balée. "Flannery O'Connor Resurrected." *The Hudson Review* 47, no. 3 (Autumn 1994). Copyright © 1994 by Susan Balée.

Wendell Berry. "Writer and Region." *The Hudson Review* 40, no. 1 (Spring 1987). Copyright © 1987 by Wendell Berry.

Thomas M. Disch. "My Roommate Lord Byron." *The Hudson Review* 54, no. 4 (Winter 2002). Copyright © 2002 by Thomas M. Disch.

Joseph Epstein. "The Pleasures of Reading." *The Hudson Review* 48, no. 4 (Winter 1996). Copyright © 1995 by Joseph Epstein.

Dana Gioia. "Learning from Robert Fitzgerald." *The Hudson Review* 51, no. 1 (Spring 1998). Copyright © 1998 by Dana Gioia.

Jeffrey Harrison. "Listening to Virginia." *The Hudson Review* 65, no. 2 (Summer 2012). Copyright © 2012 by Jeffrey Harrison.

Seamus Heaney. "'Apt Admonishment': Wordsworth as an Example." *The Hudson Review* 61, no. 1 (Spring 2008). Copyright © 2008 by Seamus Heaney.

An excerpt from "Little Gidding" by T. S. Eliot is reprinted in "'Apt Admonishment': Wordsworth As an Example" by Seamus Heaney from *Four Quartets* by permission of Houghton Mifflin Harcourt Publishing Company. Copyright 1936 by Houghton Mifflin Harcourt Publishing Company; copyright © renewed 1964 by T. S. Eliot. Copyright 1940, 1942 by T. S. Eliot; copyright © renewed 1968, 1970 by Esme Valerie Eliot. All rights reserved.

Extracts from "Snake" by D. H. Lawrence are reprinted in "'Apt Admonishment': Wordsworth As an Example" by Seamus Heaney from *The Complete Poems of D. H. Lawrence*, edited by Vivian de Sola Pinto & F. Warren Roberts, by permission of Viking Books, an imprint of Penguin

Publishing Group, a division of Penguin Random House LLC. Copyright © 1964, 1971 by Angelo Ravagli and C. M. Weekley, Executors of the Estate of Frieda Lawrence Ravagli, and by permission of Pollinger Limited (www.pollingerltd.com) on behalf of the Estate of Frieda Lawrence Ravagli.

Richard Hornby. "*Who's Afraid of Virginia Woolf?*: A Memoir." *The Hudson Review* 66, no. 1 (Spring 2013). Copyright © 2013 by The Hudson Review, Inc.

Barbara Kraft. "Last Days of Henry Miller." *The Hudson Review* 46, no. 3 (Autumn 1993). Copyright © 1993 by Barbara Kraft.

David Mason. "The Poetry of Life and the Life of Poetry." *The Hudson Review* 48, no. 4 (Winter 1996). Copyright © 1995 by David Mason.

An excerpt from "New Year Letter" by W. H. Auden is reprinted in "The Poetry of Life and the Life of Poetry" by David Mason. "New Year Letter," copyright © 1941 and renewed 1969 by W. H. Auden; from *W. H. Auden Collected Poems* by W. H. Auden. Used by permission of Random House, an imprint and division of Penguin Random House LLC, and by permission of Curtis Brown, Ltd. All rights reserved.

Extract from "Notes Toward a Supreme Fiction" by Wallace Stevens is reprinted in "The Poetry of Life and the Life of Poetry" by David Mason, from *The Collected Poems of Wallace Stevens* by Wallace Stevens, copyright © 1954 by Wallace Stevens and copyright renewed 1982 by Holly Stevens. Used by permission of Alfred A. Knopf, an imprint of the Knopf Doubleday Publishing Group, a division of Penguin Random House LLC. All rights reserved, and by permission of Faber & Faber, © Estate of Wallace Stevens.

Antonio Muñoz Molina. "A Double Education." *The Hudson Review* 64, no. 1 (Spring 2011). Copyright © 2011 by Antonio Muñoz Molina, used by permission of The Wylie Agency LLC.

Andrew Motion. "The Poem and the Path." *The Hudson Review* 63, no. 1 (Spring 2010). Copyright © 2010 by Andrew Motion.

"Questions of Travel" by Elizabeth Bishop is reprinted in "The Poem and the Path" by Andrew Motion from *Poems* by permission of Farrar, Straus and Giroux, LLC. Also published in the collection *The Complete Poems 1927–1979*. Copyright © 2011 by The Alice H. Methfessel Trust. Publishers Note and compilation copyright © 2011 by Farrar, Straus and Giroux, LLC.

"Questions of Travel" by Elizabeth Bishop is reprinted in "The Poem and the Path" by Andrew Motion from *Poems* by Elizabeth Bishop, published by Chatto & Windus. Reprinted by permission of The Random House Group Limited.

"The Shore Road" by Norman MacCaig is reprinted in "The Poem and the Path" by Andrew Motion from *The Collected Poems of Norman MacCaig* with the permission of the publisher Polygon.

Judith Pascoe. "Before I Read *Clarissa* I Was Nobody: Aspirational Reading and Samuel Richardson's Great Novel." *The Hudson Review* 56, no. 2 (Summer 2003). Copyright © 2003 by Judith Pascoe.

Clara Claiborne Park. "Talking Back to the Speaker." *The Hudson Review* 42, no. 1 (Spring 1989). Copyright © 1989 by Clara Claiborne Park.

William H. Pritchard. "Literary Awakenings." *The Hudson Review* 69, no. 1 (Spring 2016). Copyright © 2016 by The Hudson Review, Inc.

Louis Simpson. "Waterloo, the Story of an Obsession." *The Hudson Review* 47, no. 2 (Summer 1994). Copyright © 1994 by Louis Simpson.

Irving Singer. "A Pilgrimage to Santayana." *The Hudson Review* 53, no. 2 (Summer 2000). Copyright © 2000 by Irving Singer.

George Watson. "Prophet against God: William Empson (1906–84)." *The Hudson Review* 49, no. 1 (Spring 1996). Copyright © 1996 by George Watson.

Igor Webb. "Horatio Hornblower." *The Hudson Review*, 65, no. 4 (Winter 2013). Copyright © 2013 by Igor Webb.

Extracts from *Lieutenant Hornblower*, *Beat to Quarters*, and *Commodore Hornblower* by C. S. Forester are reprinted in "Horatio Hornblower" by Igor Webb by permission of Peters Fraser & Dunlop (www.petersfraserdunlop.com) on behalf of the Estate of C. S. Forester.

Joyce Zonana. "Nell and I." *The Hudson Review* 50, no. 4 (Winter 1998). Copyright © 1997 by Joyce Zonana.

Notes on Contributors

Susan Balée's *Flannery O'Connor, Literary Prophet of the South* (1994) was the first biography of the Southern writer. She lives in Pittsburgh, Pennsylvania, where, in addition to writing, she also sculpts and paints. She wrote the introduction to the new edition of Gaston Leroux's *The Phantom of the Opera*.

Wendell Berry, a poet, novelist, and environmentalist, lives on his farm in Port Royal, Kentucky. *The Unsettling of America: Culture and Agriculture* (1977) is considered a classic among his books advocating man's harmony with nature. His numerous collections of poems include *A Small Porch: Sabbath Poems 2014*. In 2016, he was awarded the Ivan Sandrof Lifetime Achievement Award by the National Book Critics Circle as well as the Sidney Lanier Prize from Mercer University's Center for Southern Studies.

Thomas M. Disch (1940–2008), a poet, novelist, librettist, and critic, specialized in science fiction. In 1999, his book *The Dreams Our Stuff Is Made Of: How Science Fiction Conquered the World* won the Hugo Award for Best Related Work. His other works included *The Castle of Indolence: On Poetry, Poets, and Poetasters* (1995), *The Cardinal Detoxes* (a verse play, 1990), and, for children, *The Brave Little Toaster: A Bedtime Story for Small Appliances* (1986).

Joseph Epstein, the former long-term editor of the *American Scholar*, is emeritus lecturer of English at Northwestern University. He is the author of numerous collections of essays and short stories, most recently

Wind Sprints: Shorter Essays (2016) and *Frozen in Time: Twenty Stories* (2016). He lives in Evanston, Illinois.

Dana Gioia is the poet laureate of California and former chairman of the National Endowment for the Arts. He is the author of five books of poetry, including *99 Poems: New and Selected* (2016). He has also published three collections of criticism, most notably *Can Poetry Matter?* (1992), and three opera libretti. He is the Judge Widney Professor of Poetry and Public Culture at the University of Southern California. He has been a regular contributor to the *Hudson Review* for thirty-five years.

Jeffrey Harrison is the author of five books of poetry, including *Into Daylight*, published by Tupelo Press in 2014 as the winner of the Dorset Prize and selected by the Massachusetts Center for the Book as a Must-Read Book for 2015. A recipient of Guggenheim and National Endowment for the Arts Fellowships, his poems have appeared widely in magazines and anthologies.

Seamus Heaney (1939–2013), a native of Northern Ireland, lived much of his life in Dublin. In 1982, he was the recipient of the Hudson Review's Bennett Award for "his distinguished achievement in the art of lyric poetry." In 1995, he won the Nobel Prize in Literature. His books include *Opened Ground: Selected Poems, 1966–1996* (1998) and a final poetry collection, *Human Chain* (2010); his *Finders Keepers: Selected Prose, 1971–2001* (2002) received the Truman Capote Award for Literary Criticism.

Richard Hornby is emeritus professor of theatre at the University of California, Riverside, and has been the theatre critic for the *Hudson Review* for thirty years. Among the five books to his credit, *Script into Performance* has become the standard work on directing classical plays and *The End of Acting: A Radical View* is a fresh examination of the art of acting. He is also visiting professor at Rose Bruford College in England and a member of the Advisory Board of the Stanislavski Centre there.

Barbara Kraft lives in Los Angeles. She is the author of *Henry Miller: The Last Days* (2016). Her other books include *Anaïs Nin: The Last Days* (2013) and *Light Between the Shadows: A Conversation with Eugene Ionesco* (2014).

David Mason, a professor of English at Colorado College, was poet laureate of Colorado from 2010 to 2014. His poetry books include *The Buried Houses*, *The Country I Remember*, *Arrivals*, *Sea Salt*, and the verse novel *Ludlow*. He has also written two collections of essays, a memoir, a children's book, and several opera libretti.

Andrew Motion, the United Kingdom poet laureate from 1999–2009, is the Homewood Professor of the Arts in the Writing Seminars program at Johns Hopkins University. He is the author of *The Mower: New and Selected Poems* (2009), *In the Blood: A Memoir of My Childhood* (2007), and *Philip Larkin: A Writer's Life* (1993), which won the Whitbread Prize for Biography. He lives in Baltimore.

Antonio Muñoz Molina, the Spanish novelist and essayist, divides his time between Madrid and New York. In 2013, he was the recipient of both the Jerusalem Prize and the Prince of Asturias Award for Literature. In 2014, he published the novel *Como la sombra que se va*.

Clara Claiborne Park (1923–2010), a literary critic, was a lecturer in English studies at Williams College from 1975 until 1994. She was well known for her writings on autism: *The Siege: The First Eight Years of an Autistic Child* (1967) and its sequel, *Exiting Nirvana: A Daughter's Life with Autism* (2001).

Judith Pascoe is a professor of English at the University of Iowa. She is the author of *The Sarah Siddons Audio Files: Romanticism and the Lost Voice* (2011) and *The Hummingbird Cabinet* (2006). She is a recipient of Guggenheim and National Endowment for the Humanities Fellowships and also received a Fulbright Japan Lecturing Award.

William H. Pritchard first appeared in the *Hudson Review* in Summer 1967 and became an advisory editor of the magazine in 1973.

His published criticism includes critical and biographical studies of Robert Frost, Randall Jarrell, Wyndham Lewis, and John Updike. Other writings include six volumes of essays and reviews, including *What's Been Happening to Jane Austen* (2011) and a memoir, *English Papers: A Teaching Life* (1995). He is the Henry Clay Folger Professor of English, emeritus, at Amherst College.

Louis Simpson (1923–2012), born in Kingston, Jamaica, was a poet, editor, translator, and critic. In 1964, he received a Pulitzer Prize for his collection of poems *At the End of the Open Road*. In addition to literary studies of modern poets, he wrote such memoirs as *The King My Father's Wreck* (1994). His final book of poems was *Voices in the Distance: Selected Poems* (2010).

Irving Singer (1925–2015) was a professor of philosophy at Massachusetts Institute of Technology, where he taught for over fifty years. His seminal work was *The Nature of Love,* which came out in three volumes (1966–87), followed by a second trilogy, *Meaning in Life* (1992–96). He published two books on George Santayana: *Santayana's Aesthetics: A Critical Analysis* (1957) and *George Santayana: Literary Philosopher* (2000).

George Watson (1927–2013), literary critic and historian, was a fellow of St. John's College, Cambridge University, for more than fifty years. His works include *The Story of the Novel* (1979), *The Lost Literature of Socialism* (1998), *Never Ones for Theory? England and the War of Ideas* (2000), and *Heresies and Heretics: Memories of the Twentieth Century* (2013). He was also general editor of the *New Cambridge Bibliography of English Literature.*

Igor Webb is the author of *Rereading the Nineteenth Century: Studies in the Old Criticism from Austen to Lawrence* (2010). His story "Reza Says," which originally appeared in the *Hudson Review,* was selected as a "Distinguished Story" for *Best American Short Stories 2012*. He is a professor and the director of creative writing at Adelphi University.

Joyce Zonana is the author of a memoir, *Dream Houses: From Cairo to Katrina, an Exile's Journey* (2008), which she began not long after completing "Nell and I"—her transition from traditional academic scholarship. She is a professor of English at Borough of Manhattan Community College and lives in Brooklyn.